Oxford English for Careers

Nursing ②

Tony Grice and James Greenan

Student's Book

OXFORD
UNIVERSITY PRESS

Contents

1 Admission by A&E

Scrub up

1 Label the equipment that goes into the ambulance.

cardiac monitor   oxygen regulator
defibrillator   drug box
bag-valve mask   ramp
IV pump   stretcher
bags of blood   suction unit
oxygen cylinders   ambulance chair

2 Explain to a partner what each item of equipment is for.

EXAMPLE
A cardiac monitor shows what the heart is doing.

3 An elderly man has collapsed in a supermarket and an ambulance is sent out. Discuss which items of equipment will probably be needed.

4 You arrive at an accident in an ambulance with a driver and find four seriously ill people who all need to go to hospital. There are no other ambulances available and there is only room for three people in your ambulance. Discuss what you should do.

In this unit
- emergency equipment
- abbreviations
- narrative tenses
- language of triage

Listening

An emergency call

1 Work in pairs. Discuss what questions an emergency operator asks when a call comes through and in what order the questions are asked.

2 🎧 Listen to an emergency ambulance call-out. Compare your answers to **1** with what you hear.

3 🎧 Listen again and complete this record of the telephone call.

CITY HOSPITAL
Emergency call log

Time of call: 01.26 hours

Code number: (1 = non-serious, 4 = emergency) _____ 1

Caller's number: _____ 2

Caller's name: _____ 3

Location of incident _____ 4

Type of incident: (✓) 5

☐ Fall from height

☐ RTA (Road Traffic Accident)

☐ Public transport accident

☐ Fire

☐ Assault

☐ Self-harm (accidental and intentional)

☐ Illness unknown

☐ Obstetric

INFORMATION ABOUT VICTIMS

Number of injured: _____ 6

Extent of injuries:

Patient 1 _____ 7   Patient 2 _____ 8

Toxic or inflammatory materials involved in incident _____ 9

4 Discuss what is an emergency and what isn't. (Think of examples of when someone should call for an ambulance and when they should not.)

Vocabulary

Abbreviations

1 Use the abbreviations key to read the information sent to the ambulance paramedics in *Listening*.

AMBO	ambulance
AMI	acute myocardial infarction (heart attack)
ATA	actual time of arrival
BHT	blunt head trauma
C	critical
Cat	category
CPR	cardiopulmonary resuscitation
CVA	cerebrovascular accident (stroke)
DoA	dead on arrival
Dx	diagnosis
ETA	estimated time of arrival
Fx	fracture
ICU	Intensive Care Unit
N/A	not appropriate
pos	possible
pt	patient
RTA	Road Traffic Accident
SHO	Senior House Officer
S/N	Staff Nurse
UNK	unknown

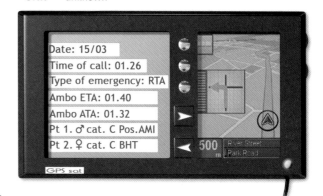

Date: 15/03
Time of call: 01.26
Type of emergency: RTA
Ambo ETA: 01.40
Ambo ATA: 01.32
Pt 1. ♂ cat. C Pos.AMI
Pt 2. ♀ cat. C BHT
500 m   River Street / Park Road
GPS sat

2 Complete this written version using full words.

The ambulance was called out on the fifteenth of March at _____ 1 to a serious _____ 2 after someone had made an emergency call. A tanker carrying petrol had crashed into the wall of a shop. The ambulance's _____ 3 was 1.40 a.m. but its _____ 4 was earlier.

There were two casualties. _____ 5 was a male. He was not moving and possibly suffering an _____ 6. He was categorized _____ 7. _____ 8 was a female. Blood from her head indicated that she was suffering a _____ 9.

A **pulse oximeter** is a probe attached to a patient's finger or ear lobe and linked to a small computer. It displays the percentage of oxygen in the patient's haemoglobin, gives a beep for each pulse beat, and calculates heart rate.

In what situation(s) would a pulse oximeter be unreliable?

Tests

Triage assessment

1 Complete the description of triage categories with the words and phrases below.

a grave	e satisfactory
b immediately threatened	f seriously impaired
c inappropriate	g stable
d life-threatening	h worsening

Critical (cannot wait)
Patient is dying or in a _____[1] condition
A very _____[2] situation that requires top priority

Urgent (see within thirty minutes)
Acute disorders, but patient is in a _____[3] condition at the moment
Requires attention soon or risks _____[4] body functions and parts

Semi-urgent (see within one hour)
Suffering from minor illnesses, but life is not _____[5]
Will need to re-triage later in case of _____[6] condition

Non-urgent (discharge)
_____[7] condition which does not present cause for concern
_____[8] attendance in emergency department

2 Use the triage categories in **1** to classify these patients who are all in A&E at the same time.

1 Male found lying face-up on the pavement. Not able to speak. No bleeding. Vomited in ambulance several times. Deeply unconscious
2 Woman (30s) 'splitting' headache after party the previous day
3 Boy (15), arm very twisted and out of shape. No pain, but numbness
4 Woman (20s) has taken ten paracetamol. Very depressed and tearful
5 Man (20s) black eye after a fight, alcohol intoxication
6 Child requiring inoculation
7 Female (50s) overweight, drove to hospital, severe pains in chest that come and go, breathlessness, back pain
8 Elderly woman (90s) chief complaint: constipation – abdominal pains for several hours

● Language spot

Narrative tenses

1 Match sentences a–h with descriptions 1–4.

a It**'s crashed** into a shop.
b There **was** this terrible noise.
c A tanker carrying petrol **had crashed** into the wall of a shop.
d He **was not moving**.
e Blood from her head indicated that she **was suffering** a …
f A wall **has fallen** on her.
g The emergency call **was timed** at 1.26 a.m.
h … someone **had made** an emergency call.

1 A past event that is still relevant now
2 A complete event in the past
3 Something in progress at a point in the past
4 An event before a point in the past

2 Underline the correct form of the verb.

1 When the ambulance arrived, he *had already taken / already took* twelve painkillers.
2 She *had / has had / was having* a baby last year.
3 He *saw / has seen* fifteen patients already, and it's only ten o'clock.
4 The family *were sitting / sat / have sat* around his bed when he woke up.
5 He recovered consciousness on Tuesday, but for the previous two days everyone *has been / had been / were* really worried.
6 The pain *has spread / spread* to my arms, and I thought I was having a heart attack.
7 The man *has woken up / woke up / was waking up* and is asking where he is.
8 The emergency call *had made / was made* and the ambulance sent to the scene of the accident.

>> Go to **Grammar reference** p.116

A triage nurse usually assigns each patient with a **chief complaint** rather than a diagnosis.

Which of the following is a **chief complaint**?

a loss of consciousness

b overdose

c stable condition

Writing
Accident report

1 🎧 Listen to a police officer talk to a nurse about the RTA in *Listening*. Take notes about what happened.

2 Write a report about the accident. Describe what happened (draw a diagram if necessary).

Include in the report your own opinion about whether or not the driver should have been driving. Say what, if anything, could have been done to avoid the accident. Make recommendations for what should be done to reduce the number of RTAs in your country.

It's my job

1 Without looking at the list of abbreviations in *Vocabulary* on p.5, say which of these abbreviations are medical problems and which are medical staff.

Fx   SHO   S/N   CVA

2 Read the text and answer the questions.

1 Why does Heidi not mind the stress of her job?
2 Why is 'triage nurse' a suitable job title?
3 What is Heidi's rank?
4 What is the A&E doctor's rank?
5 What does Heidi like best about the job?
6 Why will the patient with the eye problem not be keeping his medicines in his desk drawer in future?

3 Have you heard any stories of strange or stupid accidents and emergencies? Tell your partner.

Heidi Vettraino

A repetitive job is my idea of a nightmare, which is why I work in A&E. It's stressful, sometimes shocking, and often very upsetting, but I wouldn't change it for anything.

I specialize in emergency triage. 'Triage' means sorting and that's what I do. I sort out patients in A&E according to the nature and severity of their illness so that the doctors see the most severe cases first and we don't waste precious time on non-emergencies. You could say that's like specializing in everything. You don't know what's going to pop up next – it could be an accident with multiple fx, a sick baby, or a CVA. The day before yesterday a farming accident came in – a man had cut his hand off with a chainsaw. When the ambulance brought the patient in, he was haemorrhaging badly and we had to open up an airway and get him on a ventilator immediately. He's OK. He's in ICU, but not on the critical list any more. That was the same day a woman came in complaining of terrible pain in her feet. I was the S/N on duty and I categorized her as a non-emergency. She sat waiting for four hours before finally seeing the SHO. You'll never guess what the problem was. Her shoes were too tight!

The best thing about A&E work is the people you work with. Everyone pulls together, we're all equal, and everyone shares the same sense of humour, which is essential. Sometimes you've got to see the funny side or give up all hope for human beings. Last week, for example, an ambulance brought a man in who was unable to open his eyes. Being short-sighted, he had reached for his eye drops and didn't see that he had picked up a tube of superglue instead. Poor man! We bathed his eyes for an hour and very slowly separated his eyelids. He was able to laugh about it with the A&E staff afterwards, but in the future he won't be keeping his medicines in his desk drawer.

In 1917, an Australian outback farmer seriously injured himself in a fall. Because the nearest doctor was 3,000 km away, the local postmaster operated on the farmer's bladder using a penknife whilst receiving Morse code instructions by telegraph. The patient survived the operation, but not the journey to hospital later.

What famous Australian medical service was created because of incidents like this?

Reading

Air ambulance

1 Discuss with a partner the advantages of air ambulances like the one in the picture.

2 Read the text and compare your ideas with what the article says.

3 Read the text again and choose the correct answer.

1 The idea of an air ambulance came from the need to
   a limit a patient's movements
   b move treatment fast to sick people
   c move patients fast but gently.

2 Letting wounded soldiers die is
   a cheaper than evacuating them by helicopter
   b economically necessary
   c inefficient.

3 The first medical rescue by helicopter was
   a a response to an accident
   b a military exercise
   c after a battle.

4 The equipment in a Sikorsky YR-4 helicopter is
   a elementary
   b sophisticated
   c complex.

5 The main problem for helicopter pilots is that they
   a cannot see where they are flying
   b cannot fly when they cannot see
   c cannot use VFR.

6 Air ambulances are best employed for patients who
   a are non-emergencies
   b will probably die
   c may live.

RESCUE FROM THE AIR

When you cannot move treatment fast to sick people, you have to move sick people fast to treatment. The problem is that when someone is severely injured, movement can kill and so anything that can both speed up the journey and minimize the shock is a life-saver. This is why, over a hundred years ago, a long time before the development of aircraft, someone came up with a design for an 'air ambulance'. The idea was to put wounded people on a stretcher which was held in the air by balloons and pulled along by horses.

Warfare has encouraged progress in ambulance technology. It is expensive and wasteful to let soldiers die on a battlefield and saving their lives justifies the expense of using aircraft (particularly helicopters) to transport casualties to hospital. In fact, the first time a helicopter was used for a medical rescue was in Burma in 1945 by the American military. A soldier on a jungle-covered mountain accidentally shot himself with a machine gun. There were no medics and the area was so wild that it would have taken ten days for a rescue party to reach the wounded man. A Sikorsky YR-4 helicopter – very basic by modern standards – was sent out. It had no radio and navigated by flying low over the treetops, but the pilot completed his mission and the soldier's life was saved.

Even today, helicopters are limited by weather and darkness. Unlike aeroplanes, which have radar and computers, many helicopters have only essential flight equipment and pilots have to fly VFR (Visual Flight Rules) which means they can only fly when they can see. However, the great value of a helicopter is that it can land and take off vertically and provide speed and comfort, which are not luxuries when it comes to saving lives and a helicopter can make a huge difference in a rural area where response time is normally slow. Air ambulances can increase the chances of survival of patients whose injuries are severe but survivable; an important factor to consider when sending one out.

Speaking

Triage dilemmas

Work in pairs. Read the scenarios and answer the questions. Then compare your opinions and decisions with other students in your class.

1 You are about to save a patient's life with a large dose of a scarce drug – the patient will *certainly* die without it. It is the only supply of the drug that the hospital has. Suddenly three more patients are brought in to A&E. Each one needs one third of the drug and without it they will *probably* (though not definitely) die. Who should have the drug?

2 The ICU is full, but there is one patient who is relatively stable though still requiring ICU for optimum care. A new patient is brought in. These are his notes.

CLINICAL RECORDS

Patient: 32-year-old man
Dx: meningitis
Presenting symptoms: unconscious, extremely low blood pressure, evidence of renal failure. Grave condition – urgently requires intensive care

---

There is a bed in an ICU in another hospital 80 kilometres away but moving a patient from an ICU early increases risk of complications and death. Should you transfer the new patient to the other hospital or move the existing patient out of ICU?

3 In a high-speed car chase, a criminal crashes into a police car. The police officer suffers a fractured femur. The criminal hits the windscreen with his head – a serious BHT. The air ambulance has room for one. Who should it be?

Project

Research one of the following subjects and give a short presentation to the other students.

- START (Simple Triage And Rapid Treatment)
- advanced triage
- what to do when there are mass casualties
- battlefield triage

Checklist

Assess your progress in this unit. Tick (✓) the statements which are true.

- I can name emergency equipment
- I can understand some medical abbreviations
- I can complete a written report about an emergency call-out
- I can discuss triage

Key words

Adjectives
blunt
critical
grave
optimum
semi-urgent
stable
survivable

Nouns
casualty
complaint
ramp
self-harm
stress
witness

Verbs
collapse
haemorrhage

Look back through this unit. Find five more words or expressions that you think are useful.

2 Admission by referral

Scrub up

1 Read the ward notice and say if you think the rules are good ones.

> ### NOTICE TO PATIENTS
>
> We want to make your stay on the ward as pleasant as possible and we believe that every patient is an important individual regardless of race, religion, or age.
>
> **However, all patients must obey the following rules:**
>
> - No pets are allowed within the hospital
> - No smoking anywhere in the hospital
> - No alcohol
> - Visitors are only allowed during visiting hours (6.30 p.m. – 8.30 p.m.) unless on children's ward (under the age of 12)
> - No excessive noise
> - No mains-powered electrical equipment

2 Decide if it is fair to make these patients obey the hospital rules.

Frances has terminal cancer and is expected to live only a few weeks. There is no one to take care of her at home and her pet cat Billy is the most important thing in her life.

Dave is thirteen and is in hospital for about a month. The most important things in his life (in order of importance) are: his girlfriend, who he is in love with, his electric guitar, and his mates.

Pierre needs to smoke (he *has* tried several times to give up) and if he doesn't have a drink, he shakes, sweats, and is sick. He is in hospital for treatment unrelated to his addictions.

Vocabulary

Collocations

1 Join the words to make collocations.

1	dietary	a	care
2	hearing	b	consent
3	informed	c	difficulties
4	medical	d	effects
5	overnight	e	examination
6	physical	f	history
7	presenting	g	infection
8	round-the-clock	h	requirements
9	side	i	stay
10	wound	j	symptoms

2 Complete this case history with collocations from **1**.

Mr Aguilera injured himself with a saw and five days later went to his doctor with _____¹ of jaw discomfort. It is more than ten years since his last tetanus booster and the patient has no significant _____². There were also no significant findings from a _____³ of head and neck and his lungs were clear.

The diagnosis was 'tetanus with secondary _____⁴' so the wound was cleaned and hydrogen peroxide applied. The patient's doctor referred him for an _____⁵ in hospital for observation.

After the treatment was explained to him, the patient signed a form which gave his _____⁶ and he was then given anti-tetanus immunoglobulin. He responded well and there were no _____⁷ or complications. The patient said that because he was a vegetarian, he had special _____⁸ and could not eat hospital food. Also, he lived with his mother who is severely disabled, with _____⁹, and needs _____¹⁰. Mr Aguilera asked to be discharged and Dr Hashim gave his authorization.

In this unit
- getting information politely
- getting informed consent
- reporting what patients say
- understanding a letter of referral

Patient care

Polite phrases

Replace each underlined phrase in the dialogue with an alternative polite phrase from the list.

would you mind if I asked you to ___

it's important to know about ___

can you tell me how you are ___

could you tell me if you take ___

I'm sorry, I can't remember _1_

I need to know if you have ___

can you let me have ___

I'd like to check ___

may I ask why ___

I have to ask ___

Nurse	I've forgotten[1] your name.
Mrs Stein	It's Mrs Stein.
Nurse	Of course, Mrs Stein. Give me[2] your letter of referral.
Mrs Stein	Here it is.
Nurse	Thanks. So, Mrs Stein, you've come in for removal of varicose veins?
Mrs Stein	Yes. The operation is this afternoon.
Nurse	Confirm[3] one or two things. First, are you on[4] any medications?
Mrs Stein	Yes, I take Venlafaxine.
Nurse	What for[5]?
Mrs Stein	I take it for depression.
Nurse	OK. Now, tell me[6] about your lifestyle. Report[7] any alcohol or drug problems you have.
Mrs Stein	None, I don't drink and I don't take drugs.
Nurse	Also, tell me if you have[8] had any contact with HIV in the past six months.
Mrs Stein	I haven't had any contact with HIV, no.
Nurse	Fine, and who's[9] paying for treatment?
Mrs Stein	I'm covered by medical insurance.
Nurse	Great, and lastly, you must[10] take off your make-up and your rings.

Listening

Getting verbal consent

1 Work in pairs. Discuss these questions.

1 When is it necessary to get a patient's verbal 'informed consent'?
2 When should a patient sign a consent form and when is it not necessary?
3 Listening to a heart beat through a stethoscope is a medical procedure – does this need the patient's informed consent?

2 Listen to nurses informing four different patients about medical procedures. Identify which nurse (a–d) is

1 listing the possible risks of a procedure   ___
2 describing alternatives to a procedure   ___
3 explaining the possible benefits of a procedure   ___
4 getting agreement with the patient.   ___

3 Listen again. In which situation (a–d) is the nurse talking to

1 a patient who has a melanoma?   ___
2 a patient who has been in an accident?   ___
3 a patient who has psychiatric problems?   ___
4 a patient who is going to have major surgery?   ___

4 Discuss this situation with a partner.

A 64-year-old woman with MS is admitted. The doctor thinks she should be placed on a feeding tube. In the morning the patient is confused. A nurse talks to her about the feeding tube and she consents. However, later in the day when the tube is going to be placed, the patient says she doesn't want it in.

The following morning, the patient is vague and the nurse tries once more and again the patient consents to the procedure.

Is the patient able to decide? Should the nurse place the feeding tube or not?

Hippocrates, the 'father of medicine', would not have agreed with the idea of 'consenting to treatment'. He thought that giving information to patients was harmful, and advised doctors to 'conceal most things from patients, turn their attention away from what is being done to them, and reveal nothing of their future or present condition.'

Do you think there are ever times when it is necessary to lie to patients or not tell them certain things?

Speaking

Getting a patient's informed consent

Work in pairs. Student A, you have been suffering chest pains on and off for the past three months. You don't know what's wrong and the recommended test is cardiac catheterization. Go to p.110, where you will read about details of yourself as well as your doubts about this test.

Student B, you are a nurse. You must first check that the information you have about the patient below is complete and correct. Then you must give the patient information about cardiac catheterization and answer any questions before getting consent for the procedure. Information about the test is on p.112.

The consent form must be fully understood and agreed before it is signed.

CITY HOSPITAL
Patient's details

Name:

Age:

Address:

Family history: Father has heart disease

Patient's medical history: Childhood asthma. Appendectomy at age 18. Non-smoker

---

CONSENT FOR MEDICAL AND SURGICAL PROCEDURES

I have been given full information about my condition. I understand why cardiac catheterization is the recommended procedure and what the alternatives are. I understand what the procedure is and that it involves risks.

I authorize this procedure to be performed.

Signature of patient

● Language spot

Reported speech

1 Study the cartoons and complete the dialogues.

1 **Present tense reporting**

Nurse	Dr Weston says she's sending a patient for observation.
Ward manager	We have a bed available.
Nurse	The ward manager says they _____ [a].
Dr Weston	Good, thank you. I suspect he has concussion.
Sarah	The doctor says _____ [b].

2 **Past tense reporting**

The next day

Nurse	Last night she told me she was in pain.
Doctor	Where did she have the pain?
Nurse	_____ [a] in her chest.
Doctor	How bad was it?
Nurse	_____ [b] unbearable.
Doctor	Were there any other symptoms?
Nurse	Yes, _____ [c] stomach-ache as well.

My consultant once took a man who had been complaining about waiting to the resuscitation room and showed him five beds full of five exceedingly ill patients, and demanded to know: 'Which of these five people would you like me to boot out so we can urgently deal with the lump on your wrist?'

Dr Michael Foxton *Confessions of a Junior Doctor*

3 **Reporting *yes* / *no* questions**

11.00

Nurse	He asked if I could help him get out of bed.
Doctor	I see. Did he ask for any more help?
Nurse	Yes, he asked me _____ ᵃ get dressed.
Doctor	I see, and then?
Nurse	He asked me _____ ᵇ open a bottle of medicine.

4 **Reporting *wh-* questions**

4.00

Patient	He asked me what my date of birth was.
Visitor	Did he? What else did he ask you?
Patient	He asked me where _____ ᵃ.
Visitor	So you told him your address. Anything else?
Patient	Yes, he asked me when _____ ᵇ. I told him that I first became ill in July.

2 🎧 Listen to a patient giving information on admission to hospital. Take notes of what the patient says and write a report using reported speech.

The first sentence of the report is given as an example.

> The patient said her name was Akiko Tanaka and that she was 23. She said that ...

≫ Go to **Grammar reference** p.117

Signs and symptoms

General symptoms

Complete the sentences by forming an adjective from the noun in brackets.

1 The bandages were all _____ (blood) and needed changing.
2 He felt _____ (nausea) from the medication.
3 Her finger was _____ (swelling) and sore.
4 After her husband's death, she became _____ (apathy) and lost all interest in life.
5 An _____ (infection) wound is dangerous.
6 If your child is _____ (fever), take him to a doctor immediately.
7 Yes, it's _____ (pain) when I cough.
8 I have a _____ (burn) sensation when I go to the toilet.
9 People with _____ (phobia) disorders have irrational fears.
10 You must not scratch it even if it feels _____ (itch).

Hand-held computers

These are now in common use in hospitals. Although they can be used for recording progress and procedures performed on patients, a survey in 2004 showed that almost no medical staff used them for that purpose. They did, however, use them to get information on drug dosages, formulae, and practice guidelines.

Do you use them? Do they have disadvantages as well as advantages?

Reading

Letter of referral

1 Work in pairs. Discuss what you would expect to read in a letter from a GP when referring a patient to a specialist at a hospital.

2 Read the referral letter and check your answers.

3 Which of these problems does the patient definitely suffer from?

asthma	nervousness
depression	obesity
heart disease	poisoning
HIV	suicidal tendencies
irregular heartbeat	

4 Use the information in the letter to complete this admission form.

CITY HOSPITAL
Admission form

Name of patient: _____ ¹ Age _____ ²

Siblings: _____³

Relevant family medical history:

_____ 4

Purpose of referral:

_____ 5

Presenting symptoms:

_____ 6

Other symptoms and conditions:

_____ 7

BMI: _____ 8

Past treatments:

_____ 9

Present medication:

_____ 10

Beeches Medical Practice
Market Lane, Midtown, Sussex SR5 7JU

13th May **My ref** EAPM/RH

Re patient: Michael Marcuccilli, 21 years of age

To: Dr J.K. Nayar

I am referring this patient to you for assessment. He is suffering from attacks of palpitations and breathlessness.

The patient is a student. He has suffered from anxiety since he was thirteen. He told me that when he was a child, he was very afraid that his parents would die.

He came to see me six months ago. He expressed fears about having heart disease. These fears are based on the fact that both his brothers and his father have heart conditions.

When things are going badly, he eats too much. Consequently he is overweight with a BMI of 32, which partly explains his breathlessness. Urine analysis indicates the onset of type 2 diabetes. He said that he had gained weight recently as a result of the shock of losing his part-time job. It brought on severe palpitations, hyperventilation, and panic attacks and he had to be sedated.

He believes he was 'stupid' to become engaged to his girlfriend because she has emotional and personality problems. He regrets this relationship and they have frequent rows which make his symptoms worse.

In the past the patient has been treated with the antidepressant Lofepramine even though there are no clear symptoms of depression. It is possible that weight gain and tiredness are side effects of the antidepressants so I have advised him to stop taking them.

Other physical symptoms include joint pains, chest pains, muscle pains, and dizziness. He told me that he has morbid thoughts, but I do not think he has suicidal intentions.

He is receiving Diazepam 2 mg t.d.s. for anxiety. Because he has a history of asthma, I have not tried beta blockers.

Yours sincerely

R O'Brien

Dr. R. T. O'Brien

5 Decide with a partner where to send the patient – the coronary unit, the psychiatric unit, the renal unit, weight loss and exercise classes, or home.

Checklist

Assess your progress in this unit. Tick (✓) the statements which are true.

I can get information politely

I can obtain informed consent

I can report what patients say

I can understand a letter of referral

Writing

An email requesting information

Read the following scenario.

A female head injury patient is transferred from another hospital to an ICU at your hospital. In the process, her records have disappeared. She is very ill and unable to communicate.

Write an urgent email to Dr Van Rijn at the other hospital explaining the situation and requesting information about the patient: personal details, medical history, family details, and history of the presenting problem.

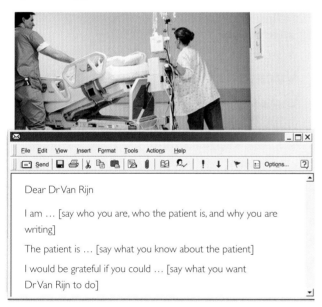

Dear Dr Van Rijn

I am … [say who you are, who the patient is, and why you are writing]

The patient is … [say what you know about the patient]

I would be grateful if you could … [say what you want Dr Van Rijn to do]

Key words

Adjectives
apathetic
compulsory
dietary
feverish
harmful
round-the-clock
significant

Nouns
authorization
breathlessness
consent
palpitations
presenting symptoms
referral
tendency

Verb
sedate

Look back through this unit. Find five more words or expressions that you think are useful.

Project

Research one of these issues and report back to the rest of the class, giving statistics.

- deaths from medical errors
- emergency admissions compared with planned admissions for adults and children
- most common reasons for admitting children to hospital
- most common reasons for hospital admissions in your country
- compulsory admission to hospital
- admissions because of physical violence

3 Obstetrics

Scrub up

1 Work in pairs. Find the following features in the pictures. Write a–j.

1 amniotic fluid _____
2 cell division _____
3 embryo _____
4 fertilization _____
5 foetus _____
6 ovum _____
7 amniotic sac _____
8 sperm _____
9 umbilical cord _____
10 cervix _____

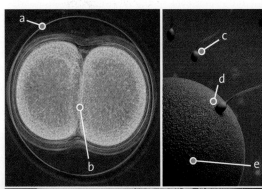

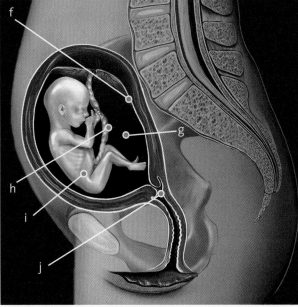

2 Describe what is happening in each picture.

3 Discuss at what stages of pregnancy you think the following events happen. For each one, choose a number of weeks from those below.

number of weeks: 3   7   12   18   22   34

a The lowest number of weeks at which a premature baby can survive. _____

b The foetus's fine covering of hair, called lanugo, begins to disappear. _____

c Arm buds and a tail are visible. _____

d The embryo measures 30 mm in length. _____

e Male and female genitals appear well differentiated. _____

f The foetal heartbeat can be heard with a stethoscope. _____

Vocabulary

Verbs for pregnancy and childbirth

1 Read Marie's birth story quickly. What complication was there with her birth?

We started *trying for / making*[1] a baby three years ago. When I didn't *get / go*[2] pregnant after two years, we *made / had*[3] tests, which showed that my husband had a low sperm count. We had IVF, and six weeks later I found I was *waiting for / expecting*[4] a baby. I was nervous when I *had / did*[5] my scan at twelve weeks, but everything was fine.

My waters broke in the middle of the night and I *went into / entered*[6] labour a couple of hours later. The midwife *made / did*[7] a vaginal examination and found that the baby was breech. I'd thought about a home birth, but was now glad I was *having / giving*[8] birth in hospital. As it turned out, though, the medical team weren't needed. The midwife *made / put*[9] a small cut and I managed to *push out / remove*[10] the baby's legs and torso fairly easily – it was a girl! Then I *made / gave*[11] a big push and the head came out. Lilia *gave birth / was born*[12] at 6.28 p.m. I was sobbing as the midwife *handed / delivered*[13] her to me.

2 Underline the correct form of the verbs in *italics*.

3 Tell a true story about a pregnancy and birth.

Listening

From pregnancy to birth

1 🎧 Listen to five short conversations between the midwife and Hannah, a first-time mother. Decide whether each one takes place

  1 pre-birth   2 during birth   3 after birth.

  a _____   c _____   e _____

  b _____   d _____

2 Compare your answers in pairs. Say what clues you heard.

3 🎧 Complete the sentences with the words below. Then listen again and check.

a miscarriage	dilated	forceps
an epidural	induce	presentation
birth plan	gas and air	
contractions	waters	

  1 My _____ broke last night, and I started getting strong _____ early this morning.

  2 Well, you're seven centimetres _____ now, so I don't think we'll need to _____ you.

  3 Now, on your _____ you've said you'd like _____ as pain relief, yes?

  4 Yes, but if I can't bear the pain, I'd like _____.

  5 That's normal when _____ are used.

  6 I've had _____ before, so they thought I should have a scan.

  7 The baby's _____ is perfect, with the head down.

It's my job

1 Before you read the interview, guess the answers to these questions.

  1 When does Nicky feel extremely happy?
  2 What makes her feel awful?
  3 In what ways does Nicky prepare women for birth in her weekly antenatal classes?

2 Read the text and see which of your guesses match what Nicky says.

3 Discuss with a partner whether you would like to do Nicky's job. Explain your reasons.

Nicky Cox

Q What do you enjoy about being a community midwife?

A The job has great highs. After I have delivered a baby, I often feel elated. I've smiled to myself on many occasions and thought, 'And I'm getting paid to do this!' It has its downsides too, though. When a birth doesn't go to plan, say, it is very prolonged and the heart monitor shows the baby is in distress, it can be very stressful. And of course – very, very rarely, thankfully – when there is a stillbirth or a baby is born with a deformity, it makes you feel awful for days or even weeks.

Q What are the qualities of a good midwife?

A Number one is people skills. Of course you need a lot of knowledge, but perhaps more than any other nursing job, a midwife must be good at getting on with people. When a woman gives birth, she feels very vulnerable and at the same time, it is an intensely personal experience you are sharing with her. I try to develop a strong relationship with my mothers during pregnancy when they come for their ultrasounds and physical examinations.

Q What are your views on a natural birth at home?

A It's all about choosing the right type of birth for you. I think giving birth without pain-controlling drugs in the comfort and familiar surroundings of your own home can be a wonderful experience. But my job is to explain objectively to each woman her options and let her decide. I run a weekly antenatal class for parents-to-be in which I explain the ins and outs of hospital birth, home birth, and water birth, as well as covering issues such as breastfeeding, the mother's diet during pregnancy, and how the father can help during labour.

The highest national birth rate is 49, in Niger.

● What does this mean?
● Guess which country has the lowest birth rate.
● How many babies do you think were born in the world today?

In 1972, the fertility rate worldwide was six children per woman. What do you think it is now?

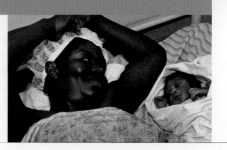

● Language spot

Modals and expressions for giving advice

1 🎧 Listen to Emma, a midwife, getting advice from another midwife and from a doctor. Answer these questions with a partner.

1 Why is Emma worried about Mrs Dent's baby?
2 What does Nina advise Emma to do?
3 How often does the doctor advise her to monitor?
4 What measurement does he suggest taking?
5 What three things does the doctor suggest to raise the baby's heart rate?

2 🎧 Work in pairs. Try to remember the missing words. Then listen again and check.

1 I think you **ought to** _____ the doctor.
2 **It's** always **a good idea to** _____ help if you're concerned.
3 **You'd better** _____ continuously from now on …
4 **I'd** _____ Mrs Dent some oxygen too – that won't do any harm.
5 And **try** _____ her to lie on her left side too.
6 If it's a little slow, but over 100, **you may want to** _____ about amnioinfusion …

3 Two of the **bold** verbs and expressions are only used to give strong and urgent advice, while the others can be used for more general or polite advice. Which are the strong two?

>> Go to **Grammar reference** p.117

4 Complete the conversation with the words below.

'd	may	should
better	oughtn't	try

Nurse Any problems, Marian?

Marian I had a bit of bleeding after my aerobics class. I thought maybe I'd _____[1] stop exercising.

Nurse Well, it's a good idea to exercise, but you _____[2] to do aerobics if it causes bleeding. You _____[3] want to try swimming, or something gentle like that.

Marian I know. I _____[4] buy myself a swimming costume. Another thing is, I can't get comfortable at night.

Nurse _____[5] putting a pillow underneath you – that should help.

Marian OK – I'll try that. I'm also a bit worried about these stretch marks on my tummy.

Nurse I _____[6] rub cream or oil into it – that's very good for stretch marks.

Marian Oh, right. I'll get some today.

5 Work in pairs. Discuss what you could do to help these problems in pregnancy.

● backache
● constipation
● indigestion
● insomnia
● spots on the face
● swollen ankles

Pronunciation

a, e, and i

1 Work in pairs. Decide which pronunciation the **bold** vowel in each word has.

a	e	i
/a/	/e/	/ɪ/
pathogen	benefits	visible
/ei/	/i:/	/aɪ/
patient	prenatal	survive
~~pathogen~~	~~benefits~~	~~visible~~
~~patient~~	~~prenatal~~	~~survive~~
basal	frequency	dilated
labour	genitals	jaundice
national	medical	umbilical
perinatal	stethoscope	vagina

2 🎧 Listen and check.

3 Look through the glossary with your partner. Find a word for each of the six columns above. Dictate your words to another pair.

forceps and **ventouse**

devices for gently pulling the baby's head to assist with difficult births. The **forceps** grip the sides of the head, and the **ventouse** attaches to the top of the head by suction.

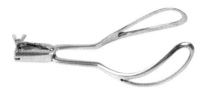

Reading

Advice for pregnant women

1 Without looking at the text, tick (✓) the things you think are safe in pregnancy. Put a cross (✗) next to the things you think are not safe, and a question mark (?) if it depends on the situation. Compare your answers with a partner.

	your opinion	advice in text
1 a lot of calcium		
2 a lot of tuna		
3 folic acid tablets		
4 four cups of tea a day		
5 gardening		
6 hard cheese, such as cheddar		
7 herbal medicines		
8 immunization against chickenpox		
9 liver		
10 one small glass of red wine a day		

2 Read the text, and put a tick, cross, or question mark according to the advice it gives.

3 Find words in the text that match the definitions.

1 a liver disease
2 two sexually-transmitted diseases
3 a metal that is poisonous in large amounts
4 three conditions caused by allergy
5 illegal drugs
6 drugs sold in a chemist's

4 Discuss the questions with a partner.

- Did any of the advice surprise you?
- Do you know of any other advice that is not included here?
- In your country, what foods do pregnant women
  - eat to help their baby develop healthily?
  - avoid?

Project

Choose one of the conditions below. Research how it is caused or transmitted, and its effects on a foetus or newborn baby.

- HIV
- spina bifida
- syphilis
- toxoplasmosis

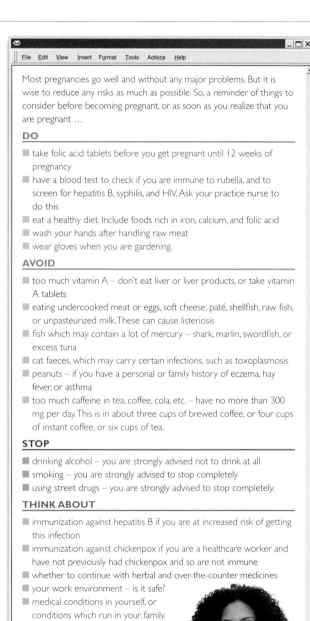

Most pregnancies go well and without any major problems. But it is wise to reduce any risks as much as possible. So, a reminder of things to consider before becoming pregnant, or as soon as you realize that you are pregnant …

DO

- take folic acid tablets before you get pregnant until 12 weeks of pregnancy
- have a blood test to check if you are immune to rubella, and to screen for hepatitis B, syphilis, and HIV. Ask your practice nurse to do this
- eat a healthy diet. Include foods rich in iron, calcium, and folic acid
- wash your hands after handling raw meat
- wear gloves when you are gardening.

AVOID

- too much vitamin A – don't eat liver or liver products, or take vitamin A tablets
- eating undercooked meat or eggs, soft cheese, paté, shellfish, raw fish, or unpasteurized milk. These can cause listeriosis
- fish which may contain a lot of mercury – shark, marlin, swordfish, or excess tuna
- cat faeces, which may carry certain infections, such as toxoplasmosis
- peanuts – if you have a personal or family history of eczema, hay fever, or asthma
- too much caffeine in tea, coffee, cola, etc. – have no more than 300 mg per day. This is in about three cups of brewed coffee, or four cups of instant coffee, or six cups of tea.

STOP

- drinking alcohol – you are strongly advised not to drink at all
- smoking – you are strongly advised to stop completely
- using street drugs – you are strongly advised to stop completely.

THINK ABOUT

- immunization against hepatitis B if you are at increased risk of getting this infection
- immunization against chickenpox if you are a healthcare worker and have not previously had chickenpox and so are not immune
- whether to continue with herbal and over-the-counter medicines
- your work environment – is it safe?
- medical conditions in yourself, or conditions which run in your family.

Igor Charkovsky ran pioneering 'birth camps' in the Black Sea from the 1960s. He believes that humans' ancestors lived mainly in water, and that it is unnatural and harmful to be born out of water. What do you think?

In the UK, 98% of births take place in hospital. Is the situation similar in your country?

Signs and symptoms
Pregnancy and labour

1 A pattern of signs often alerts a woman that she may be pregnant. A different pattern of signs occurs when labour begins at the end of the pregnancy. Work in pairs to complete the list of signs using the words below.

bloating	morning	pelvis
contractions	mucus	rupture
discharge	need	strength
fatigue	nipple	temperature
mood	~~period~~	trembling

1 You will miss a menstrual _period_.   _P_

2 False, 'Braxton Hicks' _____ occur.   ___

3 _____ and sleepiness are common.   ___

4 Contractions become more rhythmic and increase in _____.   ___

5 Some women feel abdominal _____.   ___

6 _____ swings and stress are often reported.   ___

7 You notice an increase in pink or white _____.   ___

8 You may experience _____ sickness.   ___

9 Your basal body _____ will be elevated. ___

10 There may be a 'show', which is the release of a _____ plug from the cervix.   ___

11 You may feel the _____ to urinate frequently.   ___

12 The baby's head engages – that is, it lowers into the _____.   ___

13 It is common for the area around the _____ to darken.   ___

14 Shivering or _____ without reason is common.   ___

15 Your waters break, which is the _____ of the amniotic sac.   ___

2 Decide if each sign in **1** indicates pregnancy or labour. Write *P* (pregnancy) or *L* (labour).

Speaking
Discussion for and against

1 Work in two groups. Read the sentences below. Group A, think of arguments *in favour of* the statements. Group B, think of arguments *against* the statements. Then join with the other group to discuss the statements.

- Couples should have the right to know the sex of their baby.
- There should be an age limit for fertility treatment for women.
- The best age to have children is 20–25.
- Schools should teach baby care.

2 Now read these sentences. Group B, think of arguments *in favour*. Group A, think of arguments *against*.

- Mothers should be allowed to choose whether or not to have a Caesarean.
- All foetuses should be tested for conditions such as Down syndrome and spina bifida.
- Women should be left to decide for themselves whether to breastfeed or bottle-feed.
- Abortions should be allowed up to twenty weeks.

Writing
Discursive essay

1 Read the essay on the advantages and disadvantages of water birth. Write the letter of the paragraph where the writer makes each point below. Put a cross (✗) if the point is not included in the essay.

1 Nurses have a greater risk of infection with water births.   _C_

2 Water birth is becoming more widely available. ___

3 The mother's anxiety is reduced in water.   ___

4 Water births cause delays if emergency treatment is needed.   ___

5 Women who have given birth in water often choose to again.   ___

6 There is a risk of the baby breathing water into its lungs.   ___

7 Bleeding is difficult to monitor.   ___

8 The mother can change position more easily in water.   ___

A	Water birth is becoming increasingly popular and more and more hospitals are making this option available to women. **However**, it is important for women to be aware that there are potential problems as well as benefits before opting for a water birth.
B	The main benefit of a water birth is that it makes labour more comfortable. It is easier for the woman to move around, which gives her a feeling of control and **therefore** makes her feel more relaxed and less anxious. The reduced pain of water birth also lowers anxiety. **For this reason**, being in water lowers the blood pressure, which avoids a range of complications.
C	On the negative side, it is difficult to monitor the woman accurately during a water birth, so it is not suitable for high-risk pregnancies. **Also**, it is easier for waterborne pathogens to be transferred from mother to baby – or to medical staff. **In addition to this, although** being in water reduces the mother's pain, it can also weaken the contractions. Another drawback is the risk of hypothermia unless water temperature is carefully monitored. Finally, the risk of heavy blood loss is increased in water, **as** bleeding is difficult to measure underwater.
D	**Despite** these disadvantages, both patients and medical staff are very positive about water birth and many women opt to do it again for subsequent children. With more training and facilities, the limitations of water birth could be reduced.

2 Connectors are used to join ideas together. Write the **bold** words and phrases in the essay under the three headings.

ADD	CONTRAST	REASON
in addition	however	therefore

3 Write an essay of 200–250 words with the title *The advantages and disadvantages of home birth*. Before you begin, brainstorm ideas with a partner. Write the essay in four sections, as in the example.

A Introduction
B Advantages
C Disadvantages
D Conclusion

Checklist

Assess your progress in this unit. Tick (✓) the statements which are true.

I can describe the processes of pregnancy and birth

I can give advice using a range of verbs and expressions

I can describe the signs and symptoms of pregnancy and labour

I can write an essay about advantages and disadvantages

Key words

Pregnancy
amniotic fluid
embryo
foetus
miscarriage
placenta

Labour
contractions
dilated
rupture
waters

Birth
birth plan
breech
Caesarean
epidural
induce
presentation

Look back through this unit. Find five more words or expressions that you think are useful.

4 Pharmacy

Scrub up

1 Study these pharmaceutical products and choose the right one for each customer at the pharmacy counter.

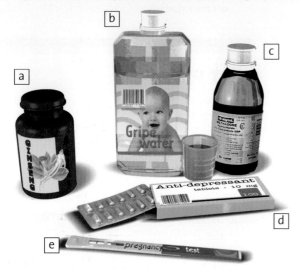

1 'They help me get through the day. Without them, life wouldn't be worth living.'

2 'The whole family suffers when she has wind. Nobody gets any sleep.'

3 'I'm late again this month. I hope it's not going to be bad news.'

4 'I don't believe in chemicals – they poison the body and mind, but I do need a pick-me-up.'

5 'I'm dealing with it and this is the only way to stop the cravings.'

2 Discuss these questions.

- Should all medicines be free?
- Can you think of any reasons why it should be illegal to sell medicines online?
- Should pharmaceutical companies be banned from aggressive advertising of new drugs and giving presents to doctors?

Vocabulary

Dosages

Complete the sentences with words from the list.

cubic centimetres	per cent
double dose	ratio
extra strength	score
half dose	teaspoon
junior strength	units
milligrams	

1 Measure out one ordinary household _____ of cough mixture.

2 If you miss one, you can catch up with a _____ later.

3 Give the child two of the new orange-flavoured, _____ aspirins.

4 He is a big man and needs an _____ analgesic.

In this unit
- units of measurement for medicine
- talking about the effects of medication
- mathematical expressions
- describing a chart

5   The drug is very strong; even just a _____ can make you drowsy.

6   Make the solution with 100 _____ of insulin.

7   Make up a suspension in a _____ of 10:1.

8   Put 3.6 _____ of the powder into a litre of water.

9   Make a 20 _____ solution with 20 grams of soluble solid and add enough water to make 100 ml.

10 The patient has a _____ of 9 on the ranking scale for reactions to drugs.

11 Use a syringe with a volume of 25 _____.

Patient care

Monitoring the effects of medication

1   Complete the dialogue using the verbs below in the correct form.

build up	react	stand
discontinue	re-evaluate	suffer
go away	renew	tolerate
notice	report	worry
put on	run out	

Nurse	I want to review your medication, Mr Thomas. How are you getting on with the new tablets?
Mr Thomas	They're a big improvement.
Nurse	Your notes say we started you on Atenolol, but you stopped taking it. Did you _____[1] badly to it?
Mr Thomas	Yes, I felt tired all the time.

Nurse	So the doctor tried something different and you were _____[2] an alternative regime. Is that right?
Mr Thomas	Yes, I was. That was Captopril. It was no good either.
Nurse	No? Did you _____[3] an allergic reaction? A lot of people _____[4] having breathing difficulties with that drug.
Mr Thomas	Yes. My mouth and throat swelled up – like I was swallowing a tennis ball.
Nurse	I see. How about the new medication? Do you _____[5] any changes in your body from taking it?
Mr Thomas	Well, yes. It is affecting my sex life.
Nurse	I see. Well, we can't ignore that. We probably need to _____[6] your medication regime and it may be necessary to _____[7] this treatment as well and think about a different one. In the meantime, how are the headaches? Do they _____[8] when you use the new painkillers?
Mr Thomas	The capsules you gave me for the headaches are great. They're very powerful and fast-acting.
Nurse	Have you _____[9] of them?
Mr Thomas	Yes. They're all gone.
Nurse	I know they are good, but people who take them _____[10] a tolerance quite quickly so they no longer work after a while. Are you able to _____[11] the headaches when they come?
Mr Thomas	Honestly, I can't, they're unbearable.
Nurse	If you can't _____[12] the pain, I think you'd better go back to the specialist before we _____[13] your prescription. I am starting to _____[14] about all these contraindications.

2   Make a list of expressions the nurse uses

1   to ask about side effects

2   to ask about medication history

3   to describe what might happen in the future.

James Lind first introduced 'control' groups into experiments in 1747. He studied sailors with scurvy. The control group was given their normal food. Other groups were given their normal food plus supplements. Lind found that the group receiving oranges and lemons recovered. What causes scurvy?

● Language spot

Mathematical expressions

1 Complete the mathematical expressions with these prepositions.

by   from   of   to

1 Five per cent _____ 50 is 2.5.

2 One teaspoon is approximately equivalent _____ 5 millilitres.

3 How much is 7.2 kg divided _____ 15?

4 Subtract 4 litres _____ 13.

5 BMI equals height divided _____ weight squared.

6 What do you get when you subtract 52 _____ 100?

7 150 mg is added _____ 500 mg to make a total dose of 650 mg.

8 Three quarters _____ 100 litres equals 75.

2 In the mathematical expressions above, identify one conversion and one formula.

3 🎧 Listen and match what you hear with the sums written below. Write a–h. Each sum has two spoken versions.

1 3 mg + 6 mg = 9   ___ ___

2 $\dfrac{36\ ml}{4\ ml} = 9$ ___ ___

3 13 litres – 4 litres = 9   ___ ___

4 3 mg x 3 mg = 9   ___ ___

4 🎧 Listen and write what you hear in numbers and symbols.

a _____   e _____

b _____   f _____

c _____   g _____

d _____   h _____

5 Work in pairs. Read aloud mathematical expressions for your partner to write down in numbers and symbols.

Student A, go to p.110.

Student B, go to p.113.

≫ Go to **Grammar reference** p.118

Reading

Drugs testing

1 Do this questionnaire on attitudes to drugs testing and compare your responses with other students.

	strongly agree	agree	disagree	strongly disagree
Testing drugs on animals is unnecessary and wrong.				
Before testing them on others, researchers should test new drugs on themselves.				
Scientific progress is more important than the lives of a few people.				

2 Read the text and answer the questions.

1 One reason why there is a constant need to develop new drugs is because new illnesses are appearing all the time. What are three other reasons?

2 In a clinical trial, first the drugs are tested on animals. What are the next two main steps?

3 What is the basis of the Nuremberg code?

4 Which two groups of people may not always be able to make a free choice over participating in clinical trials?

5 There are risks for sick people participating in clinical trials, but what are the benefits?

6 What ethical problems may arise when scientists believe very strongly in the importance of their research?

3 Think about the principle of informed consent and discuss the questions.

1 Why do most clinical trials exclude pregnant women?

2 There's scientific evidence that a positive attitude is necessary for any cure to work. If there is only four per cent chance of benefiting from a drug being trialled, should you inform trial participants of this?

Ethical dilemma: when you are faced with a moral choice. For example, a student nurse sees a very senior colleague break a basic hygiene rule. The student nurse faces an ethical dilemma. Should he do something or stay quiet?

Do something ☐   Stay quiet ☐   Depends ☐

Ethics and the search for cures

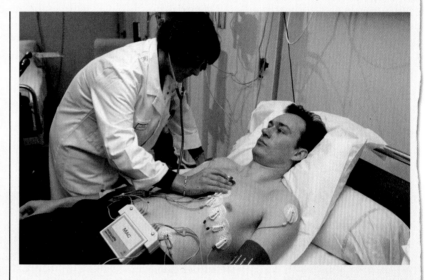

There is a constant need for new drugs. This is because there is a lot we don't know about human biology, there are still many illnesses we cannot cure, and new illnesses appear all the time while existing medicines lose their effectiveness. New drugs are tested on animals, but because animals' bodies work differently from ours, if a drug works on a caged rat, it does not mean that it will do the same for a human being. The only way to really know about a new medicine is to test it on people in a clinical trial. This is done by first giving it to healthy people to see if it is safe, and then giving it to sick people to see if it works.

Anyone participating in a clinical trial must understand the risks and give their informed consent. This is a principle of the Nuremberg code resulting from the cruel experimentation done in prison camps during the Second World War. Informed consent prevents abuse of people in the name of science, but the problem is that if you apply the principle literally, you cannot do research on children, people with Alzheimer's disease, and the mentally ill.

Prisons provide controlled environments and constant supplies of participants for drugs trials. However, the fact that prisoners often agree to do things they would not normally do (such as being deliberately infected with dangerous diseases) in

exchange for certain rewards, raises the question of whether they make genuinely free choices. The same goes for people living in extreme poverty whose need for money may blind them to the risks involved.

Sick people participating in a trial benefit by being the first to get a new treatment and a lot of attention. However, there are risks. By taking a brand new medicine, they enter an unknown area in which it is possible for things to go badly wrong. When little is known about them, the use of some drugs like Thalidomide, and more recently TGN1412, can lead to disablement and death.

The other ethical issue concerns the judgement of the doctors and nurses working on trials. As healers, their primary concern is for the well-being of their patients, but there may be times when, convinced by the importance of their work and the benefits it could bring to society, they give the experiment greater importance than the patients. In one famous study in America, hundreds of men with syphilis were left untreated, even after a cure was discovered, in order that researchers could study the effect of the disease right up until death.

Speaking

Ethical dilemmas and medicine

1 Student A, go to p.110. Student B, go to p.113. You will each read two situations which set ethical dilemmas. Answer the questions.

2 Make a prediction of how your partner would answer the same questions.

3 Work in pairs. Close this book. Set the ethical dilemmas you have read for your partner. Ask the same questions and find out if your predictions were right.

4 Explain why you made your predictions and explain your own responses to the ethical dilemmas.

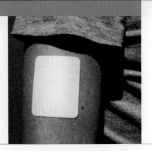

During a follow-up appointment, a practice nurse asked a patient how he was getting on with his medication patches. 'The doctor told me to put on a new patch every six hours and now I'm running out of places to put them,' he said. The nurse asked him to undress and saw that the man had fifty patches stuck on his body.

Write one sentence that gives instructions for using the medication patches that could not be misunderstood.

Listening

A clinical trial

1 🎧 Listen to a participant in a clinical trial talk to a nurse who is monitoring responses to a new drug. Answer the questions.

1 Which (a, b, or c) is the patient's self-monitoring chart?

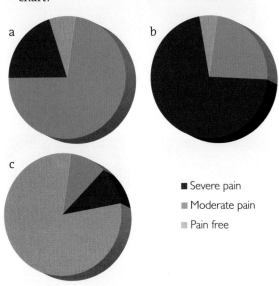

■ Severe pain
■ Moderate pain
■ Pain free

2 What are the eligibility criteria for participating in this trial?
3 How is the trial inconvenient for the participant?

2 🎧 Listen again and complete the monitoring form.

CITY HOSPITAL
Monitoring form

Patient's name: _____ [1]

Disorder: _____ [2]   Dosage: _____ [3]

Improvement / deterioration [4] in symptoms? (circle one)

Note specific details

_____ [5]

List any side effects

_____ [6]

Is the patient happy to continue with the trial? Yes / No [7]

Tests

Side effects

1 Study the chart showing side effects experienced by participants testing a sedative in a clinical trial.

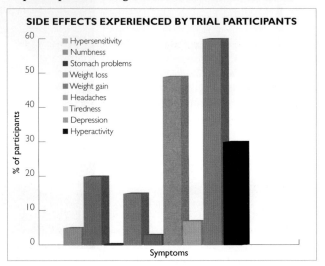

SIDE EFFECTS EXPERIENCED BY TRIAL PARTICIPANTS

■ Hypersensitivity
■ Numbness
■ Stomach problems
■ Weight loss
■ Weight gain
■ Headaches
■ Tiredness
■ Depression
■ Hyperactivity

y-axis: % of participants
x-axis: Symptoms

2 Complete the description of the chart with the names of side effects.

The most common side effect was _____ [1]. This was reported by sixty per cent of the participants, double the number who experienced periods of _____ [2].

Half the total number of participants suffered _____ [3] and out of every hundred participants, twenty complained of _____ [4]. This is four times the number who experienced periods of _____ [5].

The number of participants who experienced _____ [6] was statistically insignificant. A number of participants experienced changes in their BMI. _____ [7] was the most common at a ratio of five to one with _____ [8].

3 Read the information about two more symptoms and add blocks to the chart.

Reports of drowsiness came from forty-five participants in every hundred. This was nine times as many people who reported hallucinations.

Project

Research one of the following plants and explain in a class presentation what treatments derive from them.

- citrus fruits e.g. pineapple, oranges, lemons
- betel nut palm (Areca catechu)
- deadly nightshade (Atropa belladonna)
- poppy (Papaver somniferum)

Writing

Describing a chart

1 Study the chart, which compares the effectiveness of herbal extract *Hypericum perforatum* (St John's Wort) with the synthetic drug Imipramine on patients with depression.

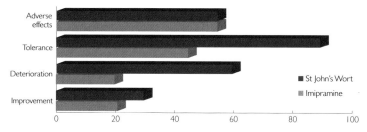

2 Say where these phrases could be used for describing the chart.

a ratio of 3:2	half the number
an equal number	one in two
double the amount	three times as many

3 Complete the description of the chart using the phrases to help you.

20% of patients taking Imipramine showed improvement.
Compared to St John's Wort, this is a ratio of 3:2.
A similar percentage of patients on Imipramine experienced
deterioration of symptoms, but three times as many ...

Checklist

Assess your progress in this unit. Tick (✓) the statements which are true.

I can talk about units of measurement

I can talk about the effects of medication

I can use mathematical expressions

I can debate ethical issues

I can describe a chart

Key words

Adjective
soluble

Nouns
clinical trial
contraindication
dosage
eligibility
ethical
participant
ratio
regime
score
synthetic
tolerance

Verbs
build up
re-evaluate
run out

Look back through this unit. Find five more words or expressions that you think are useful.

5 Ophthalmology

Scrub up

Look at these optical illusions. Then discuss the questions with a partner.

1 Which ones did you find most surprising?
2 Can you explain how any of them work?

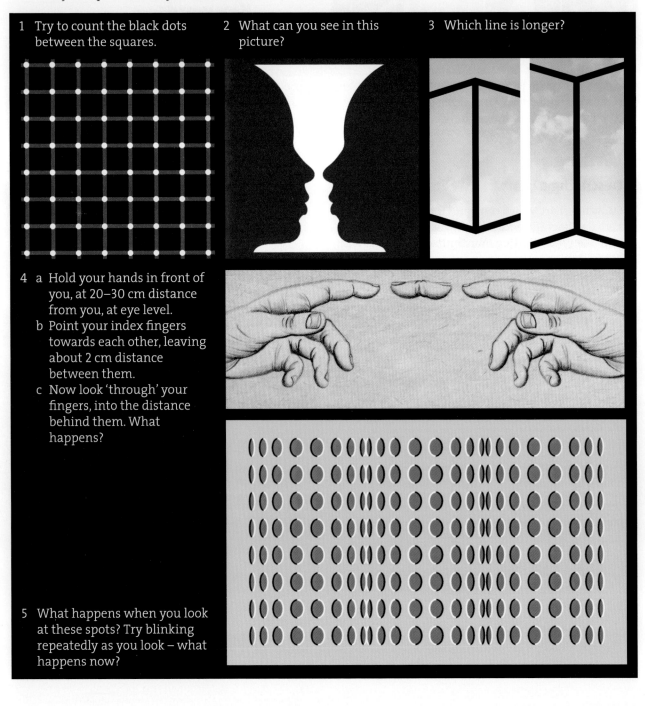

1 Try to count the black dots between the squares.

2 What can you see in this picture?

3 Which line is longer?

4 a Hold your hands in front of you, at 20–30 cm distance from you, at eye level.
  b Point your index fingers towards each other, leaving about 2 cm distance between them.
  c Now look 'through' your fingers, into the distance behind them. What happens?

5 What happens when you look at these spots? Try blinking repeatedly as you look – what happens now?

In this unit
- describing how the eye works
- describing eye conditions
- expressing ability
- stress in two-part nouns
- directing patients

Body bits

The eye

1 Label the parts of the eye using the words in the list.

cornea
iris
lens
macula
optic nerve
pupil
retina
vitreous humour

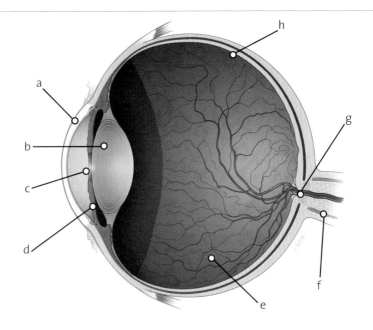

2 Complete this description using the words and phrases below.

black circle	light waves
clear dome	point
clear gel	sensitive part
electrical signals	visual image
image	

How the eye works

Actually, we don't see with our eyes, we see with our brains. When you look at things, _____[1] from them enter the eye through the cornea, which is a _____[2] at the front of the eye. The light then goes through the pupil, the _____[3] in the centre of the coloured iris. The light then bends to a _____[4] behind the lens. There, the _____[5] is reversed and upside down. The light travels on through a _____[6] called the vitreous humour and then to a focus on the retina. In the centre of the retina is the macula, which is a very _____[7] of the retina. It is used when we read or stare at something. The retina converts the light to _____[8] which travel along the optic nerve to the brain, which turns them back to a _____[9].

3 Look at the diagram again. Complete any remaining labels based on the description.

Vocabulary

Eye conditions

1 Work in pairs. Match each eye condition with a picture.

a cataract   c glaucoma
b conjunctivitis d eye trauma

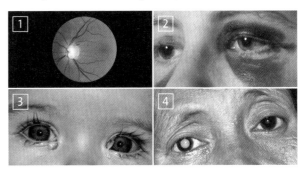

2 Match each of these symptoms with one or more of the eye conditions a–d above.

1	a bloodshot eye	8	double vision
2	haloes around lights	9	a dull pupil
3	blurred vision	10	irritation
4	bruising of the eyelid	11	sensitivity to light
5	bulging eyes	12	swollen eyelid
6	clouding of the lens	13	vision loss
7	discharge	14	watering

The **ophthalmoscope** is a hand-held instrument with lenses. It shines a light into the eye and enables ophthalmologists to examine the cornea, lens, and retina. The ophthalmoscope plays an important role in diagnosing eye diseases and preventing blindness.

Listening

Four patients

1 🎧 A student nurse is having a training session with an ophthalmologist. Listen to four conversations and decide which patient has which of the eye problems a–d. Write 1–4.

   a cataract   _____

   b conjunctivitis _____

   c glaucoma   _____

   d eye trauma   _____

2 🎧 Listen again and answer the questions.

   Dialogue 1
   1 What must the patient not do to his eyes?
   2 Who in his family has the same problem?

   Dialogue 2
   3 How did the patient injure his eye?
   4 Where is the foreign body?

   Dialogue 3
   5 What two problems does the patient have with her vision?
   6 What effect of the condition can the ophthalmologist see?

   Dialogue 4
   7 How do things look when the patient closes his left eye?
   8 What does the right eyeball look like?

3 Discuss the questions with a partner.

   • Do you know anyone who has suffered from any of these conditions?
   • What treatment did they have?
   • What was the outcome?

Project

Research one of the following eye conditions and make a short presentation to describe the signs and symptoms of the condition, and explain what causes it and how it can be treated.

   • blepharitis   • iritis
   • detached retina   • keratoconus
   • dry eyes   • macular degeneration
   • ectropion

● Language spot

Ability

1 Match each example sentence 1–6 with a description a–f.

   1 I **managed to** read all the letters on the card.
   2 When I was younger, I **could** read the fine print in newspapers.
   3 I **couldn't** find my glasses this morning.
   4 **Can** you see my fingers?
   5 You **won't be able to** see very well when the bandages first come off.
   6 I**'ve never been able to** see things clearly in the distance.

   a a general ability in the past
   b a description of ability at an unspecified time before now
   c an occasion in the past when something was successful
   d a description of future ability
   e a description of senses or sensations
   f an occasion when something was unsuccessful

   ≫ Go to **Grammar reference** p.118

2 Complete these sentences using expressions from **1**.

   1 I _____ see as well as I used to.
   2 For about a year, I _____ read in low light.
   3 Don't come by car, because you _____ drive home after your surgery.
   4 I _____ come to my appointment because I was ill.
   5 It took a long time, but in the end I _____ find my glasses.

3 Complete these questions with the verbs in brackets in the correct form. If *can* is not possible, use *be able to*.

   1 _____ (you / can) see well enough to get around the house?
   2 _____ (your husband / can) come and pick you up if you phone him?
   3 _____ (you / can) speak to the ophthalmologist yesterday?
   4 For how long _____ (you / not / can) read the newspaper?
   5 _____ (you / can / ever) see well enough to drive?

Can you read the words?
Does **colour-blindness** affect more men or more women?
What percentage of the population do you think is colour-blind?
What two colours can most colour-blind people not distinguish?

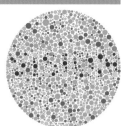

4 Discuss the questions with a partner.
- How good is your eyesight?
- When did you last have an eye test? What kind of tests were used? How did you do?
- If you have a problem, when did you first notice it?
- Does anyone in your family have vision problems? What kind?

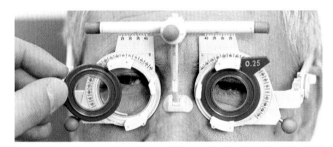

Pronunciation

Stress in two-part nouns

1 The main stress in a two-part noun can be on the first or second word. In adjective + noun combinations, the main stress is on the second word, and in noun + noun combinations it is on the first word.

adjective + noun

optical illusion (main stress on *-lu-* in *illusion*, secondary stress on *op-* in *optical*)

noun + noun

depth perception (main stress on *depth*, secondary stress on *-cep-* in *perception*)

🎧 Listen and repeat the words.)

2 Work in pairs. Decide where the main stress and the secondary stress (if there is any) goes in the following two-part nouns. <u><u>Double underline</u></u> the main stress and <u>single underline</u> the secondary stress.

1	light waves	9	vision problems
2	diabetic retinopathy	10	optic nerve
3	electrical signals	11	pupil response
4	eye condition	12	retinal detachment
5	blood vessels	13	surface membrane
6	blurred vision	14	eye test
7	reading glasses	15	visual acuity
8	ocular movement		

3 🎧 Listen and check.

Patient care

Directing patients

1 🎧 Listen to two tests being performed by a practice nurse, and decide which feature of vision a–d each one is testing.

1 _____ 2 _____

a ocular movement   c visual acuity
b pupil response   d visual field

2 🎧 Work in pairs. Student A, you are the practice nurse. Student B, you are the patient. Listen again and perform the actions as you listen.

3 🎧 Try to remember the missing words from the dialogues. Then listen again and check.

1 **Nurse** You _____[1] six metres from the chart, so _____[2] here, please? Right, now I _____[3] your right eye. Good. Now, I _____[4] the smallest line of letters that you can.

Patient P, E, C, F, D.

Nurse Fine, _____[5] the other eye _____[6]? This time, _____[7] the same line of letters backwards?

Patient D, F, C, E, P.

Nurse Right, now _____[8] both eyes. Try and read the next line down ...

2 **Nurse** Right, so I _____[9] my finger in front of your nose, like this ... about ten centimetres. Now I _____[10] at the wall behind me, please. OK, now look at my finger ... and at the wall again. That's fine. Now _____[11] at my finger ... I _____[12] it towards your nose ... and out again – keep looking at it – in ... and out ... right, that's fine. Now can you cover one eye ...

4 Take turns to do the same tests on each other. Keep talking to the patient.

Speaking

Performing eye tests

You are going to perform more eye tests. Student A, go to p.110. Student B, go to p.113.

The **Snellen chart** measures a person's eyesight according to which line they can read from 20 feet (6 metres). 20 / 20 (or 6 / 6) vision is normal. 20 / 40 (or 6 / 12) is roughly half as good, and 40 / 20 (12 / 6) twice as good as normal.

Lea symbols are often used to assess visual acuity in children who cannot read.

Do you know of any other ways of measuring visual acuity?

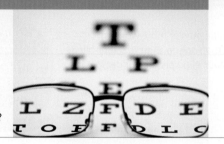

Reading

Glasses

1 Discuss the questions with a partner.

- For you, is wearing glasses positive or negative?
- What is the price range for glasses with lenses in your country?
- Imagine there were no glasses or contact lenses. How many of the people who you work with every day would not be able to work?

2 Read the text. Match these titles with paragraphs A–F. One title is not needed.

1 The social effects of glasses   _____
2 How glasses are made   _____
3 Sight in the developing world   _____
4 The invention of glasses   _____
5 How glasses work   _____
6 An important invention   _____
7 The limited life of eyes

3 Decide whether these statements are true (T) or false (F).

1 Most people of 45 need reading glasses.
2 Scientific progress in the Renaissance led to the invention of glasses.
3 Haloes are an example of an aberration.
4 A squint is a focusing problem.
5 People with hyperopia need glasses for reading.
6 Glasses doubled the hours that people could work in a day.
7 Cheaper glasses would help the economies of developing countries.

4 Do you know of any charity that helps restore vision to people in the developing world? Tell the group about it.

THE IMPORTANCE OF SEEING CLEARLY

A

If you had to make a list of ten inventions that have changed the world, glasses would be on it.

B

Most people's eyes can work efficiently for only about 35 years, and after that they may need reading glasses. 800 years ago there was no such thing as correcting sight and early in life almost everyone became disabled by failing eyesight.

C

Glasses were invented in the fourteenth century and very quickly spread throughout the world. Their invention was vital to the creative and intellectual progress of the Renaissance – a period of rapid development in mathematics, science, commerce, medicine, and art.

D

Spectacle lenses correct focus, and can be used to correct other problems too, such as aberrations (seeing ghost images, haloes, waves, or rainbows) and squints (strabismus), when the two eyes do not point in the same direction. However, their most common use is to correct long-sightedness (hyperopia) – where you cannot focus on near objects, short-sightedness (myopia) – where you cannot focus on distant objects, and the loss, through ageing, of the eye's ability to change focus (presbyopia).

E

The invention of glasses freed people from the effects of ageing. At the point in their lives when their knowledge and skills were at their highest level, people could continue to read, do accounts, write, and do small-scale, detailed work. Glasses have effectively doubled the length of time one can expect to live a productive life.

F

The link between glasses and poverty can be seen in developing countries today. The World Health Organisation says that 28 million people in developing countries, where a pair of glasses can cost several months' salary, are blind from treatable conditions. Educated people like engineers and teachers have to retire early, and millions never learn to read, simply because they cannot see.

Writing

Nursing a blind person

1 Work in pairs to perform this role-play. Student A, you are a blind student and should keep your eyes closed. Student B, give Student A some help to reach another part of the room.

2 Discuss the experience of helping or receiving help.
- How did the 'blind' person feel?
- How did the helper feel?
- What tips would you give somebody for helping in a polite way?

3 Work in pairs to decide what problems you would have doing the following everyday things if you were blind.
1 Getting dressed
2 Eating and drinking
3 Shopping
4 Communicating face to face
5 Bringing up children

Add more things to the list.

4 Make a list of strategies that help a blind person deal with each of the situations mentioned in 3.

EXAMPLE

Getting dressed – only buy clothes of the same colour so that they don't clash – make sure the label is on the inside

Filling a cup with a hot drink – feel the weight of the cup and listen to the sound. Place a ping-pong ball inside the cup to show when the cup is full.

5 Write about your experience of nursing a blind person. If you don't have experience of this, imagine doing so. Write a paragraph for each of the questions.
- How did / would it make you feel?
- What special needs did / would they have as patients?
- How did / would you have to change your way of working?
- What did / would you find rewarding?
- What did / would you find frustrating?

Checklist

Assess your progress in this unit. Tick (✓) the statements which are true.

- I can describe the anatomy and working of the eye
- I can describe common signs and symptoms of eye conditions
- I can talk about ability in different tenses
- I can give patients instructions in an appropriate way

Key words

bloodshot
blurred vision
colour-blindness
depth perception
discharge
eyesight
halo
long-sightedness
ocular
pupil response
sensitivity
short-sightedness
vision
visual acuity
visual field

Look back through this unit. Find five more words or expressions that you think are useful.

6 Dermatology

Scrub up

Discuss the questions in pairs.

1 What physical functions does the skin perform?
2 What artificial things do men and women commonly do to their skin in your culture? Why?

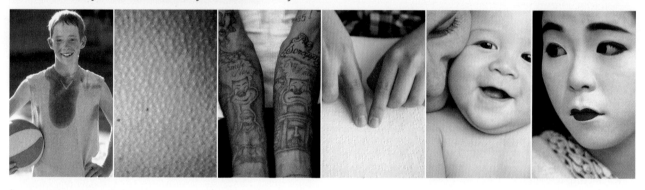

Listening

Skin conditions

1 Work in pairs. Look at these pictures of skin conditions and discuss what you know about them.

1 What is each of the conditions called in your language?
2 What are the possible causes of each one or the risk factors for developing them?

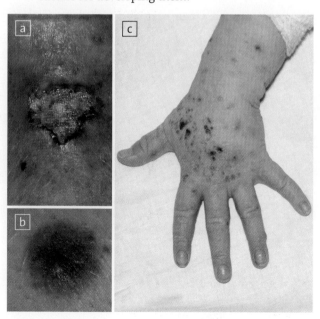

2 Which condition(s) in **1** would you expect these adjectives to be used for? Write *a*, *b*, or *c*. Use your dictionary to help you.

1	inflamed	_____	5	irregular	_____
2	sore	_____	6	crusty	_____
3	flaky	_____	7	itchy	_____
4	cracked	_____	8	scaly	_____

3 🎧 Listen to dialogues a–c and check which dialogue the adjectives are used in.

4 🎧 Listen again and tick (✓) the items on the list that are mentioned.

Dialogue a

☑ sitting down	☐ exercise
☐ bandage	☐ sleep
☐ compression stockings	

Dialogue b

☐ blood test	☐ biopsy

Dialogue c

☐ food	☐ sweat
☐ baths	☐ fingernails
☐ moisturizing cream	☐ clothes

5 🎧 Listen again and try to remember why the doctor mentions each one. You can make notes to help you remember.

In this unit
- describing skin conditions
- modifying an adjective
- phrasal verbs
- writing an essay describing a disease

● **Language spot**
Modifying an adjective

1 Look at these sentences.

That looks **quite sore**.
Today is **by far the most painful** it's been.
That will also make it **a bit less swollen**.
It's **absolutely essential** that you change the bandage every day.
It's **extremely itchy**.
This is **easily the itchiest** it's been.
It's **really awful**.
Is it going to get **a lot worse**?

2 Complete a–d with the adverbs below. Note: some adverbs will go in more than one place.

a bit / a little / a little bit	far
~~a lot~~	much
absolutely	pretty
~~by far~~	quite
easily	really
extremely	slightly
fairly	very

a Used with comparatives, e.g. *more painful, worse*
 a lot

b Used with superlatives, e.g. *the most tender, the hardest*
 by far

c Used with gradable adjectives, e.g. *sore, itchy*
 extremely

d Used with non-gradable adjectives*, e.g. *unbearable, terrible, fantastic*
 absolutely

* You can have more or less of a gradable adjective. You can't have more or less of an ungradable adjective.

» Go to **Grammar reference** p.119

3 Decide if the adverb makes the adjective stronger or weaker. Write *S* or *W* next to each.

4 🎧 Underline the adverbs that best complete the dialogue. Then listen and check.

Doctor	Mm, your scalp's still *a lot / a bit*[1] inflamed, but actually it's *much / by far*[2] better than it was.
Patient	Yes – it's my neck that's *really / much*[3] sore. It's *extremely / absolutely*[4] itchy too, and it's got *really / a lot*[5] worse this week. It was *absolutely / slightly*[6] unbearable last night – *far / easily*[7] the worst it's been.
Doctor	You've got to resist the urge to scratch, though, or it can get infected.
Patient	I know, I know. It's *very / a lot*[8] dry – that's the problem. I've tried creams from the chemist, but they don't seem to work.
Doctor	I'll prescribe you Topicon.
Patient	Is that a barrier cream?
Doctor	Yes. It's *really / very*[9] wonderful stuff. It's *a little bit / by far*[10] the best I've come across – fast-acting too.
Patient	Let's hope so.

Pronunciation
quite, *fairly*, and *pretty*

1 The words *quite*, *fairly*, and *pretty* modify an adjective in different ways depending on the intonation that is used. They can make the adjective **weaker** or **stronger**.
It's quite painful. = It's just a bit painful. (weaker)
*It's quite **painful**. = It's surprisingly painful. (stronger)*

2 🎧 Listen to these sentences and decide whether the adverb makes the adjective weaker or stronger. Write *W* or *S*.

1 _____	3 _____	5 _____
2 _____	4 _____	6 _____

3 With a partner, write a dialogue based on the words below. Add a variety of adverbs from this section and from *Language spot* to make the dialogue as expressive as possible. Practise saying the dialogue with exaggerated stress.

Nurse	how / eczema?
Patient	terrible! / itchy / red
Nurse	using / new cream?
Patient	worse than last week

About 85% of teenagers suffer from some form of acne.

- Does it tend to be more severe in males or females? Why?
- What treatments do you know of for acne?
- What foods can make acne worse?

Body bits

The skin

Read the text and label the diagram with the **bold** words.

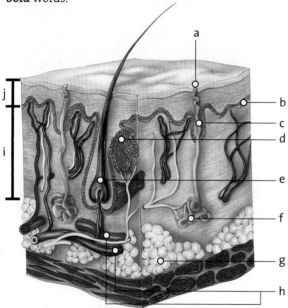

The thin outer layer of the skin is the **epidermis**, which is made of tough, flat cells. Dead cells at the surface form a scaly protective layer, and as these are lost, new skin cells are forming in the **basal cell layer** at the bottom of the epidermis. Also in this bottom layer are melanocytes, which produce the hormone melanin, which gives the skin its colour and protects it from UV light.

The skin's inner layer, the **dermis**, is made of strong, elastic tissue. It contains nerve endings and small **blood vessels**.

Sebaceous glands produce sebum, an oil that rises to the surface of your epidermis to keep your skin lubricated and waterproof.

Sweat is produced in **sweat glands**, and comes up through **sweat ducts** to the surface of the skin from where it comes out through tiny **pores**. Body hairs grow in **follicles** in the dermis.

Under the skin is a layer of **subcutaneous fat**. This keeps the body warm, absorbs shocks, and helps hold your skin to all the tissues underneath it.

Speaking

Describing skin conditions

Work in pairs. Student A, go to p.111. Student B, go to p.114.

Vocabulary

Phrasal verbs

1 Read this letter to a magazine. Work with a partner and write three pieces of advice for the letter-writer.

> I've had acne since I was thirteen. Sometimes it's better and sometimes worse, but it never goes away completely. I know that the next time I need to look my best I'll **break out** in nasty spots. I've tried out every product on the market, but they've all just been a waste of money. Is there a natural way to **deal with** acne?

2 Read the reply. Is any of the advice the same as yours?

> Acne happens when excess sebum – the skin's natural oil – blocks your pores. As skin cells **die off**, they also clog the pores, allowing bacteria to **build up**. This forms an open 'blackhead', or a covered 'whitehead'.
>
> As far as food goes, you don't need to **cut out** fat from your diet altogether, but if you can **cut down on** deep-fried food, it should help.
>
> Wash your face gently twice daily with a mild soap, taking care to **rinse** it **off**. If you wear make-up, make sure you **take** it **off** completely at night. And don't squeeze spots! If you burst a pimple, it may **turn into** a deep and painful cyst.

3 Match the **bold** verbs in the text with these meanings.

1 to take action to solve a problem _deal with_
2 to collect in a place _____
3 to suddenly have marks, spots, etc. cover an area of skin _____
4 to eat or do less of something _____
5 to remove something that you are wearing _____
6 to remove something using clean water _____
7 to stop eating or doing something _____
8 to die, one by one _____
9 to become something different _____

dermabrader
an electrical device that removes the top layer of skin with fine sandpaper or wire brushes, for example to flatten scars or to remove dead skin from burns

Writing

Describing a disease

1 Read the student essay on impetigo, and match the headings below with paragraphs A–H.

1 Prognosis   _F_
2 Diagnosis   ___
3 Prevention   ___
4 What it is   ___
5 Transmission   ___
6 Treatment   ___
7 Causes   ___
8 Signs and symptoms   ___

2 Complete the essay with the expressions below.

affected by
avoided by
based on
caused by
characterized by
effective against
likely to
resolves without
spread by
treated with

3 As part of your studies, you have been given an essay to write. The title is 'Describe the etiology, signs and symptoms, and management of athlete's foot'. Using the notes on the right, write 200–250 words. Use the same paragraph topics as in **1**.

DESCRIBE THE ETIOLOGY, SIGNS AND SYMPTOMS, AND MANAGEMENT OF IMPETIGO

A Impetigo is a contagious skin infection which usually occurs in children aged two to six. It is also common in people of any age who play contact sports.

B It is usually _____[1] the same Streptococcus bacteria that causes strep throat. It can also be caused by Staphylococcus aureus. Skin that has already been _____[2] cuts, insect bites or other trauma, or by an allergic reaction is more _____[3] develop impetigo.

C The infection is _____[4] direct contact with lesions or with nasal carriers. The incubation period is one to three days. Scratching the lesions can spread the infection to other parts of the body.

D Impetigo is _____[5] small, pus-filled blisters surrounded by reddened skin, which is often itchy. After four to six days, the blisters break down and form a thick crust.

E Diagnosis is made _____[6] the typical appearance of the skin lesion. A culture of the skin or mucosal lesion usually grows Streptococcus or Staphylococcus.

F Impetigo usually _____[7] sequelae within two weeks if left untreated. Complications, which are rare, include permanent scarring to the skin and kidney damage.

G Good hygiene is the most effective preventive measure. Scratching a sore or rash, which can lead to impetigo, can be _____[8] keeping the nails short.

H The infected area should be washed with soap and water and allowed to dry in the air. Impetigo can be _____[9] bactericidal ointments that are _____[10] impetigo, such as Fucidin and Bactroban. Severe cases can be treated with oral antibiotics such as Floxapen or Erythrocin.

* fungal infection of the skin, usually between toes
* fungus on everyone's skin – feeds on dead skin
* people with sweaty feet more likely to get it
* contagious – direct skin-to-skin contact, through towels, shoes, floors, etc.
* scaling, flaking, itching
* possibly blisters and cracked skin → can lead to exposed raw tissue, pain, inflammation
* can spread to armpits, knees, elbows, groin
* diagnosis from appearance

* skin lesion biopsy examination may show presence of fungus
* usually responds well to treatment
* risk of re-infection if preventive measures not taken
* complications rare – e.g. secondary bacterial skin infections, lymph gland infection
* prevention – keep feet clean and dry (e.g. cotton socks, leather shoes)
* talcum powder or antifungal powder useful
* severe cases – topical creams, e.g. Ketoconazole or Terbinafine

Burns are graded according to their depth.

● **First-degree** burns damage only the outer layer of skin
● **Second-degree** burns damage the outer layer and the layer underneath
● **Third-degree** burns damage or destroy the deepest layer of skin and tissues underneath

Reading
Treating burns

1 Have you ever worked with patients with severe burns? Talk about the experience.

2 Read the texts and write the letter of a treatment (A–E) next to each description. Which treatment

1 reduces tissue damage by increasing blood flow to the burn? _____

2 involves spraying skin cells on to a burn? _____

3 shows images of cold weather to distract the patient from pain? _____

4 prevents the formation of raised scars? _____

5 uses a dressing coated with metal? _____

6 reduces scarring by getting new skin to grow quickly? _____

7 requires regular wetting? _____

8 involves wearing a device shaped to fit your face? _____

9 produces new skin that does not shrink? _____

10 allows fewer pain signals to reach the brain? _____

3 Imagine you are judging these five treatments in a competition for the most imaginative technology. Give each one a mark from 1 (minimum) to 5 (maximum). Then form small groups and explain your decisions.

A _____   D _____

B _____   E _____

C _____

CUTTING-EDGE TREATMENTS FOR BURNS

A Laser technology has been developed to produce an exact image of the shape of the face quickly and easily. This is then made into a transparent mask, which keeps the skin flat and prevents raised scars from forming. The tight-fitting mask, which greatly reduces disfigurement, is worn for 23 hours a day for a year or more.

B During daily wound cleaning, burn survivors experience excruciating pain and often relive the trauma of the fire. A software company has developed a virtual reality movie called *Snow World*, where the viewer is flying through snowy landscapes and frozen water. Patients report large drops in pain while watching. MRI scans suggest that fewer signals actually reach the brain while the patient is involved in the movie.

C A doctor in California discovered that the drug Heparin, when applied on to and underneath a burn, keeps blood flow to the burn high. This stops the damaged area from spreading and reduces pain. The new skin that grows is close to the original skin in colour and texture, and also does not contract – usually a great problem with burns. Added to this are the benefits of less surgery, shorter hospitalization, and the need for less medication.

D Australian researchers have pioneered a technique for culturing small samples of the patient's skin in the laboratory and spraying them on to burns. Here they continue their growth and are added little by little until the area is completely and smoothly covered. Previous techniques involving cultured skin took around three weeks to cover a major burn, whereas this technique takes just five days, greatly reducing scarring.

E A new technique for treating burns has been developed in Australia that reduces the number of painful skin grafts by half. The treatment involves a silver-coated dressing, which helps prevent infections. The bandage needs changing less frequently, which means the patient suffers less pain, and the nurses have more time. A system of tubes allows the patient to keep the dressing moist at home, without the need for a nurse.

Patient care

Assessing pain

1 Read the dialogue between a nurse and a burns patient. What procedure is the nurse doing?

Nurse   _____[1] the donor site been?

Patient   It was pretty good last night. A lot better than the night before.

Nurse   Good. OK, _____[2] clip away the dead skin. _____[3] hurt a bit ... How's that – really painful?

Patient   Absolutely excruciating, actually.

Nurse   Sorry. _____[4] rate the pain from one to ten, with ten being the worst pain?

Patient   I'd say eight.

Nurse   OK – _____[5] give you a little more analgesic _____[6] carry on.

2 Complete the dialogue with the words below.

before I	how would you	I'm just going to
how has	I'll	it's going to

3 Work in pairs. Role-play a dialogue where a nurse is asking questions to assess a patient's pain. Take turns playing the patient. Before you do so, imagine the pain you are feeling.

Nurse   how / burn on leg?
Patient   painful last night
Nurse   take off bandage / have a look / going to sting
Patient   Ouch!
Nurse   how / rate / pain?
Patient   five
Nurse   OK / local anaesthetic / take off rest of bandage

4 Discuss the question in pairs.

1 Why is it important to assess pain?
2 With what groups of patient are questions not the best method for assessing pain?

Project

Research one of the following methods for assessing pain. In the next class, tell the other students about it.

- ABCDE
- PQRST
- CHEOPS pain scale
- NIPS pain scale
- FLACC pain scale
- NPASS pain scale

Key words

Adjectives
contagious
crusty
flaky
inflamed
scaly

Nouns
acne
biopsy
disfigurement
moisturizing cream
pus
scarring
skin graft
topical cream

Verbs
rinse off
turn into

Look back through this unit. Find five more words or expressions that you think are useful.

7 Oncology

Scrub up

1 Work in pairs. Discuss what you think each picture shows and how it relates to cancer.

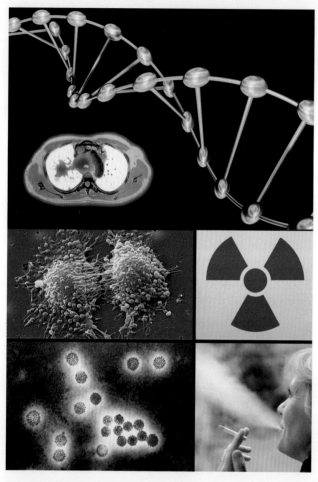

2 Work in pairs. Complete the sentences and answer the question.

1 In 2005, _____% of deaths worldwide were from cancer.

2 _____% of cancers could be cured if detected early and treated adequately.

3 In the USA and other developed countries, cancer is responsible for around _____% of all deaths.

4 Worldwide, what are the five most common types of cancer that kill men and women?

When you have finished, look at the answers on p.131. Which statistics surprise you?

Vocabulary

Cancer

1 Complete the text using the words below.

biopsy	invasion	radiotherapy
carcinogens	lymph nodes	remission
cell division	metastasis	sites
chemotherapy	mutation	staging
DNA	prognosis	

Cancer is characterized by uncontrolled _____[1], and the ability of these cells to spread, either by _____[2] of adjacent tissue, or by being carried to distant parts of the body by _____[3].

Cancer is usually diagnosed by _____[4], where a sample of cells is taken for examination. The _____[5] depends on the type of cancer and how far it has developed. _____[6] measures the severity of the cancer based on tumour size, number of _____[7] affected, and whether it has spread to distant _____[8]. Cancer is usually treated with a combination of surgery, _____[9], which uses anticancer drugs, and _____[10], which attacks cancer cells using x-rays or similar. A patient clear of cancer may be cured or may just be in _____[11], which means that the cancer will recur later.

The unregulated growth of malignant cells is caused by damage to _____[12], resulting in _____[13] to genes that control cell division. This damage can be caused by radiation, by chemicals or physical agents that cause cancer – which are called _____[14], or by viruses that can insert their DNA into the human genome.

2 Work in pairs. Student A, you are a patient. Choose one of the questions below to ask the nurse. Ask for an explanation of anything that is unclear.

Student B, you are a nurse. Without referring to the text, give a brief and very simple answer to the patient's question. Then change roles for another question.

- What is cancer?
- What causes cancer?
- How does cancer spread?
- How do you test for cancer?
- How do you treat cancer?
- Do people usually die of cancer?

In this unit
- the vocabulary of cancer
- sounding sympathetic
- articles
- describing a tumour

It's my job

1 Olivia Deans is a Macmillan nurse who specializes in nursing people with cancer. Before you read, write three questions that you would like to ask Olivia about her job.

2 Read the text. Does it answer your questions?

Olivia Deans

As a Macmillan nurse, I see patients throughout their cancer 'journey' – from the time they are diagnosed right through to their recovery – or their death. I help them make informed decisions about their treatment and make sure they know about all the services that are available to them. Cancer patients often get their treatment in different departments, so they need to have one person that they know will always be there.

Cancer affects more than just the body. Patients often feel that they are not themselves any more, so we are trained to care for the whole person, and not just the disease. We help them find ways to cope with their new life, and also give them an outlet for their emotions, worries, and questions.

You become very close to people, and I used to find the emotions involved in caring for someone who was facing death overwhelming. But now I find it very rewarding when I know I've made a difference to a patient and helped them get through the most difficult experience of their life as best they can.

To become a Macmillan nurse, you need to be a Registered Nurse with at least five years' experience, including two or more years in cancer or palliative care. You have to take specialist courses in managing pain and psychological support. I would say the most important things for a Macmillan nurse to have are qualities like kindness, warmth, compassion, and genuineness.

Pronunciation

Sounding sympathetic

1 🎧 Listen to the dialogue. How is Maria, the patient?

2 🎧 Listen again. For each sentence or expression, tick whether you think the nurse's intonation stays about the same, goes up at the end, or goes down at the end.

	Intonation		
	–	↗	↘
1 Did you sleep better last night?			
2 Did it?			
3 Oh dear.			
4 Where was the pain?			
5 We'll give you more pain relief tonight.			

3 Match the sentences and expressions 1–5 in 2 with the descriptions.

a a *yes* / *no* question _____

b a *wh-* question _____

c an expression showing sympathy _____

d a question tag _____

e a statement _____

4 Work in pairs. Think about how the nurse might say her part. Then practise the conversation, taking turns to be the nurse.

Nurse How are you feeling this morning?
Patient A bit low, to be honest.
Nurse Are you? Aah. Would you like a chat about it?
Patient Well, I suppose so. Do you think it would help?
Nurse I think so. You can tell me if anything's worrying you.
Patient OK, then – that would be good.

5 🎧 Listen to the conversation. Was your version similar?

6 Stand up and walk around. Ask other students how they are. Invent problems when someone asks you. Be sympathetic when you hear a problem.

The ancient Greek physician Hippocrates used the word **karkinoma**, meaning 'crab', for cancer, because he thought that tumours and the swollen blood vessels around them looked like a crab. *Cancer* is the Latin word for crab.

● Language spot

Articles

1 Look at the sentences and answer the questions with a partner.

    a **Radiotherapy** usually makes you tired.
    b Your tiredness is a result of **the radiotherapy** you've just had.
    c ~~We're going to give you a **radiotherapy**~~.

  1 Which sentence talks about radiotherapy in general?
  2 Which sentence talks about a particular example of radiotherapy?
  3 Why is *c* wrong?

    a I've got **a lump** under my arm.
    b When did you first notice **the lump**?
    c ~~I can see **lump**~~ at the back of your mouth.

  4 Why is *c* wrong?
  5 Which sentence mentions a lump for the first time?
  6 Which sentence talks about a lump that we already know about?

    a We're worried about **the tumours** on your kidney.
    b **Tumours** on the brain can be hard to remove.

  7 Which sentence talks about tumours in general?
  8 Which sentence talks about tumours we already know about?

2 Work in pairs. Underline the correct options.

  1 *Skin / The skin* around your mouth looks quite sore.
  2 *The tumour / Tumour / A tumour* is about four cm in diameter.
  3 Have you ever had *a biopsy / biopsy / the biopsy* before?
  4 Let me have a look at *the sore / a sore / sore* on your leg.
  5 *Herceptin / The herceptin / A herceptin* is a drug used to treat breast cancer.
  6 I have *moles / the moles* on my hand – look.
  7 We'll tell *a surgeon / the surgeon* if the bleeding starts again.

3 These sentences show special uses of articles. Look at *Grammar reference* p.119. Then write *a, the,* or – (no article).

  1 I'm _____ nurse. I work in _____ A&E.
  2 I'm working in _____ oncology department.

  3 This man needs to go to _____ hospital quickly!
  4 Mr Wright's in _____ theatre having an operation.

4 Complete the text using *a / an, the,* or – (no article).

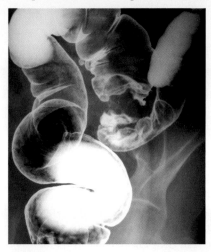

I woke up one night with _____¹ terrible pains in my stomach. I went to see _____² doctor the next morning, and had _____³ x-ray the same day. _____⁴ radiologist showed me _____⁵ x-ray. You could clearly see _____⁶ big shape in _____⁷ colon, which he told me was _____⁸ large tumour. I was shocked to hear I had _____⁹ cancer. I had to have _____¹⁰ surgery immediately. In _____¹¹ seven-hour operation, they removed _____¹² large section of bowel. I was told I would have to have _____¹³ chemotherapy for six months. I did have _____¹⁴ side effects from _____¹⁵ treatment, but it wasn't too bad. I had _____¹⁶ scan a year after being diagnosed, which was clear.

Reading

Coming to terms with terminal illness

1 How would you feel if you were told tomorrow that you had six months to live? Spend five minutes writing down words that come to mind. Then explain your thoughts to a partner.

2 Read the text and name the five phases that palliative care experts talk about.

  1 _____   4 _____
  2 _____   5 _____
  3 _____

Dr Susan Dorr Goold teaches ethics at a medical school in the USA. In one class she role-plays a patient, and students have to tell her that she has rectal cancer. Her anus and rectum will have to be surgically removed and a colostomy bag will become a permanent part of her life.

'Am I going to die?' she asks.

How would you answer?

---

3 Read the text again and match the feelings a–j to one of the phases 1–5 in **2**.

  a They may speak to the illness as if it is human. _____

  b They often don't allow doctors to treat them. _____

  c They stop fighting the idea that they are going to die. _____

  d They don't want their friends to run away from them. _____

  e They make their family's lives hard. _____

  f They try to get control of the situation. _____

  g There are times when they do and feel nothing. _____

  h They make plans for the end of their life. _____

  i They spend a lot of time alone. _____

  j They pretend they are not really ill. _____

4 Answer the questions.

- Imagine you want to become a palliative care nurse. Decide the order in which you would read these articles on a website about nursing the terminally ill. Write 1–5.

    _____ Communicating with the patient

    _____ Helping the patient's family

    _____ The phases of terminal illness

    _____ Ethical issues

    _____ Dealing with different cultures and religions

- Compare your order with a partner, explaining your reasons. Then together make a list of four more articles you would like to see on the website.

The phases of grieving

As many people still feel healthy when diagnosed with a terminal illness, the news comes as an enormous shock. Different personalities respond to it in different ways, and feelings and attitudes change as the time draws closer. Experts in palliative care say that patients generally go through five phases when coming to terms with the knowledge that they are about to lose *everything*.

Commonly, the initial reaction to the news is to refuse to believe it – it's just a terrible dream. Patients in denial carry on with their lives as if there is nothing wrong. Some look for a second opinion that will contradict what they've been told. There are complex reasons for doing this. People who are going to die sense the fear of death in others, and because they are deeply afraid of being abandoned, they avoid direct discussion of the situation. Some patients never move from this phase.

Those who reach the next phase start to feel anger at all the healthy people in the world whose lives will continue. They may attack medical staff verbally or physically, especially those who have given the bad news. They become very difficult to live with and to treat. They are really grieving for what they have lost – the healthy, happy years that are past, the lost years of the future, and the loss of their loved ones.

In the third phase, dying people will often cope by bargaining with the illness or with God. They accept their coming death, but they set conditions on it such as, 'If I can just live to see my grandchildren born,' or 'If I can see the place where I was born just once more.' In this way people feel they get some control over the situation and can delay things.

The fourth stage is a feeling of depression as the reality of the situation sinks in. The sufferer's sadness at what they will lose is typically expressed by crying, withdrawal, and lethargy. The bouts of sadness may alternate with periods of emotional numbness.

Personality types who fight until the end will not reach the final phase of acceptance because for them that would be the same as giving up. Fatalists – the ones who say 'it is out of my hands' – have the best chance of coming to terms with the situation, planning their own funerals, and saying goodbye.

American doctor Jerri Nielsen discovered she had breast cancer while working at the South Pole. While she waited four months until a flight could rescue her, she performed a biopsy on herself and treated herself with chemotherapy.

Tests

Staging

1 Complete the text with the adjectives below.

curable	involved	localized
distant	malignant	present
incurable	local	primary

Staging of a _____[1] tumour at diagnosis is the biggest predictor of survival and helps decide what treatment is required. The two most common ways to express this are Overall Stage Grouping (OSG) and TNM (Tumour, Node, Metastasis).

Overall Stage Grouping
This system uses numerals I, II, III, and IV to describe the progression of cancer.

- Stage I cancers are _____[2] to one part of the body. They are usually _____[3].
- Stage II and stage III cancers have spread to _____[4] lymph nodes.
- Stage IV cancers have often metastasized and are usually _____[5].

TNM

- **T** describes the size of the _____[6] tumour, using numbers 0–4.
- **N** represents the extent to which local lymph nodes are _____[7] and can also be ranked from 0–4.
- **M** refers to metastasis. 0 indicates that no metastasis has occurred, and 1 that metastases are _____[8].

A T1N2M0 cancer would be a cancer with a small (T1) tumour, which has spread to local lymph nodes (N2), but has not spread to_____[9] parts of the body (M0).

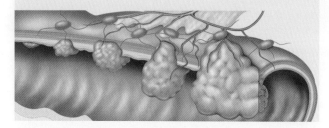

2 Read the text again and discuss the questions with a partner.

1 Who has the better chance of survival, a patient with a stage II tumour or a patient with a T2N2M1 tumour?

2 Using these systems, how would you refer to
   a a very large tumour that has not spread?
   b a small tumour that has spread throughout the body?

Listening

Treatment options

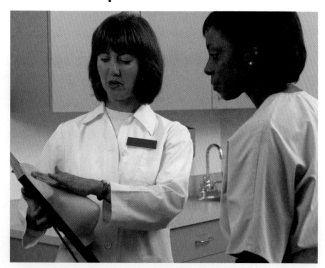

1 🎧 Layla Hart went to her GP when she found a lump in her right breast. A biopsy revealed a malignant tumour. She had surgery three days ago to find out the extent of the cancer. Listen to her find out the results from the surgeon. How would Layla's tumour be described using the OSG and TNM systems?

2 🎧 Listen again, and decide if the sentences are true (T) or false (F).

1 Layla will certainly need to have a breast removed.

2 No lymph nodes are removed in a lumpectomy.

3 With a lumpectomy, she would have both chemotherapy and radiotherapy.

4 The symptom she doesn't want to have is constant tiredness.

5 Layla can't think of any questions immediately.

Checklist

Assess your progress in this unit. Tick (✓) the statements which are true.

I can describe the cancer process

I can sound sympathetic

I can use the indefinite and definite article correctly

I can describe location of tumours or disease in the body

I can describe the diagnosis and treatment of cancer

Key words

Nouns
carcinogen
chemotherapy
DNA
invasion
lymph nodes
metastasis
prognosis
radiotherapy
remission
site
staging

Adjectives
incurable
malignant
metastasized
terminal

Look back through this unit. Find five more words or expressions that you think are useful.

Speaking

Asking about treatment options

You are going to role-play a cancer patient asking a specialist cancer nurse questions about their treatment.

Student A, look at this page. Student B, go to p.115.

Student A

1 You are Layla Hart (the patient in *Listening*). Below is a diagram of your treatment options. You have the chance to ask the nurse (Student B) questions about the treatment. Decide what you would like to ask.

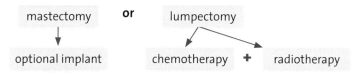

Writing

Dealing with difficult situations

1 Discuss the questions with a partner.

When a patient has just received bad news, what is the best way to handle the situation
- when the patient cries?
- when the patient gets angry?
- when relatives demand to know all the details from you?
- if you think that the patient does not really understand the situation?

2 Write a paragraph giving your opinion on each question. Where possible, give an example from your own nursing experience.

Project

Research to find out about one of the following.
- a new treatment that is being developed for cancer
- an alternative therapy that is used for treating cancer
- a food that is believed to prevent cancer

8 Gastroenterology

Scrub up

1 Here are some things student nurses say they have found embarrassing to do. How would you feel about them? Grade them 1–5 (1 = not embarrassing at all, 5 = extremely embarrassing).

Talk to Lal Bibi about her uncontrollable flatulence.

Examine Jim Pear's penis because of pain he has in it when defecating.

Shave Hapreet Singh's genitals to prepare him for an operation.

Give Miss Weinberger a rectal examination.

Talk to Charmaine Peterson about her encopresis (faecal soiling of underwear).

2 Work in pairs. Discuss the questions.
- Can you add any experiences of your own?
- If you were the patients, would you grade the experiences in the same way?
- Explain your grades and say whether the age, race, or gender of the patients affects them.
- Why is it harder to speak with patients about certain basic things that we all do, than with fellow medical professionals?
- Do you use words in your own language to talk with non-medical people about body parts, toileting, and death? If so, what are they?

Patient care

Euphemisms

Read the dialogue between a nurse and an elderly male patient. Match the euphemisms 1–15 in **bold** with words and phrases a–o.

a navel _____   i anus _____ *1*
b bowel / intestines _____   j defecate _____
c faeces _____   k urinary system _____
d toilet _____   l urine _____
e genitals _____   m ill _____
f make unconscious _____   n parasite, virus, etc. _____
g injection _____   o bowel evacuation _____
h urinate _____

Nurse Are you worried about Thursday?

Patient Well, yes, I am. It's the idea of someone pushing a tube up my **back passage**[1]. Do I really have to go through it?

Nurse We need to find out what's making you feel so **poorly**[2] and a colonoscopy is a good way to look inside your **stomach**[3]. It's a routine medical procedure which we do all the time and there's really no need to be embarrassed.

Patient I can never get used to it, nor to doctors and nurses examining my **private parts**[4].

Nurse I know, I know. But try to relax about it. It will be over within half an hour.

Patient Will you give me something to **knock** me **out**[5]?

Nurse We'll give you a sedative. It's just a little **jab**[6] and it'll make you sleepy. You may feel a little pain behind your **belly button**[7]. Nothing more. Today though, we're going to take a sample of your **stools**[8] for analysis. We want to see if you have a **bug**[9]. Oh, and the lab wants a sample of your **pee**[10].

Patient But there's nothing wrong with my **waterworks**[11], is there?

Nurse Probably not, but a urine test can tell us such a lot about what's going on inside. When you feel the need to **pass water**[12], go to the **loo**[13] and collect a sample in this container. Before you have the colonoscopy, you'll need a good **clean out**[14], so on Wednesday I'll give you a laxative which means you'll probably have to **move your bowels**[15] a few times.

In this unit
- understanding euphemisms
- vocabulary of the digestive system
- explaining purpose and cause
- understanding pathology reports

Reading

Getting medical information from faeces

1 Discuss this question with a partner.

- When a hunter is looking for animals, the faeces he finds on the ground give very important information. What do they reveal?

2 Before you read the text about getting medical information from faeces, discuss and note down what you already know about the subject. Read the text and compare what you read with your own knowledge.

3 Match headings 1–4 with paragraphs A–D.

1 Typical stools _____
2 Faeces and communication _____
3 Classifying faeces _____
4 Faecal odours _____

4 Complete the chart using information in the text.

Observation of faeces	indicate	
yellow-green infant faeces	1	_____
hard and dry faeces	2	_____
runny faeces	3	_____
small quantities of blood in stools	4	_____
faeces that float	5	_____
very smelly flatulence and faeces	6	_____

5 Discuss these questions.

1 Archaeologists get a lot of information by examining fossilised faeces (called coprolite analysis). What would they find out about ancient people in this way?
2 Why have humans developed a disgust for the appearance and smell of faeces?
3 Why do we avoid defecating and urinating in public places?

WHAT FAECES REVEAL

A Eliminating the waste products of metabolism is an essential process for all forms of life. Defecating is as natural as breathing and it is one of the first things we do when we are born. However, we grow to dislike our own excrement and flush it away as soon as we produce it. Other animals don't worry so much. The way that cats, hippopotami, and bears, for example, use faeces and urine has been compared to writing – providing information without actually being present and 'reading' it by smell and taste.

B In contrast, humans generally leave the job of examining faeces to medical professionals who analyse its contents as well as its appearance, smell, frequency, and quantity to get information about illness. The faeces of healthy babies are a yellow-green colour and many people rather like their smell. However, as they are weaned, babies' faeces become brown and acquire that nasty smell of bile and bacteria. Healthy adult faeces are 75 per cent water. The rest is bacteria, indigestible food matter, fats, inorganic substances, and protein. They should be semi-solid and coated with mucus.

C Abnormal faeces are assessed using the Bristol Stool Scale which puts them into seven groups ranging from severe constipation ('separate hard lumps') to diarrhoea (watery, no solid pieces). Faeces can be analysed to screen for cancer using the Faecal Occult Blood Test (FOBT). In this test, chemicals are added to a small sample of stool in order to identify the existence of microscopic amounts of blood which may indicate a cancer somewhere in the bowel. Faeces with a high fat content tend to float and usually indicate disease of the pancreas or small intestine.

D It is perfectly normal to produce a lot of gas, and nervousness which causes us to swallow more air creates more flatulence. The distinctive smell of flatulence is hydrogen sulphide and the more sulphur in our diet, the stronger our flatulence smells. However, very smelly faeces and gas indicate that fat is not being digested because enzymes are blocked from getting into the intestines and there is something wrong.

The word '**stomach**' is widely used when referring to **all** of the digestive system, but in fact the stomach is only one part of it and it is located a little to the left in the upper abdomen. How well do you know the location of your organs? Work with a partner and point to your

- liver
- kidneys
- colon.

Vocabulary

The body's processes

1 Complete the table.

noun	verb
absorption	*absorb*
consumption	1 _____
contraction	2 _____
conversion	3 _____
detoxification	4 _____
elimination	5 _____
expansion	6 _____
ingestion	7 _____
secretion	8 _____
stimulation	9 _____

2 Complete the sentences with the correct form of words from **1**.

1 The sight, smell, and taste of food _____ glands to produce saliva.

2 A major role of the digestion process is the _____ of waste from the body.

3 Food is _____ through the mouth.

4 The pancreas is involved in the _____ of enzymes that break down food molecules.

5 Nutrition is when the body _____ food substances into energy.

6 The digestive system breaks down food and transports it for _____ and defecation.

7 The muscles in the oesophagus make wave-like _____ which push the food along.

8 Too much _____ of certain foods can overload the digestive system.

9 The stomach can _____ as it fills with undigested food.

10 Digested products travel to the liver, which _____ blood of harmful substances.

Body bits

The digestive system

1 Label the diagram using the words below.

anus
appendix
colon
duodenum
gall bladder
liver
oesophagus
pancreas
rectum
salivary glands
small intestines
stomach

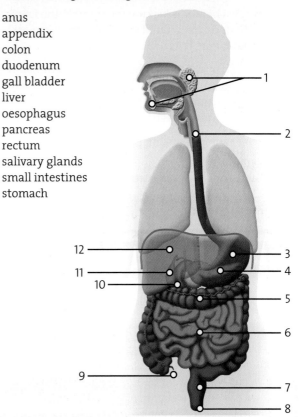

2 Order these steps in the process of digestion by numbering them 1–7.

a Salivary glands in the mouth produce enzymes. _1_

b Food in the stomach is attacked by digestive juices which include a powerful acid. ___

c When the food is in the small intestine, juices from the pancreas and bile from the gall bladder dissolve undigested fat. ___

d Food, in a liquid paste form, enters the colon where water is removed. ___

e Faeces are expelled by a bowel movement. ___

f The first swallow starts the muscle action and pushes food through the oesophagus. ___

g The food, now in a semi-solid state, slowly empties into the small intestine. ___

Almost everyone has heard that chewing gum is indigestible or that it stays in the stomach for seven years, but it's not true. **Chewing gum** does contain a fibre that can't be digested, but it is eliminated as waste by our digestive systems just like anything else we swallow.

Were you told untruths about your body and its functions when you were a growing up?

● **Language spot**
Explaining purpose and cause

1　Read these two sentences and say which explains a purpose (the intention behind something) and which explains a cause (the reason why something happens).

  1　Your weight loss shows you are not absorbing nutrients, **so** we're going to have a look at your intestine.
  2　We will not give the patient laxatives **because** she may have an internal obstruction.

2　Match the beginnings and the ends of the explanations to make sentences. Say which sentences explain purpose and which explain cause.

  1　He has a bowel problem,
  2　The whiteness of your fingernails
  3　We are going to do a colonoscopy
  4　Cut down on heavy or spicy food,
  5　You mustn't eat for four hours before the ultrasound,
  6　As **a result of** the stool test
  7　Do not give the patient aspirin,
  8　**The cause of** ulcers

  a　**in order to** find the cause of the bleeding.
  b　we have decided surgery is the best option.
  c　is **due to** the liver damage.
  d　**resulting in** weight loss.
  e　**so that** your gall bladder can be seen in the scan.
  f　**as** it would make the bleeding worse.
  g　is a bacterium called H. pylori.
  h　**to** allow your stomach to recover.

3　Complete this dialogue between a community nurse and a mother, using **bold** words and expressions from **1** and **2**. (Sometimes more than one option is possible.)

  Nurse　What's the problem?

  Mother　My little boy's got a stomach upset. He's got diarrhoea and a high temperature, and he was vomiting a lot until yesterday. I'm worried _____[1] he's not eating much.

  Nurse　These symptoms are _____[2] gastroenteritis. Lots of children at the school have got it.

  Mother　What's gastroenteritis?

  Nurse　Gastroenteritis is _____[3] an infection, which makes the stomach and intestines inflamed. There's a virus going round at the moment.

  Mother　Will you give him antibiotics?

  Nurse　_____[4] the infection is viral, not bacterial, antibiotics would have no effect. It will clear up on its own within a couple of days, _____[5] I don't think you need to worry.

  Mother　Is there anything I can give him?

  Nurse　Not really. Make sure he drinks plenty of fluids _____[6] he doesn't become dehydrated.

  Mother　Just water?

  Nurse　Water's fine. And you could give him a glucose drink _____[7] keep his energy up. But keep him off school until he's completely better, _____[8] this will avoid spreading the virus.

4　Work in pairs and by sharing your knowledge, write two sentences about each of the conditions and procedures in the lists below. Your sentences about conditions should explain their causes and contain expressions used in **1** and **2**.

EXAMPLE
Food poisoning is a result of …

Your sentences about procedures should explain their purposes.

EXAMPLE
A colonoscopy is performed so that …

Conditions

food poisoning	indigestion
constipation	obesity

Procedures

colonoscopy	liver biopsy
appendectomy	enema

>> Go to **Grammar reference** p.119

Endoscopy means **looking inside** and an **endoscope** is a thin, lighted fibre-optic tube with a tiny camera on the end. The endoscope used for looking at the inside of the stomach is called a colonoscope. A colonoscopist uses it to see any abnormalities, and can take a biopsy by pinching off bits of tissue with forceps attached to a cable running through the colonoscope.

Writing

Describing a process

Study the diagram of the stomach and write a description of what happens to food between the time it is swallowed and the time it passes into the duodenum.

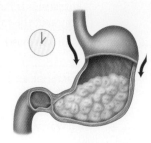

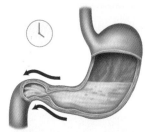

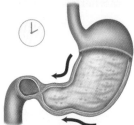

Listening

Biopsy results

1 🎧 A path lab report has come through to the Gastroenterology department. Listen to a nurse mentor as she explains to a student what it means and delete the incorrect information to complete the record.

CITY HOSPITAL
Path Lab Report

Patient name: Nadine Hartmann

Specimen analysed: polyp of *sigmoid / descending*[1] colon

Specimen size: 0.6 × 0.4 × 0.3

Specimen shape: (✓)[2]

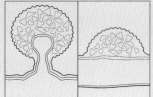

Results: *evidence / no evidence*[3] of stromal *hyperthecosis / invasion*[4]

Summary: Colon, sigmoid, *endoscopic / arthroscopic*[5] biopsy: *tubular carcinoma / adenoma*[6]

---

2 Complete this letter to the patient using the phrases below.

did an analysis
discuss treatment options
examine your colon
inform you of the results
is a benign tumour

is no evidence
made an appointment
performed a biopsy
run a risk
show an adenoma

13th February

Dear Mrs Hartmann

I am writing to _____[1] of the colonoscopy done on the 20th of January to _____[2]. During this procedure, the doctor _____[3] in which he took a sample from your lower colon for analysis. The sample was a polyp and the pathologist _____[4] of it.

This shows that there _____[5] of cancer; however, the biopsy does _____[6] in your lower colon.

An adenoma _____[7]. This means that though you do not have cancer, you _____[8] of it some time in the future. I have _____[9] for you to see Dr Monroe who will answer any questions you have and _____[10].

Yours faithfully

Jane Brown

Jane Brown

Project

Research one of the following and give a presentation to explain their contribution to the study of gastroenterology.

- Rudolph and Gabriella Schindler
- Philip Bozzini
- Basil Hirschowitz
- William Beaumont and Alexis St Martin
- Professor Barry Marshall

Checklist

Assess your progress in this unit. Tick (✓) the statements which are true.

I can understand medical euphemisms

I can communicate with patients about sensitive and embarrassing things

I can explain purpose and cause

I can describe a biological process in writing

I can understand a path lab report

Key words

absorption
anus
bile duct
colon
defecation
elimination
enema
flatulence
ingestion
mucous membrane
oesophagus
pancreas
salivary glands
secretion
stool

Look back through this unit. Find five more words or expressions that you think are useful.

Speaking

Discussing a case history

1 Read this case history of a woman who died from colon cancer because she did not get medical treatment early enough.

Mrs Jobarti was an immigrant who spoke very little of the language of the country she lived in. She was a shy woman who was not well-educated and came from a culture and a generation of women who do not communicate easily with men about personal matters.

She was suffering frequent abdominal pains and one day she noticed blood in her stools. However, she was afraid of the 'foreign' doctors at her local clinic and was too embarrassed to talk to them about bowel habits. She visited a local healer from her own country who told Mrs Jobarti that she had a potentially fatal illness, but encouraged her to stay away from 'Western' medicine, gave her herbal preparations, and performed a healing ceremony.

Finally, Mrs Jobarti found the courage to go to a doctor. The patient and the doctor (a man) did not understand each other and the doctor, who did not use an interpreter, briefly examined her, took a sample of her blood, prescribed laxatives, and recommended a change in diet.

The blood test was negative, but Mrs Jobarti's symptoms got worse over the next six months. She was eventually referred to a local hospital. There was a very long waiting list to see a specialist and the hospital did not make her a priority. Mrs Jobarti did not make a fuss, but suffered in silence. Samples of her stools got lost in Pathology. She had to repeat the tests and it was another four months before she was diagnosed with advanced colon cancer. It was too late to do anything and she died within a month.

2 Think about the factors that contributed to the delay in getting treatment. Who or what was most to blame? Put these things into what you think is their order of importance.

- the culture she was living in
- the doctor
- the healer
- the hospital
- the patient herself
- the patient's culture
- the patient's husband

3 Explain and discuss reasons for your choices to a partner and then discuss them with the rest of the class.

Admin bank

1 Emergency telephone call log

1 Study the logs of one day's emergency telephone calls and match each picture with a log. Which log is not illustrated?

2 Answer the questions.

1 Which emergency call is made by a healthcare professional already on the scene?

2 Which emergency involves a possible crime?

3 Which caller's information is not accurate?

4 How many accident victims died that day?

5 Which emergency call was not justified?

6 Which emergencies did not result in hospital admission?

7 In which emergency was the ambulance delayed?

8 Which emergency is attended by all emergency services?

3 Find words and abbreviations in the log that mean

1 the time the ambulance arrived

2 summary of events

3 the part of a large vehicle where the driver sits

4 child

5 death

6 recovery.

PHONE CALLS

1 Log Book   Time of call 06.50

Location of emergency	14 Friars Walk
Name of caller	Staff nurse Jenny Lewis
Nature of emergency	Suspected cardiac arrest
Synopsis	Victim is caller's 56-year-old male neighbour. Caller reports victim has abdominal pains and is sweating and vomiting.
Action taken	Ambulance is dispatched. ETA: 07.10
Follow-up	Heavy traffic and so ATA was 07. 50. Victim DoA at hospital

2 Log Book   Time of call 09.23

Location of emergency	2 km north of motorway junction 17
Nature of emergency	RTA
Synopsis	Lorry driver is trapped in his cab but no other vehicles are involved
Action taken	Police and fire service are notified and ambulance dispatched
Follow-up	The driver was released and transferred to hospital. He had no serious injuries and was discharged later.

3 Log Book   Time of call 14.20

Location of emergency	Central park north side perimeter fence
Name of caller	Mr Fred Thomas (park keeper)
Nature of emergency	Juvenile trapped in park railings
Synopsis	Victim has put her legs through railings. They have become swollen and she is unable to free herself. Caller reports no bleeding and the victim is fully conscious.
Action taken	Fire service is notified. Ambulance is dispatched.
Follow-up	Ambulance was not required. Fire officer used hydraulic equipment to force open the railings and free the girl. Hospital attendance was not necessary.

4 Log Book   Time of call 22.10

Location of emergency	High Street outside Lock Building
Name of caller	Male caller refuses to give his name.
Nature of emergency	Possible suicide attempt
Synopsis	Caller reports seeing victim 'jump from the roof of the building.'
Action taken	Ambulance is dispatched and police are notified
Follow-up	Police officer reported fatality. Foul play is suspected and a murder investigation has been opened.

5 Log Book   Time of call 00.00

Location of emergency	332 Rio Road
Name of caller	Shareen Heslop
Nature of emergency	Non-emergency
Synopsis	Caller reports injured wild bird
Action taken	Animal rescue notified
Follow-up	The bird was taken to an animal sanctuary for treatment and rehabilitation

2 General medical admission form

1 Study the admission form and say if these sentences are true (T) or false (F).

1 The patient was admitted in the morning.

2 The patient has cramping pain in her legs.

3 There is pain but no blood.

4 The patient has come in for an operation.

5 The patient's pregnancy is advanced.

6 The patient has a stable relationship.

7 The hospital gave her Aldomet for the first time today.

8 The patient has one child.

9 She was given Nifedipine intravenously.

10 The patient is an only child.

2 Tick (✓) the general causes of premature labour which may apply in this case.

a abdominal surgery

b alcohol use during pregnancy

c genital tract infections

d haemorrhage

e high blood pressure

f mother over forty

g smoking

h stress

i underweight

j very young mother

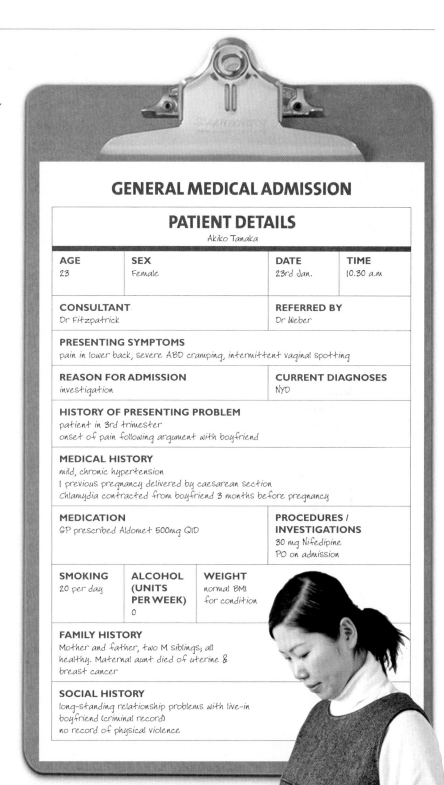

GENERAL MEDICAL ADMISSION

PATIENT DETAILS

Akiko Tanaka

AGE	SEX	DATE	TIME
23	Female	23rd Jan.	10.30 a.m

CONSULTANT	REFERRED BY
Dr Fitzpatrick	Dr Weber

PRESENTING SYMPTOMS
pain in lower back, severe ABD cramping, intermittent vaginal spotting

REASON FOR ADMISSION	CURRENT DIAGNOSES
investigation	NYD

HISTORY OF PRESENTING PROBLEM
patient in 3rd trimester
onset of pain following argument with boyfriend

MEDICAL HISTORY
mild, chronic hypertension
1 previous pregnancy delivered by caesarean section
Chlamydia contracted from boyfriend 3 months before pregnancy

MEDICATION	PROCEDURES / INVESTIGATIONS
GP prescribed Aldomet 500mg QID	30 mg Nifedipine PO on admission

SMOKING	ALCOHOL (UNITS PER WEEK)	WEIGHT
20 per day	0	normal BMI for condition

FAMILY HISTORY
Mother and father, two M siblings; all healthy. Maternal aunt died of uterine & breast cancer

SOCIAL HISTORY
long-standing relationship problems with live-in boyfriend (criminal record)
no record of physical violence

3 A midwife's diary

1 Read the midwife's diary and say if these statements are true (T) or false (F).

1 Mrs Dichter is an assistant midwife.
2 Anna is a midwife.
3 Mrs Aziz went into labour at 07.15.
4 Mrs Cross had a false alarm.
5 Mrs Gill will give her baby extra milk from a bottle.
6 Mrs Tan's baby has stopped moving.
7 Mrs Carter's baby was born early.
8 Mrs Carter was feeling a little better.
9 Both Mrs Rowe and Miss Cross are pregnant.
10 Mrs Aziz gave birth normally.

2 Write a similar diary of your own working day.

		Monday
	06.00	I attended Mrs Dichter's home birth as assistant midwife.
	06.30	I received an emergency call from Mrs Aziz, who is 38 weeks pregnant. She thought her membranes had ruptured. I phoned my midwife partner, Anna, and asked her to visit and make an assessment.
	06.45	I received a phone call from Mrs Cross' husband who reported that his wife was bleeding and in some pain.
	07.10	Mrs Dichter's baby was born. It was a boy and weighed 2.5 kilos.
	07.15	I received a phone call from Anna. She said that Mrs Aziz's membranes had ruptured, but that she was not yet having contractions. She wanted to wait for spontaneous onset of labour.
	08.00	I left the home birth with the primary midwife still in attendance.
	08.20	I visited Mrs Cross, whose bleeding and pains had stopped by the time I arrived.
	09.00	I went to the clinic and was visited by Mrs Gill, who is a six-week post-partum discharge. Mrs Gill reported that her baby was feeding normally, but was losing weight. The baby's daily output includes soft yellow stools plus heavy urine. I recommended complementing breastfeeding.
	09.30	I received a call from Mrs Tan, who is 32 weeks pregnant. She was worried because of an absence of foetal movement. I arranged for tests and examination at the clinic.
	09.40	I reviewed incoming lab reports in my office.
	09.55	I called Mrs Carter whose baby was born mildly premature four weeks ago. Mrs Carter is tearful and suffering mood swings with feelings of guilt. GP's DX is post-natal depression. The patient told me that the Fluoxetine prescribed by her GP was having some effect.
	10.05	I made a follow-up call to Mrs Aziz and arranged a home visit tomorrow for an assessment.
	10.30	I made a home visit to Mrs Rowe, who is a three-day post-partum patient with mastitis.
	11.00	I made a home visit to Miss Cross, who is a one-week post-partum patient.
	11.30	I received a phone call from Mrs Aziz, who reported that she had been experiencing labour pains since 10.00. She had no way to get to hospital and I notified ambulance services.
	12.05	Mrs Aziz arrived at the hospital. An examination showed that the baby was in the breech position.
	13.50	Mrs Aziz's baby was delivered by CS. It was a girl and weighed 2.25 kilos.

4 Prescriptions

1 Use the abbreviations on p.124 to understand prescriptions a–d and match them with a picture of the correct medicine 1–4.

2 Match the prescriptions with their full written versions.

1 Give a six milligram bolus followed by 54 milligrams in the first hour. Then 20 milligrams per hour for two hours up to a total of 100 milligrams.

2 Give 300 to 500 micrograms (0.3 to 0.5 milligrams) intramuscularly or intradermally every day before noon. Use your own judgement after three days.

3 Shake the bottle. Give one tablespoon (three teaspoons) three times a day with food.

4 Two capsules of acetaminophen plus 30 milligrams of codeine given every four hours as needed.

3 Write out this prescription in full sentences.

> Mr. Masahiko Shizawa
> insert qs R qid: am, pm
> and after BM Rep prm

4 Write prescriptions for these orders for medication.

1 Give three 300 milligram capsules of Gabapentin with food, but not more than three times a day.

2 Administer one unit of insulin by intradermal injection every four hours.

3 Shake the bottle of cough suppressant well and give a sufficient quantity orally. Repeat when it is needed.

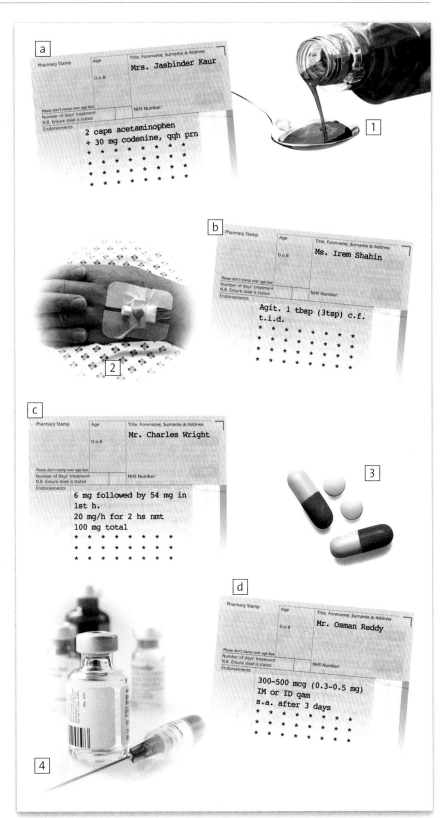

a

Pharmacy Stamp — Age — D.o.B — Title, Forename, Surname & Address
Mrs. Jasbinder Kaur

Please don't stamp over age box
Number of days' treatment
N.B. Ensure dose is stated
Endorsements — NHS Number:

2 caps acetaminophen
+ 30 mg codenine, qqh prn

b

Pharmacy Stamp — Age — D.o.B — Title, Forename, Surname & Address
Ms. Irem Shahin

Please don't stamp over age box
Number of days' treatment
N.B. Ensure dose is stated
Endorsements — NHS Number:

Agit. 1 tbsp (3tsp) c.f.
t.i.d.

c

Pharmacy Stamp — Age — D.o.B — Title, Forename, Surname & Address
Mr. Charles Wright

Please don't stamp over age box
Number of days' treatment
N.B. Ensure dose is stated
Endorsements — NHS Number:

6 mg followed by 54 mg in
1st h.
20 mg/h for 2 hs nmt
100 mg total

d

Pharmacy Stamp — Age — D.o.B — Title, Forename, Surname & Address
Mr. Osman Reddy

Please don't stamp over age box
Number of days' treatment
N.B. Ensure dose is stated
Endorsements — NHS Number:

300-500 mcg (0.3-0.5 mg)
IM or ID qam
s.a. after 3 days

5 Extracts from an ophthalmic nursing manual

1 Read the instructions to ophthalmic nurses. Match texts 1–4 with headings a–d.

a Removing something from the eye that shouldn't be there

b Removing sutures that have been used in surgery

c Managing the examination of a young child

d Using an ophthalmoscope

2 Find words in the texts that mean

1 a patient

2 to hold to prevent movement

3 to cut

4 to take out

5 to widen

6 to hurt

7 applied directly to the skin

8 damage.

3 Find a phrase which

1 gives advice (text 1)

2 gives a firm order (text 2)

3 gives a reason (text 3)

4 warns (text 4).

1

Lay the subject in the middle of a blanket so that their feet face you. Wrap the sides of the blanket around the body to restrain both arms and hold the subject firmly in a sitting position. It is best if you support their head whilst their feet are on your lap. When the examiner takes over, you will be free to hold a torch if necessary.

2

For treatment for glaucoma, 6-0 silk is used for the eyelid. It is easy to tie and has low tissue reaction properties. To remove, use forceps. It is imperative that the forceps are sterile. Gently lift the thread at the knot, clip it close to the skin, and extract it. Assess healing and swab the area with antiseptic.

3

Sit the subject up and dilate the pupils with eye drops. All eye drops sting except Fluorescin, which should be used for children. Begin at arm's length and get your patient to look at a precise spot which is away from you. Ask the patient to look directly into light if you want to see the macula.

4

Apply topical anaesthetic such as Amethocaine 1%. Position patient at the slit lamp and strap or have a colleague hold their head. Focus the slit lamp and examine the cornea, anterior chamber, iris, pupil, and lens for any distortion. Be careful about possible accidents and angle your needle away from the patient. Remove the foreign body with a 25G needle.

6 Laboratory report

1 Study the Path lab report on a biopsy done for the Dermatology department and choose a, b, or c.

1 Which of these sentences best describes the type of biopsy done on 10th October?

 a A thin slice is taken off the top of the skin.

 b A small piece of tissue is taken out using a special punch.

 c A thin needle attached to a syringe is inserted into the area and tissue removed.

2 Which of the following is the most accurate description of the appearance of the mole?

 a Soft, brown, and flat – located somewhere between the hip and the knee

 b Hard and nodular on the upper part of the leg

 c Large, flat, brown spot on the lower section of the leg

3 What does 'the mole is ulcerated' mean?

 a The mole is bleeding.

 b There is a break on the surface of the mole.

 c The mole is painful to touch.

4 'Intradermal nevus' is the medical term for a mole. In this case what does the tissue analysis of it indicate?

 a Cancer

 b No danger

 c It will get steadily worse

5 What does 'junctional activity' refer to?

 a The type of mole

 b The changing colour of the mole

 c The mole's location in the skin

6 By recommending 'clinical correlation', what is the pathologist suggesting?

 a Getting a second opinion.

 b The patient needs medication.

 c There should be a second biopsy.

2 Choose the correct news to give the patient.

 a The mole is not dangerous and you have nothing to worry about. Basically, you have a harmless skin lesion and although it is protruding, it is perfectly normal.

 b It is unlikely that the mole is malignant and so we don't think you have a cancer. However, further checks are required as the pathologist's report was not conclusive.

 c Things don't look good. We feel that you need urgent treatment because the biopsy shows the presence of atypical cells that give us cause for concern.

 d I'm afraid the biopsy has confirmed what we suspected and you have a malignant melanoma. We recommend that you come in and discuss treatment options with the doctors.

LAB REPORT

Pathology dept.

To	Dermatology
Patient name	Ashanti Jobeni
Date of report	16th October
Procedure	A shave biopsy was performed on 10th October and the sample was examined.
Description	A raised, firm, brown mole on R thigh. The mole is ulcerated and the ulceration extends to base and periphery.
Result	Tissue analysis indicates sample is consistent with benign, intradermal nevus.
Comment	Due to the surface ulceration, it is difficult to see if there is any junctional activity. Clinical correlation is recommended as the lesion is not fully evaluated.

7 Reflective writing

1 Read the student nurse's reflection on an experience and say which title a–d is the best one for each paragraph 1–4.

 a The lesson

 b The observation

 c The error

 d Reassurance

2 Decide which of the following is the most accurate summary of the student nurse's experience.

 a When I was on a placement, I observed a mistake being made. A patient was given the wrong medicine and nearly died. But it was OK in the end. The doctor saved his life and I learned how important it is to be careful when administering drugs and how easy it is to make a mistake.

 b One oncology placement I did taught me a very important lesson. I made the wrong calculation and gave the wrong quantity of medicine to a patient. I stayed calm and kept quiet and because of this everything turned out all right in the end. I learned never to panic in a crisis and always to double-check drug calculations.

 c Honesty is the best policy when you make a mistake. I learned that from the time on the Oncology ward when I gave the wrong medicine to a patient. My mistake taught me about the importance of accuracy in administering drugs and how to keep calm in difficult situations.

A MISTAKE

1 In the first few days of my Oncology placement I watched nurses doing drug calculations and administering chemotherapy. They were very helpful to me and talked me through what they were doing. I found out that though drugs are checked by the pharmacy, the ward nurses always check them again. If a patient is on a combination of drugs, then the calculations nurses do can be quite complicated, especially if the drugs are administered via a pump. Later in my placement I started to do drug calculations myself and my confidence grew.

2 Then came the time when I was on night shift. The ward was extremely busy and I assisted the charge nurse as he gave out medication. I asked if I could give out some medication myself and, when he agreed, I picked up the medicine pot for my first patient, and gave him the tablets. Almost immediately, I realised that I had given him the wrong ones. Because chemo medication is cytotoxic and potentially fatal I knew that the consequences of my mistake could be disastrous.

3 I went into a panic and started to sweat and shake. I rushed to the charge nurse and told him what I had done. He called the doctor who came within minutes. That gave me a chance to compose myself – after all, panic would not help the situation at all. In the end it was OK. The doctor said that the patient would not suffer any ill effects from this particular medication.

4 What did I learn from this? I learned how important it is to be alert and careful and about the kind of stress I will have to deal with when I am fully qualified. Perhaps my mistake would never have been noticed, but I know that I did the right thing by telling the charge nurse what I had done. If I had said nothing, I would never have learned how important it is to follow the correct procedure and check and check again.

8 Diagnostic questionnaire

1 Study the completed diagnostic questionnaire and find words and abbreviations in it that mean

1. in one place
2. spread around
3. return to normal when you press down
4. pain when touched
5. higher than normal.

2 Match the document with the correct patient history.

1. Mrs Vorster was admitted to A&E with a squeezing pain in the centre of her chest which had spread to her shoulders and neck. She vomited frequently and was sweating and short of breath. Heart rate was dangerously high. Tests confirmed cardiac arrest.

2. Mrs Vorster felt sudden, severe pain under her right shoulder after eating a meal. She felt sick and hot . Evidence of jaundice and abdominal bloating. A scan showed blockage of bile ducts though blood tests were negative for jaundice. She was diagnosed with gallstones.

3. Mrs Vorster had general pains around her stomach and felt feverish. Pain increased after releasing hand pressed down on abdomen. She felt sick but couldn't vomit because she hadn't been able to eat for twenty-four hours. Tests were inconclusive though there was a little inflammation and a slightly higher than normal WBC. Diagnosis: appendicitis.

4. Mrs Vorster felt nauseous and had suffered a sudden loss of weight. There were signs of jaundice. Her urine was dark yellow. She complained of general tenderness under her lower right rib. Tests showed an inflammation of the liver. She was diagnosed with hepatitis.

PATIENT NAME

Mrs Vorster

PAIN		
LOCATION	Localized ☐	Diffuse ☑
ABD		
PHYSICAL EXAMINATION		
Shows severe rebound tenderness in RL ABD		
NAUSEA?	Yes ☑	No ☐
VOMITING?	Yes ☐	No ☑
LOSS OF APPETITE?	Yes ☑	No ☐
VS		
TEMPERATURE	40.5°C	
PULSE	120 BPM	
RESPIRATION	27 BPM	
TEST RESULTS		
WBC	mildly elevated	
URINALYSIS	normal	
ULTRASOUND SCAN	fallopian tubes, ovaries and uterus normal, some inflammation of peritoneum	

9 Neurological observation chart

1 Read the case history and answer the questions.

1 How was Philip Boston injured?

2 When did he arrive at hospital?

3 How often was he assessed?

2 Complete the chart.

3 Study the chart and find words in it that mean

1 naturally and without being prompted

2 aware of surroundings

3 unsuitable

4 cannot be understood

5 recognizing where something is

6 bending (e.g. making a fist)

7 straightening.

CASE HISTORY: PHILIP BOSTON

Philip Boston had a minor RTA but he was still able to drive home. When he arrived, he told his wife he felt dizzy and had a terrible headache. His wife was worried and called an ambulance.

When Mr Boston came in to A&E at 22.30, observations were made to assess his level of consciousness. He was awake but quiet and watching things that were going on around him. He could respond to instructions and tell the doctor his name, but he couldn't remember the town he lived in or the date. The neurologist on duty believed he had hit his head in the RTA and was suffering a subdural haematoma (blood on the surface of the brain).

Over the next hour the patient became increasingly restless. The neurological observation chart was filled in at hourly intervals. By 23.30 the patient's condition had deteriorated. He had become vague and no longer seemed to be aware of the presence of the medical staff. He would only open his eyes when the doctor shouted into his ear. His speech became difficult to understand and sometimes he would suddenly shout single word obscenities. When asked to squeeze the nurse's hand he did it, but did not release the hand even when asked. He continued to rub the side of his head where his headache was located.

When the neurologist did an assessment at 00.30, the patient did not open his eyes to the doctor's voice until he was shaken firmly by the shoulder. He moaned but did not speak clear words as he attempted to pull the oxygen mask off his face.

OBSERVATION CHART

PATIENT _____ [1]   DX _____ [2]

		TIME		
		_____ [3]	_____ [4]	_____ [5]
EYES OPEN [6]	spontaneously (4)			
	to speech (3)			
	to pain (2)			
	none (1)			
VERBAL RESPONSE [7]	orientated (5)			
	confused (4)			
	inappropriate words (3)			
	incomprehensible sounds (2)			
	none (1)			
MOTOR RESPONSE [8]	obey commands (6)			
	deliberate withdrawal from pain (5)			
	localizing pain (4)			
	flexion to pain (3)			
	extension to pain (2)			
	none (1)			
	GCS score is given in brackets Total GCS	_____ [9]	_____ [10]	_____ [11]

10 Nursing care plan

On 27th October, Mr Hoggard had surgery for a coronary artery bypass graft and a nursing care plan was prepared.

1 Study extracts a–g from the plan and say which are observations, which are goals, and which are instructions.

a We want wounds to heal normally

b Inspect incisions for redness, swelling, drainage, and pain

c Administer spirometry and deep breathing exercises q2h

d Patient's temp. is now 36.7 °C

e Auscultation shows that lungs are clear

f Incisions are healing and there is no redness

g Patient's temp. needs to be kept within normal limits

2 Insert the extracts into the correct places in the plan.

GOALS

Goal 1. To keep the patient free of pulmonary infection

Goal 2. _____[1] (36.5–37.2 °C)

Goal 3. WBC count to be maintained

Goal 4. _____[2] and be free of drainage, redness, or warmth at wound sites

DATE	OBSERVATIONS
28th October	Patient has elevated temperature after surgery
29th October	_____[3], drainage, swelling, or foul odour VS are stable. Temp. at 0800 is now within normal range: 37 °C
31st October	Goal 1 has been met. _____[4] Respiratory rate: 20 WBC count: 10.2mg/d
2nd November	Goal 2 has been met. _____[5] Goal 3 has been met. Lab. report shows that WBC count is 9.6 mg / dL.
3rd November	Goal 4 has been met. The patient's surgical wounds are healing well. They are clean and dry with no swelling

NURSING ORDERS

1 _____[6] to promote maximal lung capacity and decrease the risk of infection. Collect sputum or respiratory secretion for culture to guide antibiotic therapy.
Encourage the patient to move at least TID. Change position q2h while in bed in order to prevent pneumonia and collapse of lungs (atelectasis).

2 Expect elevated temperature in the first 48–72 hours and assess vital signs q 2–4h.

3 Check labs for new WBC count and report any elevation of WBC count.

4 _____[7] QD and give antibiotics as prescribed.

11 Pre-op documentation

1 Read the case history and answer the questions.

  1 Exactly what part of his body will the patient lose?

  2 What feature of the patient's lifestyle is relevant to his illness?

  3 What long-term illness is relevant to the operation?

  4 What will probably happen if the patient does not have the operation?

  5 What are the patient's feelings about his coming operation?

2 Complete the patient's pre-op form with the relevant information.

CASE HISTORY: RICHARD CAMPBELL-SMITH

Richard Campbell-Smith is 55 years old. He smokes twenty cigarettes a day and has had type 2 diabetes for the past ten years. He is now suffering hardening of the arteries with foot ulceration. The hardening of his arteries has become so severe that gangrene has developed in his right foot and he is in considerable pain which he describes as 'severe, constant, and stabbing'. His life is in danger and the only suitable treatment is a 'ray' amputation to remove part of his right foot (see picture), during which he will be given general anaesthetic.

Mr Campbell-Smith is blood type A-. He has had gastroparesis (delayed emptying of the stomach) for three years and takes metoclopramide (Reglan) for this. He is allergic to penicillin.

He is very anxious about the operation and is sure he is going to die despite the surgeon's reassurances.

Normal pre-op procedure is followed; i.e. his insulin dose is halved the day before the operation and he is given a prophylactic antibiotic (Vancomycin) 1 hour before surgery. NPO from midnight. An EKG done just prior to the operation shows normal and his VS are fairly stable.

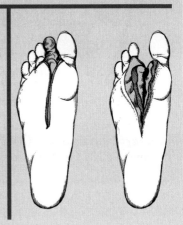

PATIENT'S NAME _____ 1	
AGE _____ 2	BLOOD TYPE _____ 3
DX _____ 4	
PLANNED PROCEDURE (including anaesthetic)	_____ 5
PATIENT HISTORY (including allergies and meds.)	_____ 6
	_____ 7
	_____ 8
	_____ 9
PATIENT'S PRESENT CONDITION (including pre-op preparation and test results)	_____ 10
	_____ 11
	_____ 12
	_____ 13
	_____ 14

12 Asepsis – list of rules

Study the list of rules which should be followed to reduce the spread of hospital acquired infection.

1 Say how often, in your experience, you have seen each rule broken.

2 Read the following accounts of incidents and decide which rules were broken in each incident.

1 A nurse was cut by a scalpel when she pressed down on a container for used sharps to make more room in it. She automatically sucked the wound and it was later found that she was infected with HIV.

2 Nurses' uniforms were examined at the end of a shift and more than half were found to be contaminated on the waist area as a result of leaning over patients in bed.

3 Porters provided a black bag for nurses to use for ward waste. The nurses used it for everything: old specimens, used needles, dirty bandages, broken glass, empty bottles, etc.

4 A ward ran out of disposable towels and whilst waiting for new ones, nurses used cloth squares cut from old sheets.

5 A ward was cleaned very carefully, the furnishings and curtains washed, etc. but still there were signs of contamination. Nobody could understand where it came from until someone pointed out that the floor polisher was often used but never cleaned.

6 A contaminated bedpan in the Intensive Care Unit of one hospital was identified as the possible source of infection in a second hospital via patient transfer.

7 A woman with a kidney stone developed septicaemia when staff did not spot that she was developing a deadly infection. She lost consciousness and died five days later.

8 A patient was given a blood transfusion and a catheter left in her arm in case she needed more blood. She developed pains and fever and phlebitis was found in the artery where the catheter had been inserted.

		QUESTIONNAIRE			
		Rule	Often broken	Sometimes broken	Never broken
	a	Frequently decontaminate hands using the correct technique			
	b	Wear protective clothing whenever necessary			
	c	Dispose of clinical waste in colour-coded bags and boxes			
	d	Always decontaminate equipment after use			
	e	Achieve and maintain a clean clinical environment			
	f	Use indwelling devices properly			
	g	Deal with accidental exposure to blood-borne viruses using the correct procedure			
	h	Ensure all staff are fully trained in infection control			

13 Record of care

1 Study the computerized record of care and decide if these statements are true (T) or false (F).

1 Aydin Gulcek is a long-stay patient in the hospital.

2 Urine tests showed clear for diabetes at the initial assessment.

3 The patient was overweight at the time of the assessment.

4 The patient leads an active life.

5 The patient reacts badly to medication.

6 The patient has been receiving care for nearly two years.

7 The patient has stopped smoking during his treatment.

8 The patient has got steadily better.

9 Mervyn Chong is a podiatrist.

10 The next step for the patient will probably be home dialysis.

2 Decide which of the following complications of diabetes the record shows.

a Diabetic retinopathy

b Loss of sensation in the extremities

c Sexual problems

d Skin disorder

e Cataracts

PATIENT PERSONAL DETAILS

Name	Aydin Gulcek
Admission status	outpatient
Date of diabetes diagnosis	24 / 5 / 06

RECORD OF CARE

Education review given by	Jane Bell	Date	13 / 2 / 08

Comment — Smoking is now significantly reduced.
Patient making good progress on self care but renal functioning is deteriorating. Follow on at home to assess potential for CAPD.

Education review given by	Mervyn Chong	Date	08 / 9 / 07

Comment — Home visit to educate patient in foot care

Education review given by	Jane Bell	Date	27 / 8 / 07

Comment — I have talked to him about foot care today. Community podiatrist will follow on at home.

Education review given by	Carl Holst	Date	03 / 1 / 07

Comment — Not always complying with recommended lifestyle changes but he understands what he needs to do. Better to concentrate on foot care next time as he reports numbness and his feet are at considerable risk

DIABETES ASSESSMENT

Assessment by	Jane Bell	Date of assessment	25 / 5 / 06

Diabetes   Type 1 ☐ type 2 ☑

Dates of diagnosis with diabetes	24 / 5

Diabetes risk assessment	High ☑

Location of assessment	Renal Unit	Date	27 / 8 / 07

Tests — All urine tests positive

PERSONAL DETAILS   Date   03 / 1 / 07

Height	155cm	Weight	88 kg	Target Weight	70kg
BMI	29	Mobility	housebound		

Alcohol consumption	25 u/wk	Smoking (no. per day)	10

INTERNAL COMMENTS

Very grave risk of future renal failure. Patient needs to make urgent lifestyle changes. Won't take ACE inhibitors as says they make him dizzy.

14 Psychiatric case history

These extracts are from the case history of a patient's illness. Read all the extracts before answering the questions.

1 Match the events with the dates.

1 4 May 1987
2 12 January 2007
3 15 January 2007
4 5 February 2007
5 15 February 2007

a The patient is discharged after a three-day hospitalization.
b Mrs Kaneiria spends a week in hospital suffering depression.
c Mrs Kaneiria tries to kill herself.
d Patient is referred for home visits.
e The patient's medication is changed.

2 Answer the questions.

1 What event is associated with the onset of Mrs Kaneiria's illness?
2 What symptoms has she suffered repeatedly from?
3 How many times has she been admitted to hospital?
4 How has she responded to inpatient treatment?
5 What example of self-harming behaviour has the patient shown?
6 What has caused her auditory hallucinations?

REFERRAL

4 May 1987
From Dr. R. Saad
City Centre Group Practice

Re: Patient Mrs J. Kaneiria
Age: 31 years
Request admission for: Post-partum depression following birth of child

HOSPITAL PSYCHIATRIC UNIT ADMISSION RECORD

Admission	Mrs Jaharna Kaneiria	Date	12 January 2007

Patient is a 51-year-old female.
Admitted following suicide attempt. Found unconscious in her car with the engine running and garage door closed. The patient had left a suicide note: 'I don't deserve to live any more.'

Presenting symptoms

Acute depressive episode: suicidal tendencies, feelings of guilt and worthlessness

History The patient suffered from depression twenty years ago with the birth of her first child. She was hospitalized for one week.

Treatment 72-hour admission to inpatient psychiatric unit for safety and stabilization. Bupropion SR (80 mg, t.i.d.) and group therapy

PSYCHIATRIC NURSE'S ASSESSMENT FOR DISCHARGE

Date 15 January 2007

On admission the patient presented as having average intelligence. She was withdrawn and did not interact with staff or fellow patients. However, following medication and group therapy her symptoms have improved significantly. She has become more sociable, and her guilt, insomnia, and decreased appetite have resolved fairly rapidly over the three days of hospitalization.

15 February 2007

Three weeks following her discharge Mrs. Kaneiria was re-admitted to the inpatient psychiatric unit. She was experiencing auditory hallucinations. According to her husband, she had been yelling and screaming at home, and hiding in a corner trying to escape from 'voices accusing her of murder'. Her husband described her behaviour as 'animal-like' and said that she had never behaved like that before.

The psychiatric evaluation indicated possible Bupropion-induced psychotic symptoms. Treatment was discontinued and the patient was started on Sertraline 100 mg qid.

Ten days following the start of her new medication regimen, her affect was much brighter. She smiled more, and showed emotion. She was more interactive on the unit with staff and peers, and her appetite and sleep had improved significantly. She denied experiencing auditory hallucinations any longer and was discharged home. Her medication is to be supervised by the community psychiatric nurse.

15 Interdepartmental communication

1 Read the emails and answer the questions.

1 What does the Neurology department think is wrong with their patient?

2 What three pieces of information did Beth Forrest give Radiology to help trace the x-rays?

3 What was the first error?

4 What was the second error?

5 What will Beth Forrest need to do if the x-rays can't be found?

2 Find words or phrases in the emails that mean

1 try to find (email 1)

2 dangerous to health (email 1)

3 referring to the brain (email 1)

4 records (email 1)

5 lost (email 2)

6 to send on (email 2)

7 mail service within the hospital (email 2)

8 x-rays (email 2)

9 for me (email 3)

10 do again (email 3).

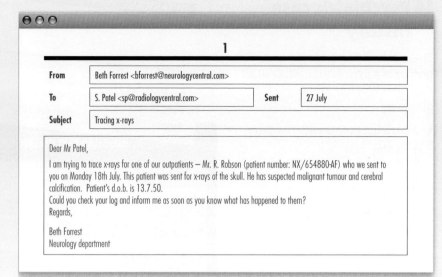

1

From	Beth Forrest <bforrest@neurologycentral.com>		
To	S. Patel <sp@radiologycentral.com>	Sent	27 July
Subject	Tracing x-rays		

Dear Mr Patel,

I am trying to trace x-rays for one of our outpatients — Mr. R. Robson (patient number: NX/654880-AF) who we sent to you on Monday 18th July. This patient was sent for x-rays of the skull. He has suspected malignant tumour and cerebral calcification. Patient's d.o.b. is 13.7.50.

Could you check your log and inform me as soon as you know what has happened to them?

Regards,

Beth Forrest
Neurology department

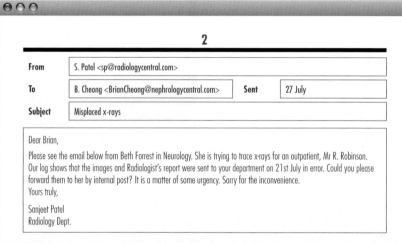

2

From	S. Patel <sp@radiologycentral.com>		
To	B. Cheong <BrianCheong@nephrologycentral.com>	Sent	27 July
Subject	Misplaced x-rays		

Dear Brian,

Please see the email below from Beth Forrest in Neurology. She is trying to trace x-rays for an outpatient, Mr R. Robinson. Our log shows that the images and Radiologist's report were sent to your department on 21st July in error. Could you please forward them to her by internal post? It is a matter of some urgency. Sorry for the inconvenience.

Yours truly,

Sanjeet Patel
Radiology Dept.

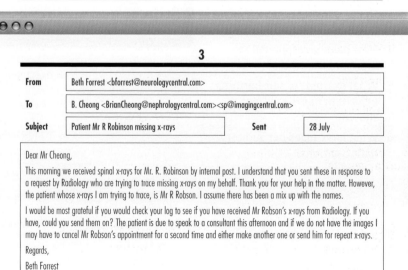

3

From	Beth Forrest <bforrest@neurologycentral.com>		
To	B. Cheong <BrianCheong@nephrologycentral.com><sp@imagingcentral.com>		
Subject	Patient Mr R Robinson missing x-rays	Sent	28 July

Dear Mr Cheong,

This morning we received spinal x-rays for Mr. R. Robinson by internal post. I understand that you sent these in response to a request by Radiology who are trying to trace missing x-rays on my behalf. Thank you for your help in the matter. However, the patient whose x-rays I am trying to trace, is Mr R Robson. I assume there has been a mix up with the names.

I would be most grateful if you would check your log to see if you have received Mr Robson's x-rays from Radiology. If you have, could you send them on? The patient is due to speak to a consultant this afternoon and if we do not have the images I may have to cancel Mr Robson's appointment for a second time and either make another one or send him for repeat x-rays.

Regards,

Beth Forrest

Admin bank key

1 Emergency telephone call log

1 a2 b1 c4 d3
5 is not illustrated

2 1 Incident number 1
2 Incident number 4
3 Incident number 4
4 2
5 Incident number 5
6 Incident numbers 1, 3, 4, 5
7 Incident number 1
8 Incident number 2

3 1 ATA
2 synopsis
3 cab
4 juvenile
5 fatality
6 rehabilitation

2 General medical admission form

1 1T 2F 3F 4F 5T 6F 7F
8T 9F 10 F

2 c, d, e, g, h

3 A midwife's diary

1F 2T 3F 4T 5T 6T 7T
8T 9F 10 F

4 Prescriptions

1 a1 b3 c2 d4

2 1c 2d 3b 4a

3 Mr Masahiko Shizawa
Insert a sufficient quantity of the medicine rectally four times a day; in the morning, in the afternoon, and after bowel movements. Repeat the treatment when it is needed.

4 1 3 x 300mg caps Gabapentin c.f. nmt t.i.d
2 1 unit insulin ID inj. qqh
3 agit cough suppressant qs PO rep prn

5 Extracts from an ophthalmic nursing manual

1 1c 2b 3d 4a

2 1 a subject   5 (to) dilate
2 (to) restrain   6 (to) sting
3 (to) clip   7 topical
4 (to) extract   8 distortion

3 1 It is best if you ...
2 it is imperative that ...
3 ... if you want to see the macula
4 Be careful about possible accidents ...

6 Laboratory report

1 1a 2b 3b 4b 5c 6a

2 b

7 Reflective writing

1 1b 2c 3d 4a

2 c

8 Diagnostic questionnaire

1 1 localized   4 tenderness
2 diffuse   5 elevated
3 rebound

2 3

9 Neurological observation chart

1 1 in a road traffic accident
2 10.30 p.m.
3 hourly

2 1 Philip Boston
2 subdural haemotoma
3 22.30
4 23.30
5 00.30
6 22.30 : 4
22.30 : 3
00.30 : 2
7 22.30 : 4
22.30 : 3
00.30 : 2
8 22.30 : 6
23.30 : 4
00.30 : 4
9 14
10 10
11 8

3 1 spontaneously   5 localizing
2 orientated   6 flexion
3 inappropriate   7 extension
4 incomprehensible

10 Nursing care plan

1 a goal   e observation
b instruction   f observation
c instruction   g goal
d observation

2 1g 2a 3f 4e 5d 6c 7b

11 Pre-op documentation

1 1 Centre section of right foot
2 Smoking
3 Diabetes
4 He will probably die
5 He is anxious and is sure he will die

2 1 Richard Campbell-Smith
2 55
3 A-
4 hardening of arteries & foot ulceration
5 right foot ray amputation under general anesthetic
6 type 2 diabetes (2 years)
7 gastroparesis (3 years)
8 Metoclopramide (Reglan)
9 allergic to penicillin
10 ½ insulin dose 24 hours pre. op.
11 Vancomycin 1 hr pre. op.
12 NPO from midnight.
13 EKG shows normal
14 VS are fairly stable

12 Asepsis – list of rules

2 1g 2b 3c 4a 5e 6d
7h 8f

13 Record of care

1 1F 2F 3T 4F 5T 6T 7F
8F 9T 10 T

2 b

14 Psychiatric case history

1 1b 2c 3a 4e 5d

2 1 Birth of child
2 Feelings of guilt
3 Three
4 Responds well
5 Suicide attempt
6 Medication – Buproprion

15 Interdepartmental communication

1 1 Suspected malignant tumour and cerebral calcification
2 Patient's name, patient number, date of birth
3 X-rays possibly sent to the wrong department
4 Mistake over the name of the patient; Robson / Robinson
5 Cancel the appointment and either make a new appointment or repeat the x-rays

2 1 trace   6 to forward
2 malignant   7 internal post
3 cerebral   8 images
4 log   9 on my behalf
5 misplaced   10 repeat

9 Neurology

Scrub up

1 Look at the map of the brain. With a partner, decide which parts of the brain a–f you would use most when doing each of the actions 1–6 below.

2 🎧 Listen to five people describing the effect of a head injury on a family member or friend. Decide which part of the brain a–f you think each person has damaged. Compare your answers with a partner before listening again.

1 _____   3 _____   5 _____
2 _____   4 _____

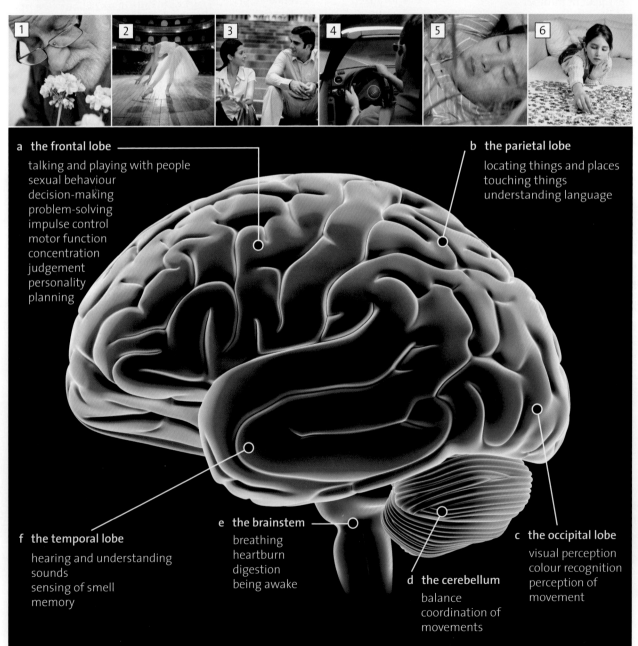

a the frontal lobe
talking and playing with people
sexual behaviour
decision-making
problem-solving
impulse control
motor function
concentration
judgement
personality
planning

b the parietal lobe
locating things and places
touching things
understanding language

f the temporal lobe
hearing and understanding sounds
sensing of smell
memory

e the brainstem
breathing
heartburn
digestion
being awake

d the cerebellum
balance
coordination of movements

c the occipital lobe
visual perception
colour recognition
perception of movement

In this unit
- First and Second Conditional
- pronouncing contractions
- common medical adjectives
- giving your opinion on medical cases

Tests

Glasgow coma scale

1 Read about the Glasgow coma scale and complete the text with the adjectives and adverbs below.

appropriately	incomprehensible
bent	random
coherently	spontaneously
deeply	verbal

The Glasgow coma scale is used for measuring how _____ [1] unconscious a patient is, in order to assess the extent of brain damage. Eye response, verbal response, and motor response are tested. For each of these tests, the patient receives a score, with the minimum being 1 for no response. The total for the three tests gives the patient's GCS score.

Eye response

a eyes opening to _____ [2] command ☐

b no eye opening ☐ 1

c eyes opening in response to pain ☐

d eyes opening _____ [3] ☐

Verbal response

a confused (the patient responds to questions but there is _____ [4], some confusion) ☐

b none ☐

c inappropriate words (_____ [5] speech, but no conversational exchange) ☐

d _____ [6] sounds (moaning, but no words) ☐

e orientated (the patient responds _____ [7] to simple questions) ☐

Motor response

a withdrawal (pulls arm away) from pain ☐

b extension (arms straight by sides) in response to pain ☐

c no motor response ☐

d obeys commands (the patient does simple things as asked) ☐

e localizing to pain (moves hand towards pain) ☐

f flexion (arms _____ [8] up to chin) to pain ☐

2 The order of responses has been mixed. Read each section and number the responses.

1 eye response (1–4) 3 motor response (1–6)

2 verbal response (1–5)

Listening

An unconscious patient

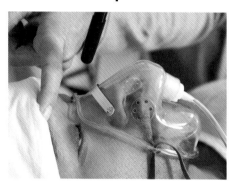

1 🎧 A 45-year-old man, Lewis Gavin, has been admitted unconscious after his wife found him collapsed on the bathroom floor. Listen to the senior nurse assess him, and work out his GCS score, using the description in *Tests* to help you.

1 Eye response = _____

2 Verbal response = _____

3 Motor response = _____

4 GCS = _____

2 🎧 Two doctors are discussing possible courses of action. Listen and make notes. Then compare your notes with a partner.

diagnosis	1
evidence for diagnosis	2
actions	3

3 Discuss the questions.

- What are the special difficulties of nursing an unconscious patient? Talk about your own experience if possible.
- Think about an unconscious patient you have nursed. What did you find challenging?

Speaking

Finding out what went wrong

Work in pairs. You are going to find out what happened to Lewis Gavin (the patient in *Listening*). Student A, go to p.111. Student B, go to p.115.

• 70–88% of all people that sustain a head injury are male.
• 10–19% are aged 65 or older.
• 40–50% are children.

What reasons can you think of to explain these statistics?

• Language spot

First and Second Conditional

1 Work in pairs. Read the two sentences, spoken by a doctor. Answer the questions that follow.

a His blood pressure would be lower if he didn't smoke.

b If we break up the clot now, that'll prevent further damage to the brain.

1 Which sentence talks about something which is possible in the future?

2 Which sentence imagines something different from the real situation now?

>> Go to **Grammar reference** p.120

2 Complete the dialogue by putting the verbs in brackets in the correct tense.

Nurse 1 How's Mr Rigg?

Nurse 2 If his operation __*goes*__ [1] (go) well tomorrow, he __*'ll make*__ [2] (make) a full and speedy recovery.

Nurse 1 It's a straightforward procedure, isn't it?

Nurse 2 Yes, he's having a haematoma evacuated from his skull. He _____ [3] (be) home by the weekend, unless something unexpected _____ [4] (happen).

Nurse 1 We spend too much time treating cyclists. There _____ [5] (not be) so many accidents if they _____ [6] (have) more cycle paths.

Nurse 2 And if cycle helmets _____ [7] (be) compulsory, there _____ [8] (be) fewer brain injuries.

Nurse 1 Yes. This patient was lucky. At least he _____ [9] (wear) a helmet when he next _____ [10] (ride) his bike.

3 🎧 Listen and check your answers.

4 Complete these sentences in a way that is true for you.
If I had more time, I …
I'll be very happy if …
If my current plan is successful, …
If I could work anywhere in the world, …

5 Work in small groups. Take turns to read one of your sentences. Ask each other as many questions as you can about each sentence.

Pronunciation

Contractions

1 🎧 Work in pairs. Listen and complete the sentences.

1 His blood pressure _____ be lower if he _____ smoke.

2 She _____ healthier if she _____ so much.

3 If we break up the clot now, that _____ further damage to the brain.

4 If his operation goes well tomorrow, he _____ a full and speedy recovery.

5 If she were in pain, we _____ her morphine.

6 I _____ at the weekend if there _____ a staff shortage.

2 Practise saying the sentences. Pay attention to the contractions (*didn't*, *'ll*, *'d*, etc.)

3 Where possible, shorten these sentences by using contractions. Then practise saying them.

1 If Mr Jones does not stop drinking, he will really affect his health.

2 I would not give Mrs Rook morphine if she did not want it.

3 She will probably die if we do not operate soon.

4 If he were not in hospital, he would be looked after at home.

5 They will not recover quickly if they do not take their medicine.

6 If George was not in hospital, he would be on holiday.

Reading

Case study – a head injury

1 You are going to read the case study of a young female patient who received brain injuries four months ago. First, read the first paragraph of the case study and tick (✓) which injuries Katie sustained.

1 a fractured skull	☐	4 a broken leg	☐
2 a broken arm	☐	5 internal injuries	☐
3 chest injuries	☐		

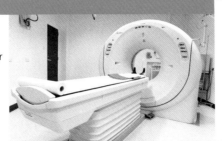

A **CT scanner** sends x-rays through the body from different angles, producing detailed 3-D images of internal structures. CT scans are especially useful for diagnosing bleeding in the brain, aneurysms, brain tumours, and brain damage.

2 Read the rest of the case study and match the headings with paragraphs A–E.

1 Cognitive skills _____
2 Psychosocial _____
3 Communication _____
4 Physical functioning and mobility _____
5 Personal and self care _____

3 Rate how well you think Katie can probably do these things. Write a number from 0 to 5 (0 = she cannot do it, 5 = she can do it without help).

1 brush her hair _____
2 control her emotions _____
3 feed herself _____
4 make decisions _____
5 recognize what things are _____
6 remember information _____
7 understand her disabilities _____
8 understand what people are saying _____

CASE STUDY

Katie Martin is a nine-year-old female who was in a car crash. At the scene her Glasgow coma scale was 3. She was intubated and transported by helicopter to hospital. She was taken to the intensive care unit due to her intracranial haemorrhage which 24 hours later resulted in evacuation. She was placed on a ventilator and a tracheostomy was performed. Katie's pre-operative diagnosis was left frontal haemorrhagic contusion and multiple skull fracture. She had a left frontal craniotomy with evacuation of the intracerebral haematoma. The dural tear and skull fracture were repaired. Additionally she suffered lacerations to the liver, face, left eyelid, and a right femur fracture. Four months after the accident, her mental and physical state have improved, as outlined below.

A Katie is able to reposition herself in bed. She can ambulate 10–15 feet with maximal assistance, but locomotes in a wheelchair. She will need physical therapy to improve coordination and balance. She requires moderate assistance transferring in and out of the bed, chair, and car. Her hearing is adequate, but she has lost the vision in her left eye. She is unable to write, but can hold a pen, so she will need physical therapy to restore her fine motor coordination and strength.

B She needs assistance for grooming and hygiene care. She will need occupational therapy to help restore her dressing, grooming, and hygiene skills. She needs assistance using the toilet. Katie shows little interest in food, but feeds herself with small bites and has a G-tube for supplemental nutrition. She has moderate problems with both her bladder and bowel management.

C Katie's frontal lobe syndrome has left her unable to produce abstract reasoning, logical concept formation, and planning. She is no longer spontaneous and creative. She does not possess the judgement and insight required to make safe or reasonable social and personal decisions. Her memory has been compromised for both auditory and visual processing of stimuli and retrieval of information. Although she is alert, she cannot sustain concentration sufficiently in order to learn. She is able to count, but has difficulty identifying objects. She can follow simple commands.

D She is more alert and oriented to person and can identify significant relationships. Katie has a basic understanding of simple conversations, but cannot produce or comprehend abstract thoughts. She is capable of expressing her basic needs. She is uncooperative and easily frustrated. She cries easily and shouts obscenities without provocation.

E Katie is emotional and cries frequently for brief periods of time for no particular reason, but is easily redirected. She argues because of her poor ability to overcome frustration and delay gratification. Katie is unaware of the extent of her impairment. It is predicted that she will become depressed and angry as she gains insight. Katie does not initiate recreational activities and entertainment.

You've probably read in *People* magazine that I'm a nice guy – but when the doctor first told me I had Parkinson's, I wanted to kill him.

Michael J. Fox, actor and Parkinson's disease sufferer

Vocabulary

Common medical adjectives

1 Adjectives relating to parts of the body, the senses, and areas of life often use Greek or Latin roots. Complete the expressions with the adjectives below.

auditory	nasal	sensory
cerebral	ocular	verbal
cranial	senile	visual
cutaneous		

1	a _____ haemorrhage	*bleeding in the brain*
2	_____ perception	*the ability to hear*
3	_____ polyps	*abnormal growths in the nose*
4	_____ skills	*the ability to use words*
5	_____ aortic stenosis	*a heart condition associated with the elderly*
6	_____ impairment	*a problem with one or more of the senses*
7	_____ anatomy	*the anatomy of the skull*
8	_____ acuity	*the ability to see things clearly*
9	the _____ surface	*the surface of the eye*
10	_____ diseases	*diseases of the skin*

2 Work in pairs and share your knowledge. How many of these adjectives can you complete?

1	weakness of the muscles	m_____ weakness
2	the body's system of veins	the v_____ system
3	cancer of the womb	u_____ cancer
4	lung problems	p_____ disorders
5	a heart operation	c_____ surgery
6	keeping the mouth clean	o_____ hygiene
7	eczema in babies	i_____ eczema
8	problems with thinking	c_____ impairment

It's my job

1 Aileen Bowles nurses children with head injuries. Before you read about her job, discuss these questions with a partner.

- What do you imagine would be interesting about the job?
- What do you imagine would be the most challenging aspect of the job?

2 Would you like to do this job? Why (not)?

Aileen Bowles

I work in Paediatric Neurology, and specialize in caring for children who have suffered trauma to the head. The training is long because you need to understand how to keep someone alive and how the brain affects every system of the body. Our care needs to be constant, even if an injury doesn't seem serious, as secondary bleeding and swelling in the brain is invisible, but very dangerous.

After the initial critical period, we start considering what therapies will help the patient regain function. Patients are usually unconscious when I meet them, and what I love about my job is seeing patients gradually become an active person again and restart their lives. They don't always make it, unfortunately, and you can never get used to the death of a child.

The most challenging and interesting part is the different types of communication. We have to try to find out what the patient is feeling, which in infants is difficult even without a head injury. We also have close contact with the patients' families – we keep them informed of what's happening at all times, and prepare them for the time when they get their child back. That's the best bit, when the child goes home.

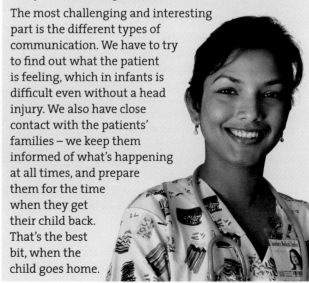

Project

1 Research one of these head injuries.

- concussion
- second-impact syndrome
- cerebral contusion
- subarachnoid haemorrhage
- subdural haematoma

2 Prepare a short talk for your next lesson, using visual aids if appropriate. Think about

- common causes
- how dangerous it is
- how it is treated
- what long-term problems it can cause.

Writing

Giving your opinion on medical cases

Work in small groups. Go to p.111. You will read three real-life medical cases. Discuss the cases and give your opinion on what you think should happen. Then write a short paragraph giving your opinion on each of the questions below.

Story A

- Should the couple have the baby?
- If they have the baby, should the hospital continue to keep it alive artificially?
- Who should have the right to decide – the parents or the hospital?

Story B

- Should the hospital remove her feeding tube?
- Who should have the right to decide in this case – the husband or the parents?

Story C

- Should the hospital remove her feeding tube?
- Who should have the right to decide in this case – the parents or the hospital?

Checklist

Assess your progress in this unit. Tick (✓) the statements which are true.

I can use conditionals to talk about possible events and actions

I can use a range of adjectives identifying parts of the body and senses

I can write about my opinion of a medical case

Key words

Adjectives
auditory
cerebral
cranial
cutaneous
intracranial
oral
senile
sensory
uterine
venous

Nouns
balance
impairment
judgement
motor response
perception

Look back through this unit. Find five more words or expressions that you think are useful.

10 Coronary

Scrub up

Do the quiz in pairs or teams. Your teacher will give you the answers.

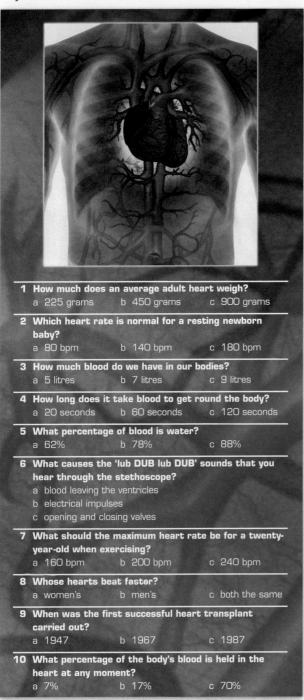

1 How much does an average adult heart weigh?
  a 225 grams   b 450 grams   c 900 grams

2 Which heart rate is normal for a resting newborn baby?
  a 80 bpm   b 140 bpm   c 180 bpm

3 How much blood do we have in our bodies?
  a 5 litres   b 7 litres   c 9 litres

4 How long does it take blood to get round the body?
  a 20 seconds   b 60 seconds   c 120 seconds

5 What percentage of blood is water?
  a 62%   b 78%   c 88%

6 What causes the 'lub DUB lub DUB' sounds that you hear through the stethoscope?
  a blood leaving the ventricles
  b electrical impulses
  c opening and closing valves

7 What should the maximum heart rate be for a twenty-year-old when exercising?
  a 160 bpm   b 200 bpm   c 240 bpm

8 Whose hearts beat faster?
  a women's   b men's   c both the same

9 When was the first successful heart transplant carried out?
  a 1947   b 1967   c 1987

10 What percentage of the body's blood is held in the heart at any moment?
  a 7%   b 17%   c 70%

Body bits

The circulation of the blood

1 Work in pairs. Look at the ECG. Try to explain what is happening in the heart at points P, QRS, and T.

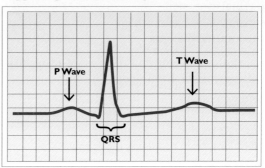

2 Complete the text using the verbs below. You will need to change the form of some of them.

cause	fill	push	relax
contract	force	reach	return

A heartbeat has three phases.

In the first, diastole, the heart _____¹ and blood _____² the atria. This appears as a flat line on the ECG.

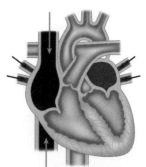

In the second phase, an electrical impulse _____³ the atria to _____⁴ and _____⁵ blood into the ventricles. This is point P on the ECG.

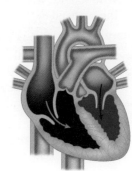

In the third phase, the electrical impulse _____ [6] the ventricles. These contract, _____ [7] blood to the lungs and to the rest of the body. This phase includes points Q, R, and S on the ECG. The heart then _____ [8] to its relaxed state, marked by point T.

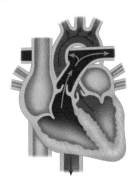

3 Before reading the text, work together to explain what route blood takes around the body.

4 Complete the descriptions 1–6 with the words below, and match them to parts a–f in the diagram.

deoxygenated   oxygen   oxygenated

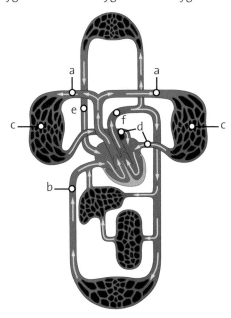

1 The aorta carries _____ blood from the heart to all parts of the body.   ___

2 The pulmonary veins carry _____-rich blood from the lungs to the left atrium of the heart. They are the only veins that carry _____ blood.   ___

3 The pulmonary arteries carry blood to the lungs. They are the only arteries that carry _____ blood.   ___

4 The superior vena cava returns _____ blood from the upper part of the body to the heart.   ___

5 The inferior vena cava returns _____ blood from the lower part of the body to the heart.   ___

6 The network of vessels in the lungs lose carbon dioxide and absorb _____.   ___

Listening

Heart failure

1 Read this information leaflet for patients. Discuss the possible answers with a partner.

Congestive heart failure happens when the heart cannot pump enough blood to the body. The problem usually starts on the _____ [1] side of the heart. This means not only that the body doesn't get enough _____ [2], but also _____ [3] escapes into the body's tissues and lungs. This is why the first sign of heart failure is often extreme _____ [4] and breathlessness, and why the _____ [5] usually become swollen.

Heart failure is often the result of damage to the heart caused by a heart attack, by coronary heart disease, or by _____ [6]. These change the shape of the heart and the thickness of its walls, which stops it working well. If your heartbeat is _____ [7], this can also make heart failure more likely eventually. Patients with possible heart failure are sent for an examination called an _____ [8]. This shows how well the ventricles are working.

Patients with heart failure are encouraged to do exercise to improve their breathing, and _____ [9] are often prescribed to reduce the build-up of fluid. The doctor will also usually prescribe _____ [10], which reduce blood pressure and make the heart's job easier, and _____ [11], which keep the heartbeat strong and steady. A device called a pacemaker may also be fitted, which sends a regular electrical impulse to the heart through _____ [12] wires.

2 🎧 Listen to a radio interview with a heart specialist, and complete the information.

In the USA, a 'do not use' list of abbreviations and symbols to do with drug dosages is published each year. The ones not to use are

U   IU   qd   qod   X.o mg   .X mg   MS

- Do you know what they mean?
- Why do you think they should not be used?
- Do you know any other confusing abbreviations or symbols?

A book has been published in the US listing 15,000 commonly used medical abbreviations, acronyms, and symbols.

According to the US Institute of Medicine, there are more than 7,000 deaths a year due to medication errors.

Vocabulary

Abbreviations

Try to work out what the abbreviations in these sentences mean. Use the words in the boxes and a dictionary to help you.

abnormal · drug · nil (=nothing) · nothing · activity · embolism · physical · acute · failure · adverse · heart · pulmonary · by · heart · rate · central · left · reaction · coronary · renal · detected · level · system · disease · mouth · nervous · ventricle

1   This patient's notes say NBM, so
    don't give him any food.   *nil by mouth*

2   This disease affects the CNS, causing speech,
    movement, and memory problems.   _____

3   The tests showed NAD, so this patient
    can go home.   _____

4   Damage to the kidneys has caused ARF. _____

5   Mrs Welsh's breathing is bad. She
    may have a PE.   _____

6   Smoking is a risk factor for CHD.   _____

7   The LV is enlarged, so the heart
    is not pumping effectively.   _____

8   The patient suffered an ADR after
    being put on new medication.   _____

9   HR is now back to 70.   _____

10 He has an office job and takes no
    exercise, so his PAL is very low.   _____

Reading

Patient notes

1 Discuss the pros and cons of using abbreviations in patient notes.

2 Match the abbreviations with the words and expressions.

1   bilat.
2   BS
3   BS
4   c/o
5   CV
6   CXR
7   DM
8   EtOH
9   GI
10 HTN
11 M/G/R
12 +
13 N
14 POE
15 RRR
16 sl
17 SOB
18 u/s

a   alcohol
b   bilaterally (= on both sides)
c   pain on exertion
d   breathing sounds
e   cardiovascular system
f   slight
g   complaining of
h   diabetes mellitus
i   gastrointestinal
j   hypertension
k   murmurs, gallops, rubs
    (= sounds that may indicate
    heart irregularities)
l   bowel sounds
m   nausea
n   present, observed
o   regular rate and rhythm
p   shortness of breath
q   chest x-ray
r   ultrasound

3 Read the patient notes and answer the questions.

1   What type of pain does the patient get and where is it located?
2   How many times has the patient had this pain?
3   How long has he been getting this pain?
4   When does he get the pain?
5   What makes the pain better?
6   Does he smoke or drink?
7   Did his GP refer him to the hospital?
8   What condition does the doctor think is most likely to be causing the pain?

The Arab physician Ibn Al-Nafis (1213–1288) was the first person to realize that blood passed from the right side to the left side of the heart via the lungs.

The English physician William Harvey (1578–1657) was the first to correctly describe how the heart pumps blood around the body.

PATIENT NOTES

Jerry Kahn

History

48 y.o. male c/o chest pain. Began last night POE (jogging). Squeezing pain, sl SOB, sl N and diaphoresis. Pain resolved spontaneously after 20 mins. No pain now. 5 similar episodes over past 3-4 mos. usually POE or after a heavy meal with some relief by antacids. Has Hx of ↑ cholesterol but no follow-up or treatment. Plays tennis weekly. Ex-smoker x 20 yrs. (40 pack/yrs.), EtOH 3 beers/day x 30 yrs. Denies unusual stress. Sister with unknown heart problem. No Hx HTN, DM but has not seen GP x 2 yrs.

Physical Examination

No obvious distress, minimizing symptoms, anxious to leave. BP of 180/90 noted.
Resp. clear BS bilat. without wheezes, rhonchi, or rales.
GI – no tenderness, BS+, no masses
CV – RRR no M/G/R

Differential Diagnosis

1 myocardial infarction

2 acid reflux

3 muscle strain

4 anxiety reaction

Diagnostic Workup

1 ECG

2 CXR

3 u/s heart

4 upper GI series

Project

Research one of the relatively new treatments for heart problems below. In the next class, explain to the group what problem it treats and how it works.

- ablation
- angioplasty
- statins
- stent grafts

Writing

Patient notes

1 🎧 As part of your training, you are observing a physical examination of a patient with a suspected heart problem. Listen and <u>underline</u> the correct information.

Marie Thomas is *45 / 35*[1]. She *has chest pains / is short of breath*[2] when she goes *upstairs / for a walk*[2]. She finds it easier when she *lies down / sits up*[4]. She's had the problem for *a year / two years*[5], and it's been bad for *six / two*[6] months. For the last *three / four*[7] weeks, she's had *shooting pains / aching*[8] down her *left / right*[9] arm. She's *sweating a lot / feeling very hot*[10]. She's *lost her appetite / got a good appetite*[11]. She takes *no / regular*[12] exercise. She weighs *48 / 92*[13] kilos. She drinks about *seven / two*[14] glasses of wine a week. She's *never smoked / smokes 20 a day*[15]. Her mother has *diabetes / angina*[16] and her father died of *a heart attack / lung cancer*[17]. There is no *diabetes / heart disease*[18] in her family. Her blood pressure is *160/80 / 120/50*[19] and has always been *low / high*[20]. Her *ankles / wrists*[21] are swollen. The doctor hears *heart murmurs / no heart murmurs*[22], and abnormal lungs sounds *on the left / on both sides*[23]. He can hear *bowel sounds / no bowel sounds*[24]. Mrs Thomas feels *tenderness / no tenderness*[25] in her abdomen. There are *masses / no masses*[26], but *some / no*[27] oedema.

2 Write the information as notes in a similar style to those in *Reading*.

PATIENT NOTES

Marie Thomas

History

Physical Examination

Differential Diagnosis

The Greeks believed that the heart held a person's spirit, the Chinese believed it was the centre for happiness, and the Egyptians thought the emotions and intellect came from the heart.

Pronunciation

Saying abbreviations

1 Pronounce each letter of the alphabet and write it in a column according to the vowel sound it has. For example, we say A /eɪ/, B /biː/.

/eɪ/	/iː/	/e/	/aɪ/	other
a	b			

2 🎧 Listen to these sentences and discuss the questions.

1 Julia is an SRN.
2 This patient has a URTI.
3 A teacher gave the child CPR.
4 The driver of the car was DoA.
5 The hospital has no A&E department.

a Which part of an abbreviation should you stress?
b How is the pronunciation of R different in SRN and CPR? Why?
c Why does sentence 1 use an and not a?
d Why does sentence 2 use a and not an?

3 🎧 Complete these sentences with a or an. Then listen and check.

1 I'm going to ask for _____ AXR.
2 The patient has _____ JVP of 5 cm.
3 She has _____ UTI and will need antibiotics.
4 Mr Musevi has _____ WBC of 45.

4 Write ten abbreviations. Dictate them to your partner.

● Language spot

Verbs followed by *to* or *-ing* form

1 Look at these sentences.

I **decided** to come and see you when it got really bad.

I **avoid** doing exercise when possible.

I **tried** walking for ten minutes a day, but it almost killed me.

I **enjoy** having a glass of wine with dinner.

Of course, I'd **advise** you to **stop** smoking.

My kids are always **asking** me to give up.

I've **tried** to stop lots of times but I haven't **managed** to kick the habit.

Some verbs are followed by the infinitive with *to*, some by *-ing* form, and some can be followed by both, sometimes with a different meaning for each form.

2 Put the **bold** verbs in the examples in 1 in the correct category.

verb + *to*	verb + *-ing*	verb + *to* / *-ing*
decide		

3 Underline the correct form of the verb.

1 Do you remember *coming / to come* here in the ambulance?
2 This patient had to give up *playing / to play* tennis because of chest pain.
3 Don't forget *writing / to write* in your diet diary every day.
4 I recommend *using / to use* nicotine patches to help you.
5 Most people don't mind *having / to have* an ECG.
6 Do you want *making / to make* an appointment for next week?
7 I'll never forget *watching / to watch* an operation for the first time.
8 The patient promised *making / to make* a big effort to stop smoking.
9 People don't feel like *exercising / to exercise* when they first leave hospital.
10 You must remember *taking / to take* your medication every morning.

4 Add the verbs in **3** to the table in **2**.

5 Complete these sentences in a way that is true for you. Then listen to another student's sentences and get them to talk about each one in more detail.

- I want to _____ this week when I have time.
- I try to avoid _____ whenever possible.
- I decided to become a nurse because _____.
- I'm trying to give up _____.
- I'll never forget _____ for the first time.
- I often forget _____.

≫ Go to **Grammar reference** p.121

Patient care

Giving an ECG

1 Here are some things a nurse might say to a patient when doing an ECG. Match the beginnings and endings of the sentences, and put them in a logical order.

1 We're nearly	a lying comfortably?	___
2 I'm just going to clean your chest so that	b try not to move.	___
	c the electrodes make good contact.	___
3 The machine's just		
4 We're going to do an ECG so that we can	d done recording now.	___
5 Are you	e look for any abnormal heart rhythms.	*1*
6 It's all done, so I'll		
7 Now just relax and	f take the electrodes off now.	___
	g printing out the recording.	___

2 Practise doing the procedure on a partner. Take turns being the nurse. Keep the patient informed and relaxed. You can chat to the patient too if you like.

Speaking

Self-help for the heart

1 You are going to give a short talk to a group of factory workers about how to keep their heart healthy. In groups, prepare a short presentation on one of the topics below.

● diet
● drinking and smoking
● exercise and stress

2 Form new groups of people who have prepared different topics and give your talks.

Checklist

Assess your progress in this unit. Tick (✓) the statements which are true.

I can describe how the heart works

I can understand and use common medical abbreviations

I can use verbs followed by *to* or *-ing* form

I can keep a patient informed during an ECG

Key words

angina
atria
beta blockers
bilaterally
congestive heart failure
diastole
electrode
embolism
exertion
heart murmurs
myocardial infarction
oedema
pacemaker
pulmonary veins
ventricles

Look back through this unit. Find five more words or expressions that you think are useful.

11 Surgery

Scrub up

1 Work in pairs. Match each word with its description. How many of the items can you find in the pictures?

1	drapes	a	a tool with a sharp blade for cutting
2	forceps	b	a scissor-like tool for gripping tissue
3	an implant	c	tubes attached to a pump for removing blood or other fluid from the surgical site
4	a swab	d	a device or artificial part that is inserted into the body, for example to replace or assist a defective part
5	retractors		
6	a scalpel	e	stitches that are inserted to close a wound
7	a scar	f	sterile covers for the parts of the patient's body not involved in the operation
8	a clamp	g	small pieces of wire that are pushed with a machine into each side of a wound to close it
9	suction		
10	sutures	h	tools that hold organs out of the way to allow access to the surgical site
11	diathermy plates	i	a mark that remains after a cut has healed
12	a gown	j	a loose, sterile piece of clothing worn by people in the operating theatre
13	an incision	k	a tool for holding a blood vessel closed to prevent bleeding
14	staples	l	tools that use heat to close the ends of blood vessels to prevent bleeding
		m	a piece of material, such as cotton, that is used to absorb blood during surgery
		n	a cut made by a surgeon to allow access inside the body

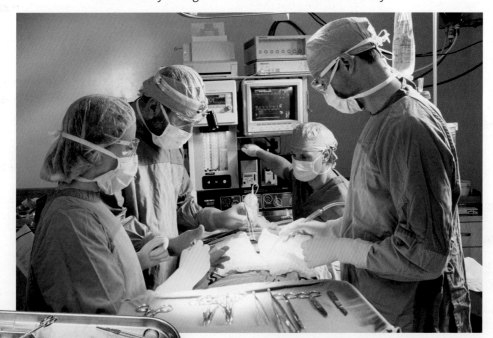

2 Talk about what is happening in the picture.

3 Tell your partner about an operation you, someone you know, or a patient of yours has had. Talk about

- the reason for it
- the anaesthetic
- what it involved
- the after-effects.
- the preparation

Listening

Preparing the patient for surgery

1 If you were having abdominal surgery, how much would the following things worry you? Mark them between 0 (it wouldn't worry me at all) and 5 (it would worry me a lot). Compare your answers with a partner.

- dying during surgery _____
- having the wrong operation done _____
- MRSA _____
- pain after the operation _____
- pain during the operation _____
- scarring _____

2 🎧 Listen to the nurse talking to a patient before her operation. Tick (✓) the things in 1 that the patient is worried about.

3 🎧 Listen again and answer the questions.

1 What operation is Tori having?
2 In what form is the pre-med?
3 How will the pre-med make her feel?
4 What will the anaesthetist ask her to do?
5 What will Tori have to control her pain post-op?
6 What is the worst pain she should have after the operation (out of ten)?
7 What does the orderly check before taking Tori?
8 What documents does the orderly take into theatre?

● Language spot

Future forms

1 Complete these sentences from *Listening* with the verbs below. Some of the verbs are used more than once.

be going to	ask	give
may	be	make
might	be able to	feel
should	let	wake up
will / 'll / won't	leave	

a I'm worried that the anaesthetic *won't be* strong enough, and I _____ in pain, but _____ speak.

b If you like, I _____ the anaesthetist to explain exactly what he does.

c It _____ quite a neat little scar actually.

d In a moment I _____ you a pre-med.

e How _____ I _____ when I _____?

f You _____ a little sick or you _____ really hungry.

2 Work in pairs. Discuss the questions.

1 Which sentences in 1 predict or imagine the future? _____
2 Which sentence states someone's intention? _____
3 Which sentence includes an offer or promise to do something? _____
4 Which modal verbs are used to mean 'possibly'? _____
5 Which modal verb is used to mean 'probably, if everything goes well'. _____
6 In which sentence is a present tense used to talk about the future? _____

3 Using the prompts below, make up a similar dialogue with your partner. Take turns as nurse and patient.

Nurse how / feeling?
Patient OK / nervous
Nurse what / worrying?
Patient anaesthetic / not strong enough / in pain / not / able to speak
Nurse I / ask / anaesthetist / explain / what / does
Patient thanks
Nurse in a moment / give / pre-med / feel / relaxed / sleepy
Patient OK
Nurse after that / theatre / anaesthetist / connect up / monitoring equipment / give / drugs / sleep
Patient how / feel / wake up?
Nurse pain relief / waking up – fully awake / little pump / only mild pain

4 Work in pairs. You are going to role-play a nurse reassuring a patient about an operation. Student A, go to p.112. Student B, go to p.113.

>> Go to **Grammar reference** p.121

In 2001, Professor Jacques Marescaux, in New York, performed the most common keyhole operation on a patient in Strasbourg, France.

Do you know what operation this is?

Reading

Keyhole surgery

1 Which of these phrases do you think will be included in a text on keyhole surgery?

1 hand–eye coordination _____
2 images on screens _____
3 oxygen therapy _____
4 one-centimetre cuts _____
5 robots' hands _____

Read the text quickly to check your answer.

2 Read the text again and answer the questions.

1 What other job did surgeons do in the past?
2 What two special skills do keyhole surgeons need to develop?

3 How many incisions are made in a keyhole heart bypass operation?
4 What four complications are mentioned that keyhole surgery reduces?
5 What advantages do robots have over human surgeons, according to the text?

3 Match the halves of these collocations. Then look at the text again to check.

1 a low   a blood clot
2 open   b instrument
3 a complex   c operation
4 a precision   d success rate
5 a potentially fatal   e surgery

4 Discuss the questions in small groups.

● Why isn't every operation done using keyhole surgery?
● How do you think surgery will be different in 50 years' time?

Surgery – the repair of a body with knives and stitches – is thousands of years old, and in the past it was performed by unqualified men whose other job was cutting hair. For a long time, surgery was limited to amputations which were performed incredibly fast, without anaesthetic, and without knowledge of microbes. Success rates were low and many patients died from shock or post-operative infections.

Despite the many innovations that have made surgery safer, open surgery has remained a bloody business which involves cutting open the body, holding it open with metal retractors, and putting both hands into the hole. However, the invention of the laparoscope – a tube for looking inside the body – has led to the development of a whole new way of doing things, commonly known as 'keyhole' surgery. Now complex operations are done through small incisions using instruments at the ends of long tubes. It is precise and delicate work and involves the minimum of invasion.

Refinements in technology mean that now surgeons don't have to hold a tube in one hand and look down it – they see images on screens made by a tiny video camera at the end of the laparoscope. The surgeon moves the precision instruments using two sets of controls like the handles of scissors. It has

been compared to painting the hallway of your house using a brush on a long stick pushed in through the letter box. It demands a lot of practice both in hand–eye coordination and in depth perception (most video screens are two-dimensional) in order to accurately navigate around the internal organs. Surgeons who grew up with computer games take to it quite naturally.

Keyhole surgery means less pain and less scarring. In conventional heart bypass surgery, for example, the surgeon has to open the patient's chest with a 30 cm long incision, whereas keyhole surgery involves just three one-centimetre cuts. Recovery time is much faster with keyhole surgery, which frees up hospital beds, and disrupts the patient's life less. There are fewer wound complications like infection, haematoma, and hernias, and because a patient is active soon after surgery, there is less risk of a potentially fatal blood clot in the veins.

Further advances in keyhole surgery are being made with robots. Robots' hands have a greater range of movement and don't shake. In a recent trial, their accuracy was measured against surgeons'. In a test to insert a needle into an exact spot in a dummy patient's kidney (the first stage in removing kidney stones), the human hand found the exact spot 79% of the time. The robots' score was 88%.

A less invasive surgery

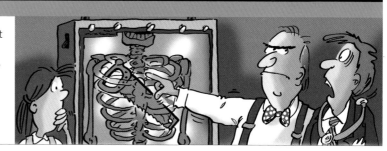

Each year in the USA, 1,500 people have objects left inside them during surgery.

- What do you think is the most common object left?
- What does the theatre nurse do to prevent this happening?

Vocabulary

Suffixes

1 Match the meanings 1–6 with the groups of words a–f.

1 cutting into
2 making a puncture in order to drain off fluid or air
3 making a passage from an organ to the skin
4 optical examination
5 surgical removal
6 surgically changing the shape

a thoraco<u>centesis</u> amnio<u>centesis</u> arthro<u>centesis</u>
b end<u>oscopy</u> gastr<u>oscopy</u> colon<u>oscopy</u>
c hyster<u>ectomy</u> vas<u>ectomy</u> tonsill<u>ectomy</u>
d trache<u>ostomy</u> col<u>ostomy</u> oesophag<u>ostomy</u>
e lapar<u>otomy</u> gastr<u>otomy</u> nephr<u>otomy</u>
f dermato<u>plasty</u> tympano<u>plasty</u> abdomino<u>plasty</u>

2 🎧 Listen and decide which of the operations or procedures in **1** is being referred to by each speaker.

1 _____ 4 _____
2 _____ 5 _____
3 _____ 6 _____

Pronunciation

Word stress

1 Work in pairs. Circle the stress pattern that represents the word.

1 colostomy	a •●••	b ••●•
2 tracheostomy	a •●•••	b ••●••
3 encephalograph	a •●•••	b •••●•
4 encephalography	a •••●••	b •●•••••
5 endoscope	a •●•	b ●••
6 endoscopy	a •●••	b •••●

🎧 Listen and check.

2 <u>Underline</u> the part of the word you think is stressed.

1 vasectomy
2 laparotomy
3 oesophagostomy
4 microbiology
5 radiography
6 cardiograph
7 cystoscopy
8 ophthalmoscope

🎧 Listen and check.

It's my job

1 Work in pairs. Write down words that you know for operating theatre equipment under the following headings.

cleaning	cutting	dealing with bleeding	clothes	other
soap				

2 Read the text and tick (✓) the items in **1** that Matthew mentions.

Matthew Binns

I'm a theatre nurse. When I start a shift, my first duty is to prepare the theatre. My team and I dust everything and check that all the electrical equipment is working. We make sure the table's set up, and that we have everything we need such as gowns, gloves, soaps and brushes, waste bags, and stocks of swabs. Then I check the operation list and prepare the equipment tray for the first one. I count all the swabs, sutures, blades – anything that could be left inside a patient – and write it all up on the whiteboard.

Our patients are all unconscious, and it's part of our job to make sure they are not injured or uncomfortable when they are on the operating table. During the operation you need to anticipate what the surgeon will need next. They generally work with forceps and scalpel, and you always need the right type of swab ready. With experience, you get to know what clamp or blade will be needed next.

At the end of the operation, we count in all the equipment that's been used, clean up the patient, and take them to the recovery room. Then it's back to the theatre to wipe down all surfaces and start all over again.

The basic job stays the same, but technology brings in new things. About half our operations here use keyhole surgery, which means we have to operate TV screens and other equipment. I've also been trained to use the laser machine, which is used for cutting or removing tissue.

The longest operation ever lasted 97 hours, when surgeons separated eleven-month-old Nepalese conjoined twins, Jamuna and Ganga Shrestha, who were connected at the tops of their heads and whose brains were partially fused together.

Signs and symptoms

Post-operative complications

1 Match the common complications 1–6 with the information about them A–F.

1 Atelectasis
2 Deep-vein thrombosis
3 Low urine output
4 Post-operative pain
5 Post-operative wound infection
6 Pyrexia

Different types of surgery have different types of complications. Generally though, patients face the following risks.

A _____ treated by antibiotics.

B _____ (fever) a symptom of infection either at the surgical site, in the lungs (for example, pulmonary oedema), or in the urinary tract.

C _____ The standard treatment is by intramuscular opioid (usually Morphine).

D _____ After surgery, there is a tendency for patients to retain fluid, and urinary output is a measure of the performance of the liver and kidneys.

E _____ This occurs when a blood clot develops, usually in the lower leg. It can cause a fatal pulmonary embolism. Early signs of clot formation include hypertension and cold feet. Heparin is commonly used as a prophylactic (a course of action to prevent a disease).

F _____ (collapsed lung) caused by blocked air passages. One of the first signs is abnormally high heart rate (tachycardia) and abnormally rapid breathing (tachypnea). Mechanical ventilation is provided to help patients breathe.

2 Use words and phrases from **1** to complete the patient care record below.

PATIENT
Isak Christiansen

AGE	DIAGNOSIS	HISTORY	SURGICAL OPERATION
79	abdominal aortic aneurism	ischemic heart disease	midline incision to repair aorta and removal of aneurism. Admitted ICU 16.00

	OBSERVATIONS	NURSING INSTRUCTIONS
0-4 HOURS POST-OP	mild _____ [1] (38°)	
	risk of _____ [2]	☐ administer _____ [3] (Cefazolin) intravenously ☐ monitor _____ [4] for inflammation & ooze ☐ send nasal swab to lab to test for Staphylococcus
	_____ [5]	provide relief by _____ [6] infusion
	low _____ [7]	fit catheter to take hourly measurements
	patient has _____ [8]	☐ give Metoprolol infusion hourly (beta blocker) to lower blood pressure ☐ cover feet with extra blankets
	risk of _____ [9]	give Heparin as a _____ [10]
12 HOURS POST-OP	abnormally _____ [11]	give Amioderone infusion to slow heart give chest x-ray
DAY 2 POST-OP	x-ray confirms pulmonary oedema falling O2 level	provide _____ [12] to assist breathing
DAY 5 POST-OP	condition stable no evidence of pulmonary oedema remaining	extubate discharge to Coronary Care Unit

Speaking

Discussing what people should do

Work in small groups. Read these situations and discuss the questions.

1 A 50-year-old woman has a slow-growing brain tumour, which doctors are refusing to operate on because they feel the operation is too risky. She wants her family to pay for her to fly to another country, where a surgeon has offered to perform the operation, but her doctor says the stress of the experience could kill her. What should her family do?

2 A man has lost his face in a dog attack. A surgeon is ready to do a face transplant as soon as a donor can be found. However, the risk of rejection is great, which would leave the man in an even worse position, without the underlying facial tissue. Should he risk the transplant?

Writing

A case study

As part of your training in the surgical unit, you have to write a case study of a patient undergoing surgery. Use the information in the patient care form to complete the account of Mr Christiansen's post-operative progress.

Isak Christiansen has a history of heart disease. He was
diagnosed with abdominal aortic aneurism. An operation
was performed to remove the aneurism.
Because of the risk of post-operative wound infection,
the patient was given an antibiotic (Cefazolin).
The surgical site was monitored for infection and a nasal
swab was sent to the lab for analysis.
The patient suffered post-operative pain and he was given …

Project

Research the procedure and pre- and post-operative care required for one of the following operations. Prepare a five-minute talk for the next class.

- cataract removal
- ectopic pregnancy
- heart transplant

Key words

Adjectives
complex
intravenous
post-operative

Nouns
accuracy
amputation
catheter
complications
conventional surgery
discomfort
haematoma
hernia
incision
keyhole surgery
precision
success rate

Look back through this unit. Find five more words or expressions that you think are useful.

12 Infectious diseases

Scrub up

1 Play the *Disease transmission game*. How long does the disease take to spread through the classroom and what proportion of people survive the epidemic?

2 How long would it take the disease to work through everyone in the building?

3 When you had the disease, did you infect your friends first? What would happen in real life?

4 Which of the following routes of transmission does the game demonstrate?

1 droplet contact (respiratory route) – through coughs and sneezes, kissing, cups, etc.
2 faecal-oral transmission – from contaminated food or water
3 direct physical contact, including sexual contact
4 vertical transmission – mother to child
5 iatrogenic transmission – due to medical procedures
6 vector-borne – carried by insects or other animals
7 indirect contact – by touching contaminated surfaces

5 Match these diseases with the routes of transmission in 4.

a athlete's foot
b chickenpox
c cholera
d HIV
e influenza
f malaria
g meningitis
h MRSA
i polio
j rabies
k syphilis

6 What examples of disease epidemics do you know?

7 Discuss how epidemics affect the running of hospitals and the lives of ordinary people.

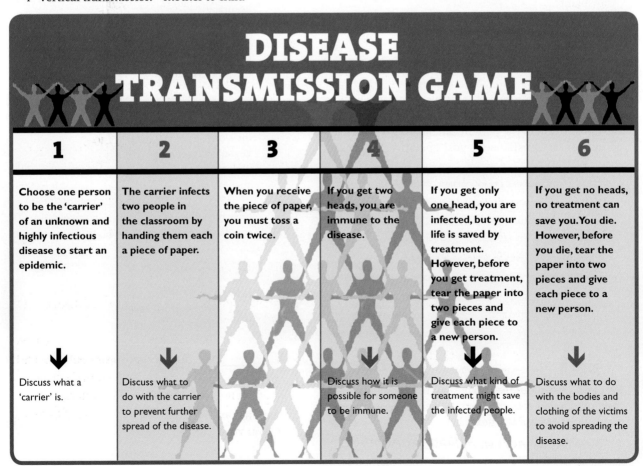

DISEASE TRANSMISSION GAME

1	2	3	4	5	6
Choose one person to be the 'carrier' of an unknown and highly infectious disease to start an epidemic.	The carrier infects two people in the classroom by handing them each a piece of paper.	When you receive the piece of paper, you must toss a coin twice.	If you get two heads, you are immune to the disease.	If you get only one head, you are infected, but your life is saved by treatment. However, before you get treatment, tear the paper into two pieces and give each piece to a new person.	If you get no heads, no treatment can save you. You die. However, before you die, tear the paper into two pieces and give each piece to a new person.
Discuss what a 'carrier' is.	Discuss what to do with the carrier to prevent further spread of the disease.		Discuss how it is possible for someone to be immune.	Discuss what kind of treatment might save the infected people.	Discuss what to do with the bodies and clothing of the victims to avoid spreading the disease.

● Language spot

Passive sentences

1 Study sentences 1–4 and say which describes
  a an action in the past that has continued up to the present
  b a past finished action
  c a future action
  d a regular activity.

  1 The wards are disinfected twice daily.
  2 The wards were disinfected, but they remained contaminated.
  3 The wards have been disinfected by the cleaning staff, but not deep cleaned.
  4 The wards will be disinfected and the germs will be destroyed.

2 Choose the correct reason *why* the sentences are passive and not active.
  1 Because the action (disinfecting) is more important than the agent (the cleaning staff).
  2 Because the agent is more important than the action.

3 Rewrite these sentences using the Passive.
  EXAMPLE
  We isolate infected patients. ⇨ *Infected patients are isolated.*
  1 Lymphocytes make antibodies.
  2 Tomorrow we will follow the disinfection schedule.
  3 We have cancelled all operations because of an MRSA outbreak.
  4 Antibiotics have improved his condition.
  5 The epidemic will probably kill millions.

Passive modals

4 Study the examples and make the sentences that follow passive.
  EXAMPLE
  This rule has to be followed at all times.
  These instruments should not be sterilized at temperatures higher than 160 °C.
  Use of gloves alone must not be considered a substitute for hand washing.
  1 The nurse on duty must write the report.
  2 You have to limit the growth of micro-organisms.

3 Someone should clean the soap dispensers every day.
4 We must all use alcohol hand-rub between patient contacts.
5 Staff must never use common towels – they are vectors for disease.

>> Go to **Grammar reference** p.122

Vocabulary

Word-building

1 Complete this table.

noun	verb	adjective
asepsis		1 _____
contagion		2 _____
contaminant / contamination	3 _____	4 _____
hygiene		5 _____
immunity	6 _____	immune / immunized
7 _____	inoculate	inoculated
pathogen		8 _____
9 _____		prophylactic
susceptibility		10 _____
transmission	11 _____	transmitted

2 Complete the sentences with the correct form of words from **1**.
  1 Gloves protect medical staff from _____ diseases.
  2 The anthrax bacterium is _____ to the antibiotic Ciprofloxacin.
  3 I think I must be _____ to chickenpox – I had it when I was a child.
  4 A disease needs a route of _____ to a host.
  5 A _____ doesn't cure disease, but prevents it.
  6 The most _____ method is to wash your hands in hot water for at least one minute.
  7 Maintain an _____ environment by killing all germs.

Disinfectant

Disinfectants kill microbes on surfaces. The most natural disinfectant is sunlight, but popular chemical disinfectants include carbolic acid, phenol, chlorine, and iodine.

Disinfectants work best on smooth surfaces like plastic, but they often do not kill all bacteria and those that survive an attack by chemicals will produce a resistant generation. Therefore, modern practice is to create conditions which discourage the growth of microbes rather than trying to kill them.

What are the differences between disinfectants, antibiotics, and antiseptics?

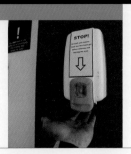

Listening

Barrier nursing

1 The aim of 'barrier nursing' is to put up a barrier to pathogenic organisms. Make a list of five things that should be done to barrier-nurse patients who have a hospital-acquired infection such as Clostridium difficile (C. difficile) or methicillin-resistant staphylococcus aureus (MRSA).

2 🎧 Mr Cohen comes to visit his mother in hospital, but she's not in her usual bed. Listen to the nurse explain why and tick the items on your list in **1** that are mentioned.

3 🎧 Listen again and complete the sentences.

1 There is a danger that Mrs Cohen's infection is highly _____.

2 Mrs Cohen is in isolation to allow the staff to _____ nurse.

3 Mr Cohen will need to follow basic _____.

4 The hand-rub contains _____.

5 Mr Cohen is not allowed to sit _____.

6 Provided he is _____, Mr Cohen is not at risk.

Patient care

Talking about changing a dressing

1 Complete the dialogue between a nurse and a patient who is being discharged. Use the words and phrases below.

be sure	it's imperative	never fail to
do not omit	keep in mind	remember to
don't forget	may want	to be avoided
don't want to		

Nurse When you get home, you will need to change the dressing every day, OK? And when you do that, you must _____[1] to have everything handy. _____[2] about preparing a clean surface to work on and you _____[3] to have a clean towel with you as well. When you've got everything ready, what is the most important thing to _____[4] do next?

Patient To wash my hands.

Nurse Right. _____[5] to keep your hands clean. Hand hygiene comes first and foremost. Touching a new dressing with unwashed hands is _____[6], because that will lower the risk of infection. Remove the old dressing and throw it away in a dustbin. Always _____[7] the fact that it is contaminated, so wrap it up in a plastic bag. OK?

Patient Yes, I've got it.

Nurse Then wash your hands again.

Patient Again?

Nurse Again. You _____[8] transfer germs from the old dressing to the new one, do you? _____[9] check the wound for any signs of infection every time you change the dressing.

Patient Redness, swelling, soreness – that kind of thing?

Nurse That's right. And apply the clean dressing. Use sterilized gauze and _____[10] the tape to hold it in place.

Patient And that's it?

Nurse Yes, except for one thing ...

Patient Don't tell me – 'wash your hands'!

2 With a partner, role-play the following situations.

● Give instructions to a patient who is being discharged about hygiene procedures in their kitchen and when preparing food.

Change roles.

● Give instructions to a patient who is being discharged about hygiene procedures in the toilet / bathroom at home.

Speaking

Staff meeting

1 Study this list of reasons for MRSA outbreaks and score them 1–4 for how important you think they are (1 = not important, 4 = extremely important).

big, overcrowded wards ——
inadequate laundry service ——
lack of information about spread of infection ——
not enough isolation wards ——
overuse of antibiotics ——
overuse of catheters ——
patients' visitors spreading infections ——
poor staff discipline ——
poor ventilation ——
staff shortages and overwork ——
use of unqualified staff ——

2 Follow the instructions in this memo to hospital staff and role-play the meetings.

CITY HOSPITAL
Internal Memo

25th February
To all staff from the hospital director

All staff should be aware that there has been an outbreak of MRSA in Wards Four and Seven. 95% of all other hospital beds are occupied and the hospital's three isolation rooms are accommodating patients with meningitis and tuberculosis.

It is imperative that we deal with the present outbreak and protect the hospital from any future outbreaks.

1. You are requested to first meet in pairs to come up with a plan of five actions to take which cover aspects of cleaning, hospital visitors, and medical staff.
2. Next, you should meet with one other pair, compare suggestions, and decide on a final action plan of the five best suggestions.
3. Your five suggestions should then be presented to a mass meeting of all staff.

Writing

A notice to patients and their visitors

Write a notice for a ward wall. The notice should

1 explain to patients what they should do to avoid spreading germs
2 explain to patients' visitors what they should do to help maintain hospital hygiene
3 give information to patients about when and when not to ask for antibiotics.

Signs and symptoms

Describing symptoms

Study sentences a–j and use the words in **bold** to complete definitions 1–10.

a The disease is gone when the patient is free from all **morbid** signs and symptoms.
b Despite all the treatment she received, the symptoms of the disease remained **persistent**.
c We didn't expect weight loss. It's an **atypical** sign and led to the wrong diagnosis.
d At first, meningitis is hard to identify, but eventually the **classic** sign of a haemorrhagic rash appears.
e The final symptomatic phase of HIV is **full-blown** AIDS.
f In the early stages of the disease, the **initial** symptoms are things like nausea and muscle pain.
g He showed only **minimal** signs of the disease for quite a long time and did not feel particularly ill.
h The symptoms are **progressive,** starting in the spinal cord and continuing to the brain.
i The **cardinal** signs of leprosy are readily recognised in countries where the disease is common.
j Early clinical presentations of ehrlichiosis are **non-specific** and resemble various other infectious diseases.

1 Signs and symptoms that do not go away are

_____ .

2 _____ signs are textbook examples.

3 A complete set of signs and symptoms are

_____ .

4 _____ symptoms indicate disease or abnormality.

5 _____ signs and symptoms appear in a number of different diseases.

6 The sign or symptom that leads to a diagnosis is known as _____ .

7 Signs and symptoms that are not usual are

_____ .

8 Symptoms that get worse are _____ symptoms.

9 _____ symptoms are often not noticed.

10 The _____ signs of an infectious disease appear early on.

Quack doctor: a fake medical practitioner who claims to have miraculous cures and who sells medicines that are unproven and sometimes dangerous. Also known as a 'snake oil salesman' (USA) because of the exotic ingredients in the 'cures'.

Sometimes quack cures actually work. Why do you think this is?

Reading

A pandemic

1 A *pandemic* is a disease that spreads to many different countries. A disease that is *endemic* is constant. Think of examples of pandemics and of diseases that are endemic.

2 Read the article and answer the questions.

1 What did the pandemic of 1347 achieve?
  a It killed 200 million people.
  b It set back social progress.
  c It wiped out the population of Europe.

2 Which of these is *not* amongst the characteristic symptoms of bubonic plague listed in the text?
  a abdominal cramps
  b swellings
  c restlessness

3 Why were long gowns and masks worn during the plague?
  a for religious reasons
  b to avoid contagion
  c to conceal identity

4 Who were the Flagellants?
  a people who did not believe in God
  b people who wanted to die
  c people who made themselves suffer in order to survive

5 Who believed they were going to die?
  a everybody
  b nuns
  c the hedonists

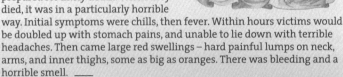

The Plague

A Over the course of human history, the bubonic plague has killed 200 million people. In one pandemic around 1347, over half the population of Europe died and along with their deaths came economic collapse, food shortages, and a breakdown of law and order. ____

B The first sign that the plague had arrived was the rats that came out into the streets to die in huge numbers. The people fled their homes, isolated themselves from other people, or prepared for likely death. When they died, it was in a particularly horrible way. Initial symptoms were chills, then fever. Within hours victims would be doubled up with stomach pains, and unable to lie down with terrible headaches. Then came large red swellings – hard painful lumps on neck, arms, and inner thighs, some as big as oranges. There was bleeding and a horrible smell. ____

C The medicine of the time could not explain it. Doctors tried blood letting – draining the illness out by cutting a vein and letting it bleed. It didn't work. Because it was obvious that you could get the disease from contact with victims and their clothing, the response of most people was to abandon anyone who caught it. There were very few qualified doctors, but there were plenty of quack doctors who would, for a very high price, care for the sick. They wore long gowns and bird-like masks filled with herbs and oils and they washed in vinegar for protection. Though strange, these measures were actually quite effective. ____

D Though it was known that survivors of an infection didn't catch it a second time, the random way that one person could be struck down by disease and another survive was explained in terms of God's will, not immunity. People believed that a loving god would not create anything so bad unless it was to punish those who had done some kind of wrong. The Italian writer Giovanni Boccaccio lived through the epidemic and described people's reactions to the death all around them. He described the Flagellants, for example, who believed that if they walked from town to town and beat themselves in public, then they would escape the disease. ____

E According to Boccaccio, many people adopted a fatalistic attitude – leaving it in God's hands. The hedonists, he said, dedicated their lives to pleasure – eating, drinking, and casual sex while they had the chance. They were going to die anyway. Others, like nuns, applied fatalism to its logical extreme and ignored the risks involved in having close contact with the dying. They actually nursed the sick. Nuns (women living in religious communities) have an important place in the history of professional nursing, and though during the plague epidemics they said they were only doing God's will and had no choice in the matter, they were much admired for their charity and courage. ____

3 Add sentences 1–5 to the end of paragraphs A–E where they fit best.

1 However, death came quickly.
2 The use of the word *sister* both as a form of address to a nun and as a nursing rank originates from this time.
3 The gowns protected them from fleas, the masks filtered the air, and vinegar disinfected them.
4 They conducted a sort of mass therapy at a very frightening time, by encouraging people to release extreme emotion.
5 At the time, nobody knew where the disease had come from or how to cure it, and it could not be stopped from attacking the towns and villages of the Middle Ages.

Project

Research one of these infectious diseases. Make a presentation: describe when and where there have been epidemics of the disease, explain the disease's symptoms, and describe its method of transmission.

- cholera
- influenza
- leprosy
- lymphatic filariasis (elephantiasis)
- malaria
- measles
- meningitis
- tuberculosis
- yellow fever

Checklist

Assess your progress in this unit. Tick (✓) the statements which are true.

I can use the passive

I can give hygiene instructions

I can write a ward notice

I can describe the signs and symptoms of some infectious diseases

Key words

Nouns
antibody
asepsis
carrier
epidemic
hygiene
inoculation
isolation
pandemic
plague
prophylaxis
transmission

Adjectives
atypical
full-blown
initial
morbid

Look back through this unit. Find five more words or expressions that you think are useful.

13 Renal

Scrub up

1 Play the *Kidney transplant game*. Work in teams of two to four. You are going to attempt a kidney transplant. Your patient is a 55-year-old man. He is a scientist researching cancer. He has end stage renal disease and needs a kidney transplant.

Teams take it in turns to toss a coin and move from square to square. In some squares, a spokesperson from the team must speak to your teacher before the team can move on.

2 When you have finished the game, present a short case study to the rest of the class. The case study should describe the progress your team made in attempting to transplant a kidney.

Kidney Transplant Game

4 Match the blood type of the patient with the donor kidney

Toss the coin once. If you get heads, you have a match. But before moving on, you must explain to the patient (your teacher) that everything is ready. When the patient understands everything, go to square 5. If you don't get heads, go back to square 2.

5 Decide which transplant to do

Before you transplant the kidney, a teenager is brought into A&E – a new kidney will save her life.

Your team must decide whether to continue with the first patient or give the kidney to the new patient. You must explain to your teacher why you made the decision.

If you decide to continue with the original transplant, go to square 6.

If you decide to transplant the kidney into the young woman, go to square 7.

3 Match the donor kidney with the patient's tissue

Toss the coin twice. If you get two heads, the tissue matches. Go to square 4.

If you don't get a match, go back to square 2.

9 Fight post-operative infection

Toss the coin twice. If you get heads at least once, the infection clears up. But before the patient (your teacher) goes home, you must tell them about taking anti-rejection medication (for life), rest, and diet and make a follow-up appointment. If you don't get heads, the patient dies. You have failed.

2 Find a donor

To find a donor, toss a coin once. If you get heads, you are in luck. But before moving on, you must get the permission of the donor's relative (your teacher). When you get permission, go to square 3. If you don't get heads, wait for your next turn and try again.

6 Resuscitate the patient after the operation

Toss the coin twice. If you get heads at least once, the patient recovers from post-operative shock. Go to square 8.

If you don't, the patient dies. You have failed.

1 Get your patient's informed consent

Your teacher is the patient. Explain what you are going to do. Explain that the tissue, blood type, and size of a donor kidney must match the recipient. Explain about the risk of rejection and get the patient's 'informed consent' before moving to square 2.

7 Match the kidney tissue, size, and blood type again

Toss the coin twice. If you get heads at least once, everything matches. Proceed with the transplant. Go to square 8.

If you don't, you have run out of time. Your new patient dies. You have failed.

8 Treat rejection of the donor kidney

For the immune system to accept the transplanted kidney, toss the coin twice. If you get two heads, the kidney is accepted. But before the patient (your teacher) goes home, you must tell them about taking anti-rejection medication (for life), rest, and diet and make a follow-up appointment. If you get heads only once, go to square 9. If you don't get heads, the transplant has failed. Go back to square 2.

In this unit
- relative clauses
- verbs for operating equipment
- answering FAQs
- debating transplant ethics

● Language spot

Relative clauses

1 Read sentences a–e and answer questions 1–4.

a Kidney transplant is a treatment **which is given to people with renal failure**.

b The on / off switch, **which is at the back of the machine**, is broken.

c Mr Jameson, **who has been on the waiting list for six months**, has an infection.

d Patients **that have dialysis at home** can get on with their lives more easily.

e The donor **whose kidney was removed** has recovered quickly.

1 Which sentences are being described?

  a These are examples of defining relative clauses. They help us to identify the person or thing we are talking about.

  b These are examples of non-defining relative clauses. They give more information, which we do not need in order to understand the whole sentence.

2 When can *that* replace *who* and *which*?

3 When do we use *where* and *whose*?

4 Which type of relative clause has commas around it?

2 Join the sentences by adding a relative pronoun (*who, which, that,* or *whose*). Add commas where necessary.

EXAMPLE

The patient needs a kidney. He has end stage renal disease. ⇨ *The patient, who has end stage renal disease, needs a kidney.*

1 John died in the car accident. He's an organ donor.

2 The donor soon recovered. Her kidney was removed.

3 The kidney is now ready. It is for Mr Mucci.

3 Make one full sentence from each of these sets of notes.

EXAMPLE

nurse / specializes in kidneys / available Mon. to Fri. ⇨ *A nurse who specializes in kidneys is available from Monday to Friday.*

1 button / controls the rate of dialysis / left of the machine

2 bags / contain dialysate / a green label

3 patient / next on the list / 45-year-old male

>> Go to **Grammar reference** p.122

Body bits

The kidney

1 Study the diagrams of a transplanted kidney and identify and label these things.

bladder	renal vein
donor kidney	urethra
donor ureter	withered kidney
renal artery	

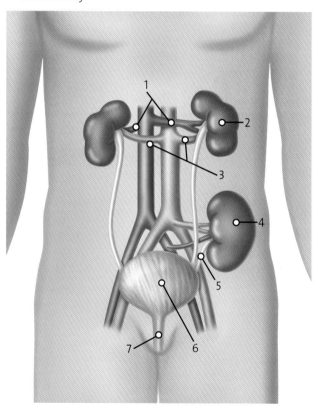

2 Complete the labels to explain what is happening in the diagram using these phrases.

a connects the new kidney with the bladder

b excretes urine after storing it

c remains in place

d takes away the filtered blood

e takes over the job of converting waste into urine

f supplies the kidneys with blood

g transports urine out of the body

Dialysis machine

The machine copies the way the kidneys work. You get access to the blood through a catheter in the arm. The blood goes through a tube into the dialysis machine. There it passes through a membrane which filters out the salts and urea before it is returned to the patient.

What is the name of the fluid that is used in a dialysis machine? How long does one exchange take?

Listening

Instructions on home dialysis

1 🎧 A patient who has dialysis at home has a problem with his machine. Listen as he gets instructions by telephone from a renal nurse. Label this diagram of his machine.

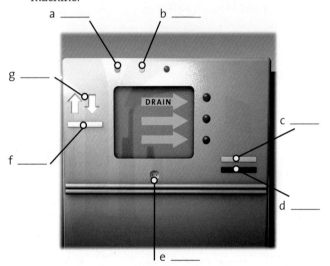

a _____   b _____

g _____

DRAIN

c _____

f _____

d _____

e _____

2 🎧 Listen again and answer the questions.
1 Why is the screen blank when the nurse begins?
2 What should happen when you press DRAIN?
3 What time is the default setting?
4 What time does Mr Mucci need to reset the machine to?
5 When the alarm sounds, what does it say on the screen?

It's my job

Read about Merja Halonen and answer the questions.
1 What symptoms of renal failure did Merja's mother show?
2 Why does Merja feel guilty?
3 What was Merja's route into renal nursing?
4 What did her mother's death teach Merja?
5 Why does Merja now have a lot of opportunities to talk with patients?

From your experience and observations, how much time do nurses spend talking with patients, carers, partners, and patients' families?

Merja Halonen

When my mother got ill, I didn't realise she was sick even though I had been a general nurse for fifteen years. For several months she had been complaining of no appetite, fatigue, insomnia, and itchy skin and looking back I remember how depressed she was. But I didn't notice any of that, nor that she had lost weight.

One morning I called in to see her. She was disoriented – calling me Jenny instead of Merja, and her blood pressure was much too high. So I drove her to hospital. On the way she started having seizures and later that day she died. Diagnosis: renal failure. I had never thought about renal failure. At the time I thought she was just showing symptoms of ageing, and I feel very guilty about that. After the funeral, I went to the hospital library and read up on Nephrology. Later I applied for specialist training and became a renal nurse.

My mother's death taught me how important it is for everyone involved in illness to talk and listen. It's true for all types of nursing, but with renal nursing, most of the patients I get to know are chronically ill so I see them over long periods of time, and we have the opportunity to do a lot of talking. Some renal dialysis patients, for example, come to the clinic three times a week, every week. I am their first port of call for help with both practical and emotional problems and I am their main source of information on medication, equipment, and diet.

I frequently counsel kidney transplant donors and recipients, but because I know from personal experience how illnesses like kidney failure affect everybody connected to the patient, I also make sure I hear about the worries and concerns of carers, partners, and family, too.

Peritoneal dialysis (PD) may be done several times a day at home. It involves filling the abdomen with a dialysate and using the natural abdominal membranes to filter toxins from the body. What are the advantages and disadvantages of self-administered treatment at home?

Vocabulary

Verbs for operating equipment

Complete these instructions to nurses for operating a haemodialysis machine. Use verbs from the list.

flash on	plug in	switch on
go off	scroll down	switch over
join up	set up	take off
load up	shut down	wash down

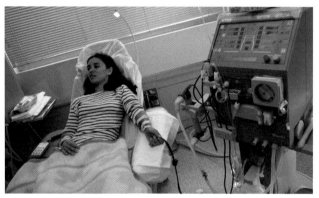

1 Ensure hygiene and _____ all surfaces before you start.

2 _____ the machine with two full bottles of dialysate fluid.

3 _____ the machine to a mains socket.

4 _____ the machine by pressing the red on / off button.

5 _____ the exit and the entry tubes with the patient's catheters.

6 Use the touch screen to _____ the machine's cycle correctly.

7 When you set the timer, the orange light will _____ and off.

8 The alarm buzzer will _____ if there is a problem.

9 The machine will _____ automatically when the cycle ends.

10 At the end of the cycle _____ the tubes from the catheters.

11 Using the touch screen, _____ to 'IDLE'.

12 _____ the machine _____ from 'FUNCTIONING' to 'IDLE' by pressing the 'ENTER' key.

Writing

Explaining treatments

1 Read the case history and study the chart of treatment options. Discuss with a partner which treatment would be best for the patient.

The patient is a 66-year-old woman with end stage renal disease. She is wealthy and lives alone in a major city. Four days a week she takes care of her grandchildren 9.00–5.00 while her daughter goes to work.

	Continuous Ambulatory Peritoneal dialysis	Haemodialysis	Transplant
Where	Any clean place	At a dialysis centre with trained professionals	Hospital
When	Patients decide when they do it, but it must be done several times a day, 7 days a week. One 'exchange' takes 30 minutes.	3 times a week at a clinic. Treatment at a clinic takes 4 hours.	Only one operation but a long wait for donor kidney
Patient education	Patients must have training. They usually need help with treatment.	None needed	None needed
Level of freedom	Patients can live normally with solution in abdomen.	Freedom on non-treatment days. No freedom during treatment.	Greatest freedom

2 Read this case history by yourself. Decide which treatment is most suitable. Write a short essay explaining the differences between the three treatment options and give reasons why your choice of treatment is most suitable for this patient.

Adult male who is moderately mentally retarded has advanced diabetes and end stage renal disease. The patient receives state benefits and does labouring work. He lives in an isolated cottage alone with his mother who is 75 years old. They have no car.

An American coroner, who ruled on a man's death, said that medical staff had removed the man's heart, liver, pancreas, and kidneys before they had proved he was brain-dead. The coroner therefore decided that the death was murder and said, 'I am not opposed to organ transplants, and I am a registered donor myself, but I want to be dead first.'

Are you a registered donor? Why? / Why not?

Reading

FAQs about organ donation

1 Think about the following situation and answer questions 1–3.

A potential kidney donor asks a renal nurse this question: 'I want to donate a kidney, but can I be sure that it goes to someone of my own nationality and not to a foreigner?' The nurse answers, 'Living donors can donate a kidney to a specific person. However, we select recipients of donated organs based on need, blood type, and genetic match.'

1 Does the nurse's answer mean 'yes' or 'no'?
2 Do you think the nurse gives a good answer?
3 Would you give a different answer?

2 Read these FAQs (Frequently Asked Questions) and discuss with a partner how to answer them.

Frequently Asked Questions

a Is it cruel to talk to a grieving family about donation?
b Is it true that I can't be an organ donor? My mother says it is because of our religion and we believe that organ transplants are immoral.
c Are surgeons more interested in transplanting organs than saving lives?
d Can I make money out of donating an organ?
e Are people who receive an organ always chosen for medical reasons?

3 Read these answers and match each one with a question.

1 Yes and no. It depends where in the world you are, but most transplant agencies are blind to things like race, gender, age, income, or celebrity status. When a famous person receives an organ there are always accusations of unfairness especially when that person has damaged their organs through drinking. Any sign of favouritism puts people off donating their own organs.

2 No. There have been studies that show that when families are not given information about donating, they feel angry and frustrated. People see organ donation as something good to come out of a tragedy especially when the death is unexpected and think of donation as a tribute to the deceased.

3 Yes, but not much. There is a worldwide shortage of donor organs and whenever there is a shortage of something, there will always be a black market, as there is for organs. In 2007, someone looking for a black market kidney could pay an agent as much as US $180,000. The donor may receive as little as $1,000 because most of the money goes to the agents. The people involved in the trade are motivated by money alone and do not have the welfare of either donor or recipient at heart.

4 Check again. Although there are faiths that believe that all of the body parts must be intact because the soul keeps a physical shape, all the major ones see organ donation as an act of charity because it restores the life of another human being. So how can there be anything wrong with it?

5 No. However, surveys show that 27% of people believe that emergency staff won't work so hard to save the life of a casualty if they know the patient is an organ donor. Doctors deny this. They insist that after doing everything possible to resuscitate, they then use formal tests to make absolutely sure that a person is dead before considering them as a donor.

4 Study the criteria for deciding who gets an available organ.

- blood type
- severity of illness
- size of organ
- time spent on waiting list
- tissue type

Use the criteria to write an answer to the following FAQ.

> Is getting an organ just a matter of luck?

Speaking

Deciding what to do

1 🎧 A man has been in a coma for nearly three months. Listen to his wife and daughter's conversation. What decision are they trying to come to? How do they feel about it?

2 You decide. Arrange these options in the order that you prefer.

1 To discontinue life support, let the patient die, and consider using his organs for transplanting to the other patient.
2 To wait. Encourage the family to look on the bright side and hope for a full recovery.
3 To prepare for the worst. Help the daughter understand that there is almost no chance of recovery. It means caring for the patient for the rest of his life in a vegetative state.
4 To expect nothing. The patient must be kept alive until he dies – no matter what, because that's the job of doctors and nurse.

3 Compare your choices with those of other students, discuss the issue as a class, and take a vote to make a final decision.

Project

Research one of the following and give a short presentation to the other students.

- homeostasis
- hormone secretion by kidneys
- nephrons
- the collecting duct system
- the renal artery and the renal vein
- the structure of the human kidney

Checklist

Assess your progress in this unit. Tick (✓) the statements which are true.

I can use relative clauses

I can give instructions for operating dialysis equipment

I can answer questions about organ donation

I can debate the ethics of organ transplant

Key words

Adjective
peritoneal

Nouns
bladder
dialysis
donor
malfunction
nephrology
organ
rejection
transplant

Verbs
drain
dwell
flash on and off
go off
load up
shut down

Look back through this unit. Find five more words or expressions that you think are useful.

14 Psychiatry

Scrub up

1 Study this 'ink blot' for a few seconds. Think about what it looks like and what it makes you think about.

2 🎧 Listen to a psychiatric patient, William, talking to a nurse about what he sees in the same ink blot.

This ink blot represents the 'self'. Tick (✓) what you think William Heron's description shows.

The patient is

anxious ☐ depressed ☐ happy ☐
creative ☐ excited ☐ unresponsive ☐

3 Work in pairs. Study this picture and make up a story about what is happening.

4 Discuss how the following people might interpret the picture.

- someone with a secret
- someone whose parent has just died
- a young person
- an old person
- someone who thinks a lot about death

Patient care

Encouraging patients to talk

1 Read the dialogue between a nurse and a psychiatric patient. Say where in the dialogue the nurse

1 prompts the patient to remember
2 gives reassurance
3 demonstrates acceptance.

Nurse … I'm sorry about the interruption, Karen. Now, you were telling me about last Thursday. Take your time and cast your mind back.

Patient I can't remember. I've forgotten what I was saying.

Nurse Well, I haven't forgotten. You were telling me about your feelings for Emily. Last Thursday, you were watching her when she was asleep. Do you recall telling me about that?

Patient Yes, I suppose so.

Nurse Can you tell me what you were thinking?

Patient I can't say.

Nurse It's perfectly all right. Anything you say in here, stays in here. I won't judge you or think you've done anything wrong.

Patient I wanted her to die. I'm sorry, I'm sorry.

Nurse That's perfectly all right. You know, Karen, most of us have feelings like that.

Patient Not about their own children! What a terrible mother I am.

Nurse Don't be so hard on yourself. You're not the first person to have feelings like that about their children and you won't be the last.

2 Work with a partner and discuss how you would respond to patients who say the following.

'I'm worthless. I fail at everything I try.'

'I can't help it, I hate everyone and everyone hates me.'

'I can't accept that my son is dead.'

'The reason why I get Ds at college is because all the other students cheat.'

'My baby sister gets all my parents' love.'

Continue the conversations for a short while by role-playing patient and psychiatric nurse (change roles so that each person plays patient *and* nurse). The nurse should encourage the patient to say more, demonstrate acceptance, and give reassurance.

Tests

Interpreting test results

1 Complete the sentences with the correct form of the verbs in the list.

assess	indicate	screen
detect	measure	see
draw	reveal	show
give		

1 When he was referred, his strange, disturbed behaviour _____ immediate hospitalization.

2 Tomorrow, the test results _____ us clearly if she is at risk.

3 Her responses to the questionnaire are helpful for us in _____ her condition.

4 Her drawing has _____ us insight into her subconscious.

5 It can be _____ from the neuropsychological examination that Mrs Wise's brain is functioning normally.

6 This procedure is often used _____ how much brain activity is going on.

7 The patient's responses enable us _____ conclusions regarding possible brain damage.

8 I have _____ serious cognitive impairment from the test results.

9 The Folstein test is used _____ for dementia.

10 People project their personality on to the ink blots and _____ hidden emotions.

2 Do the following psychological test. Read the prompts and simply say / write the first thing that comes into your head.

People I know _____

I think boys and men _____

I think girls and women _____

My father _____

My mother _____

3 Compare your responses with other students. Compare the test with the tests in *Scrub up*. Discuss which may be most effective in revealing people's personalities and problems.

Vocabulary

Word-building

1 Work in pairs to complete the table. Use your dictionary if necessary.

noun	adjective
anger	angry
1_____	creative
2_____	intelligent
3_____	lonely
4_____	obsessive
paranoia	5_____
phobia	6_____
psychiatry	7_____
schizophrenia	8_____
suicide	9_____
withdrawal	10_____

2 Complete the sentences with words from **1**.

1 He has _____ delusions that someone wants to kill him.

2 The patient has become _____, and rarely speaks to anyone.

3 Her drawings and poems show great _____.

4 She has persistent, _____ thoughts about death.

5 They looked for _____ help for their son as his behaviour became stranger.

6 Art therapy allows patients to express their _____ in a non-harmful way.

7 Her _____ of any kind of social interaction makes a visit to the shops into a major problem.

3 Rewrite the sentences using verbs instead of the **bold** nouns.

EXAMPLE
*My attempt to get the patient to talk was a **failure**.*
⇨ *I failed to get the patient to talk.*

1 The patient gives a **response** to each of the ink blots.
2 We had a **discussion** about his parents' relationship.
3 Let's hope that this course of therapy is a **success**.
4 It wasn't her **intention** to upset the patient.
5 We need to make a careful **assessment** of the patient's needs.

The song **Gloomy Sunday**, which was written in 1933 by the Hungarian Rezsö Seress, has bitter and melancholic lyrics. The song has been blamed for prompting hundreds of suicides and in 1968 the composer himself jumped to his death from his apartment. Discuss if you think music influences or simply reflects your mood. Can it control your behaviour?

Reading

Suicide

1 Work in groups. Compare your attitudes to suicide with other students. Say which of these statements are closest to your beliefs and explain why.

- When life is so terrible, death may be the only logical choice.
- All suicide is morally wrong.
- Suicide is an individual's choice and other people have no right to interfere.
- Many people are affected by suicide – there is always more than one victim.
- People who try to commit suicide should be punished.

2 Read the text. Say if the following are true (T) or false (F).

1 It is important not to raise the subject of suicide with a patient at risk.
2 The 'cry for help' type of suicide attempt is done by people who want someone to stop them.
3 Impulse suicides are often copies of other suicides.
4 Suicidal people will often reveal their plans.
5 Nurses can generally do nothing to prevent a suicide attempt.
6 Nurses should never reveal a patient's secrets to others.

3 Read the case and decide which of the three types of suicide mentioned in the text it illustrates.

Not long ago, an American woman took an overdose of barbiturates and pinned a note to herself which said, 'If you love me, wake me up.' Her husband came home, saw the note, threw it into the dustbin, and went out to a bar. When he returned several hours later, his wife was dead.

A very personal choice

The subject of suicide invokes fear, shame, guilt, and anger and it is taboo in many communities. The lack of openness about suicide makes it hard to identify people who are considering it. It also encourages myths about it such as the idea that talking about suicide encourages it.

In trying to understand the motives of people who try to end their own lives, sociologists and psychologists have classified suicide into types. There is, for example, 'rational' suicide. This is when a person, after thinking long and hard, decides to end their own life because continuing it would be too physically or emotionally painful. Another type is the 'cry for help'. It is a gesture which means, 'If you don't pay attention to me, I will kill myself and then you'll be sorry'.

The type of suicide that is the hardest to understand and therefore predict and prevent is the 'impulse' suicide. This is most common amongst young people, temporarily miserable and frequently influenced by alcohol. Impulse suicide attempts are often inspired by others, such as when the 18-year-old Japanese singer Yukiko Okada jumped to her death from a building. Over the following two weeks, 33 young Japanese people, one nine years old, killed themselves, 21 of them by jumping from buildings.

Many people who attempt suicide tell someone about their plans or give warning signs, so nurses who spend time with patients have a vital role to play in assessing risk and preventing suicide. They get opportunities to establish relationships which encourage disturbed people to reveal feelings and thoughts which they may hide from family members or doctors.

In making an assessment of risk, nurses are trained to ask open questions and to read non-verbal clues that may indicate a difference between what a patient says and what they are feeling. Sometimes a nurse may need to ask a direct question such as; 'Have you thought about harming yourself?' Sometimes they may have to break rules of confidentiality and involve other people in order to protect a patient's safety.

An **electroconvulsive therapy (ECT) machine** sends a pulse of electric current to electrodes on either side of a patient's head and the brain receives an electric shock (usually about 80 volts). Nobody really knows how it works, but perhaps the shock resets the brain like rebooting a computer. Some people say ECT is cruel and unethical, but it is often effective with depression. What psychiatric treatments do you know which have been called cruel and unethical?

Project

The sociologist Emile Durkheim identified the following types of suicide. Research and explain one of these types.

- altruistic suicide
- anomic suicide
- egoistic suicide
- fatalistic suicide
- suicide with expected reward

Pronunciation

Changes in stress

Different parts of speech belonging to the same word family can sometimes have stress on different syllables.

EXAMPLE
suicide / suicidal

1 🎧 Work in pairs. <u>Underline</u> the syllable in these words where you think the stress falls. Then listen and check.

1 therapy	therapeutic
2 psychology	psychological
3 examine	examination
4 disabled	disability
5 trauma	traumatic
6 analysis	analytical
7 symptom	symptomatic
8 personal	personality

2 Which pairs of words in *Vocabulary* on p.99 have the stress in different places?

● Language spot

Present Perfect Simple and Present Perfect Continuous

1 Study the sentences and say which ones

   a focus on a result or completion of an action
   b focus on an action 'up to now'.

   1 I'm sorry; I've forgotten your name.
   2 We've just done an assessment.
   3 She's been having difficulty sleeping.
   4 We have decided that ECT is the best option.
   5 The patient hasn't eaten for two days.
   6 She hasn't been taking her medicine.

>> Go to **Grammar reference** p.123

2 Write the questions to go with the answers.

   EXAMPLE
   Have you been waiting long? Yes, I have been waiting for two hours.

   1 How many times _____? She has refused her medication twice this week.
   2 How much _____? I have given her 10 mg of Diazepam.
   3 How long _____? I've been taking this medication for about three years.
   4 _____? No, she hasn't been assessed yet.
   5 _____? No, I have not been seeing a psychiatrist.

3 <u>Underline</u> the correct verbs to complete the student nurse's entries in a journal.

JOURNAL ENTRY		
	MONDAY 16th JULY	
5.30 p.m.	All day long the nurses on the psychiatric ward **have had / are having** ¹ problems with Mrs O'Malley. She **has refused / is refusing** ² to eat for the past two days and every time anyone **is going / has gone** ³ near her she has **been shouting / shouted** ⁴ and sworn at them.	
	TUESDAY 17th JULY	
11.00 a.m.	The problems with Mrs O'Malley **are continuing / have continued** ⁵ overnight and the staff nurse **have asked / has asked** ⁶ me to help. She says that she **did / has done** ⁷ everything possible for the woman but that now she has **ran / run** ⁸ out of patience.	
4.00 p.m.	I've done it! I **have talked / had talked** ⁹ to Mrs O'Malley. I think the problem is that she feels she **had been / has been** ¹⁰ neglected. When I said to her, 'How long **are you / have you been** ¹¹ sitting there?' at first she **has refused / refused** ¹² to answer. 'You look very uncomfortable,' I said. 'You have not been **eaten / eating** ¹³ and you must **have been / be** ¹⁴ very hungry. Why don't you let me get you something from the kitchen?' Mrs O'Malley grasped my arm. 'You're not made for this job, are you?' she said. 'What do you mean?' I asked. 'You haven't **been walking / walked** ¹⁵ away from me.' 'I can't walk away until I have **been getting / got** ¹⁶ you a little more comfortable,' I said. She smiled and for the rest of my shift she didn't swear or shout at all.	

Speaking
Mental health issues

Read the case notes and either choose a solution or think of an alternative solution. Compare your solutions with other students and explain your choice. Then make a final decision by taking a vote.

1   A 27-year-old female patient, who comes from a broken home and was sexually abused as a child, is addicted to heroin. She turns to prostitution and street robbery to get money to buy drugs. She has had psychiatric treatment in the past, but each time she has run away and returned to her old lifestyle.

There are two priorities: the patient's best interests and the interests of the community. Decide which, if any, of the following you would recommend.

a   Deal with the crimes and send her to prison
b   Give her psychotherapy
c   Address the drug addiction and send her into rehab

2   An intelligent teenage girl from a strong religious background tells an extraordinary story. She says she has been forced by Satanists to kill a child and eat its heart. She is totally sincere but there is no evidence that her story is true.

Decide how to deal with this.

a   Tell the police that a crime has been committed
b   Treat her as if she is lying
c   Pretend you believe her story

3   An aggressive child is in frequent fights at school and disrupts lessons. The head teacher suspends him. A psychologist tests the child and concludes that though he has emotional problems, he is of above average intelligence.

There are two priorities: the education of the child and the education of the other children. Decide which, if any, of the following is the best way forward.

a   Whatever happens to the boy, he should not go back to the classroom
b   Give him special (and expensive) one-to-one teaching
c   Send him back to school and make allowances for his behaviour

Writing
Journal entry

Read a student nurse's description of an experience on a psychiatric ward. Then write a description of problem behaviour you have witnessed.

JOURNAL ENTRY		**MONDAY**
	6.00 p.m.	Today we admitted a male patient following a manic episode which had resulted in him being detained by the police. When he was brought on to the ward, he was drunk and verbally abusive. He demanded to see his own 'private psychiatrist' and threatened to sue the hospital, the doctors, and the nurses. At times nobody could understand what he was saying. When he tried to walk out of the ward, I had to stand in the doorway and stop him which is when he swore at me and spat in my face. Finally the on-call psychiatrist came and did an assessment and the nurses calmed him down and talked him into taking his medication.

Listening
A psychiatric case conference

1   You are going to listen to a discussion about a patient suffering severe anxiety. Discuss what signs and symptoms you would expect to hear about.

2   🎧 Listen and complete this record of the meeting.

PATIENT NOTES

Daphne Duchamp

Age _____¹   Marital status _____²

Referred by _____³

Presenting symptoms _____

    panic attacks with feelings of _____⁴ and

    _____⁵ and _____⁶

Evidence of obsessive behaviour

    worries about _____⁷ , _____⁸ and

    _____⁹

Proposed treatment _____

    _____¹⁰ and _____¹¹

Outpatient's appointment with _____¹²

3   'Desensitization' is when you gradually introduce a phobic person to the things they are afraid of. Discuss how this patient could be desensitized.

Signs and symptoms

Manifestations of mental disorders

1 Look at the picture. Say which mental disorder it illustrates.

  1 psychosis (disturbed perception and thoughts)
  2 anxiety
  3 mania

2 Identify which of these typical symptoms is associated with each disorder in **1**.

delusions	pressured speech
euphoria	racing thoughts
auditory hallucinations	repeated checking
panic attacks	uncontrollable crying
paranoia	

3 Match sentences 1–9 with symptoms in **2**.

  1 'He talks virtually non-stop – nobody can interrupt him or even understand him.'
  2 'At those times I have so much energy and I am so high that people around me get scared.'
  3 'The thoughts just won't be quiet; they gallop around in my head so fast that sometimes I want to scream.'
  4 'The voices comment on everything I do. One of them keeps calling me stupid.'
  5 'Aliens have removed my brain and I am now under constant police surveillance.'
  6 'I know people are out to get me – you hate me too, don't you?'
  7 'Sometimes she has simply sat sobbing on a chair, her face wet with tears.'
  8 'I have made sure that the oven is turned off, and the iron is disconnected and the TV is unplugged, oh yes, and the hi-fi too. Have I checked the oven?'
  9 'The patient has been experiencing recurrent unexpected episodes of severe anxiety.'

Checklist

Assess your progress in this unit. Tick (✓) the statements which are true.

  I can talk about psychological test results

  I can make adjectives from nouns and nouns from adjectives

  I can understand an article about suicide

  I can use the Present Perfect Simple and Present Perfect Continuous

  I can discuss mental health issues

  I can describe signs of mental illness

Key words

Verbs
assess
commit (suicide)
detect
reveal
screen

Nouns
creativity
hallucination
intelligence
intention
loneliness
obsession
paranoia
phobia
schizophrenia
withdrawal

Look back through this unit. Find five more words or expressions that you think are useful.

15 Outpatients

Scrub up

1 Study this picture of an outpatients waiting room. If you could do five things to improve the waiting room, what would they be? Arrange them in order of importance and compare your list with other students. Decide on a final list of five things that could be done cheaply and easily.

2 Describe any personal experience of waiting which you found difficult or annoying (not limited to hospitals).

Vocabulary

Appointments

Use this list of words to identify the kinds of appointments described in sentences 1–12.

~~cancelled~~	initial	previous
confirmed	missed	routine
delayed	out-of-hours	successive
double-booked	postponed	vacant
follow-up		

EXAMPLE

When a patient phones up to say they cannot keep their appointment. ⇨ *This is a* <u>cancelled</u> *appointment.*

1 An outpatient's appointment after an operation
2 When two people are given the same appointment time
3 When a patient tells you they will definitely keep their appointment
4 An appointment for eight o'clock in the evening
5 When the consultant is running late
6 The first appointment
7 An appointment made for Monday, but changed to Wednesday
8 When a patient doesn't turn up
9 An appointment slot that is available
10 A regular appointment
11 Not this appointment, but the one before
12 All the appointments after this one

Listening

Appointments diary

1 In some countries, outpatients don't make appointments; they just turn up. Discuss if a 'first come, first served' system has any advantages at all compared to an 'appointments only' system.

2 🎧 Listen to an outpatients' receptionist at a meeting with a consultant and complete the appointments diary.

3 🎧 Listen again. Add information to the diary about patient Ba Ling.

APPOINTMENTS

TIME	NAME	NOTES
9.30	Natasha Alaqaiah	late for _____¹ check up. _____² 5/9 at 10.30
10.00	Serena Wilson	test results lost. New _____³ appointment made
10.30	Brigitte Hecker	has missed two _____⁴ appointments
11.00	Celestina Dubois	_____⁵ appointment. _____⁶ appointments to be weekly, starting 6/9
11.30	Ba Ling	_____
12.00	Akira Sato	_____⁷ appointment. Midwife to make _____⁸ visit
13.00	Elsa Yager	Admissions have _____⁹ vacant bed on ward.

When patients talk to nurses, they often say things which they would not mention to a doctor for fear of wasting their time or because they believe it may be irrelevant.

Sarah Collins, Lecturer in Communication

Reading

The problem of missed appointments

1 With a partner, discuss the following reasons why patients might miss a hospital appointment and arrange them in the order which, in your experience, seems to be most common.

- fear of hospitals, doctors, and bad news
- inconvenient appointment times
- mistakes made by administration staff
- patients feel better
- patients forget
- patients have other things to do
- too ill to attend

2 Read this letter to a nursing journal and tick (✓) the statements which represent the opinions of the writer.

1 DNAs have problems that are best dealt with by psychiatric services.
2 DNAs are sometimes not to blame for missing appointments.
3 There is never any good excuse for missing outpatients' appointments.

4 Persistent DNAs are problem patients.
5 Patients don't need reminders of appointments.

3 Choose the best answer to each question.

1 When can't we 'fill the slot'?
   a When patients waste time and money.
   b When patients cancel appointments well in advance.
   c When patients don't turn up.

2 When patients 'don't think twice about making emergency calls', what are they doing?
   a Considering carefully.
   b Not thinking about what they are doing.
   c Making two or more calls for an ambulance.

3 What is the writer's 'solution'?
   a Use a system of returnable deposits.
   b Charge for all medical treatment.
   c Refuse treatment to persistent DNAs.

4 Discuss whether you think the writer's idea would work or just create more bureaucracy and damage the nurse / patient relationship.

LETTER OF THE WEEK

Dear Editor

In my hospital, the average time for an outpatient's appointment is half an hour and if someone doesn't keep the appointment and doesn't tell us in advance, we cannot usually fill the slot. About one in every ten appointments is missed and patients who do not appear (DNAs) waste a great deal of time and money.

In my opinion, persistent DNAs are people with behaviour problems. They are excessively self-centred, have a total disregard for others, demand major attention for minor illnesses, and are often rude to the receptionist, but smile sweetly at the doctor. They are careless about medical services and don't think twice about making emergency calls or using out-of-hours services. They miss appointments quite freely and then complain loudly that they can't get to see a doctor. Oh yes, they know a lot about their rights, but they have no idea about their responsibilities.

It must be said that 95% of our patients are perfectly reasonable, decent people who may sometimes simply forget an appointment – we all do it from time to time and sometimes, admittedly, it's the fault of the system. I can understand why someone might forget an appointment if it's weeks or months into the future or if there is a complicated procedure for confirmations. Persistent DNAs are actually stealing time from other people and sometimes I wish I could refuse them

treatment, but I know that's not practical because it just passes on the problem to someone else. So we should make them pay. My solution is this: we provide patients with an answering service so they can leave messages and on top of this we send a text message reminding them of their appointment time. After that though, anyone who misses two appointments should deposit a sum of money before making their next appointment. The money would be returned to them if they turned up. If they don't turn up, the money would go to a local hospice.

A. Etherington (Charge Nurse)

Speaking

Deciding who should have an appointment

Work in pairs. You work in a hospital x-ray department. The next four weeks are almost fully booked, but there is one vacant slot today. Four patients want the vacancy and you must decide who gets it. Student A, go to p.110 where there is information about two of the patients. Student B, go to p.113 where there is information about the other two patients.

A 'heart sink' patient is one who brings about negative feelings in medical staff: anger, guilt, hatred, and even depression. Patients who do this have been classified under four types: the demander, the manipulator, the denier, and the self-destroyer.

Do you recognise any of these types? Describe any experience you have had with a 'difficult' patient.

● Language spot

used to do / be used to doing / get used to doing

1 Read these pairs of sentences and match them with definitions a–c.

1 I **used to work** in A&E but I moved to Outpatients last year.

We **didn't use to get** so many cancellations.

2 She**'s used to coming** to hospital all the time – she's been on dialysis for years.

I**'m not used to working** nights yet – I can't get to sleep in the daytime.

3 It took me a long time to **get used to taking** blood from patients.

I **haven't got used to booking** patients in on the phone yet.

a a process of becoming familiar with doing something

b something that happened regularly in the past which is now over

c something which is now familiar and is no longer strange, awkward, or difficult

2 Underline the correct option.

1 When I worked at the clinic, we *used / got used / are getting used* to have two days off a week.

2 Did you *getting used / use / used* to see Doctor Ho?

3 I didn't *used / get used / use* to like that nurse, but actually she is very good at her job.

4 She is *get used / getting used / use* to working nights.

5 It's taken a long time, but the staff have slowly *get used / got used / getting used* to the new hospital administrator.

3 Use the verb in brackets to complete the sentences using *used to*, *be used to*, or *get used to*.

EXAMPLE

Everything <u>used to go</u> (go) wrong with our appointments system. Things are better now.

1 I'm getting _____ (work) here and soon I will be familiar with it.

2 We _____ (see) a lot more patients in the old days.

3 We are _____ (do) things this way. We've been doing them like this for years and we don't want to change.

4 You didn't _____ (miss) your routine appointment – what's happened to change things?

5 When I was younger, I _____ (see) a different specialist.

6 I _____ (take) Largactil, but the doctor put me on Lithium instead.

7 I have gradually _____ (attend) the clinic – it's now part of my weekly routine.

>> Go to **Grammar reference** p.123

Writing

An email about an appointment

Read this email which you receive from the outpatients' receptionist. Write an email to Abdullah Nesin.

● Explain who you are and why you are writing.

● Explain why it is important for him to come to the hospital.

● Ask him if there is a problem that anyone can help with.

● Suggest a new appointment date and time.

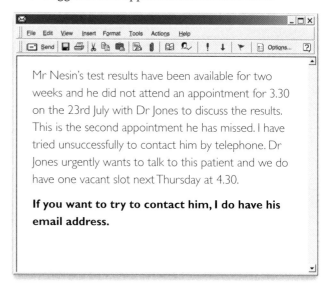

Mr Nesin's test results have been available for two weeks and he did not attend an appointment for 3.30 on the 23rd July with Dr Jones to discuss the results. This is the second appointment he has missed. I have tried unsuccessfully to contact him by telephone. Dr Jones urgently wants to talk to this patient and we do have one vacant slot next Thursday at 4.30.

If you want to try to contact him, I do have his email address.

Stethoscope As a child, René Laënnec found that he could hear the scratching of a pin through the entire length of a wooden beam and when he became a doctor, he remembered this when he had to examine a young female patient. Instead of placing his ear on her chest to listen to internal sounds (a procedure called 'auscultation'), he used a paper tube, thereby inventing the first stethoscope. Which organs can you listen to using a stethoscope?

Listening

Examining a child

1 🎧 Listen to a nurse as she examines an eight-year-old child in Outpatients and talks to the patient and her mother. Say which hospital outpatients' department they are probably in.

2 🎧 Listen again. Number the pictures in the order in which they happen.

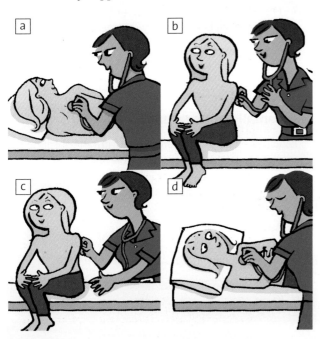

3 Say if these statements are true (T) or false (F).

1 The patient has had surgery.
2 The patient is feeling unwell.
3 The patient is not used to auscultation.
4 A year earlier the patient felt worse.
5 The patient did not have enough energy to take part in the race.
6 The nurse cannot find anything wrong.

It's my job

1 Work in pairs. Describe a patient who has had an effect on you and taught you something.

2 Discuss whether or not it is acceptable for a nurse to get upset and cry in front of a patient.

3 Read about the experience of a practice nurse and answer the questions.

1 How did she feel when she walked into the room?
2 Why didn't she try to stop the patient getting upset?
3 What did she learn from the experience?

Martha Farrell

The average practice nurse is skilled and qualified in wound management, minor surgery, and diagnosis. Yet the most important things nursing has taught me don't show up in the letters after my name.

One morning, one of the doctors I work with asked me if I could talk to a patient. He had just told her that she had a massive malignancy in her left breast which was almost certainly terminal. He said, 'The poor woman's shaking and keeps saying she doesn't know what to do. Perhaps you can get through to her.'

I gulped, nodded, silently took the report, and went into his room. An elderly woman was sitting on the bed staring at the floor. I wanted to say something profound that would somehow 'make it all better', but nothing came into my head. Instead, I took her hand and said, 'I'm Martha. I know what the doctor has just told you and I want you to know that it's OK to cry as much as you want.'

It was as if I'd given her the permission she needed. She began sobbing. I'm not embarrassed to say that I cried too and I did something else; I prayed. That was the first time I ever prayed with a patient. It seemed so little, but it was all I could do. Later, she actually thanked me!

I hope very much that her death, when it came, was as peaceful and dignified as she deserved. As for me, I took away some important lessons; that life is precious even to the elderly and how, even when looking death in the face, the human spirit fights on. I hope that I will always remember that when we cannot cure, we can at least care, and however hi-tech and sophisticated it becomes, nursing must always involve the heart.

Tests

Language that indicates levels

1 Complete the test results with the phrases below.

abnormally high
low-pitched
medium-sized
precancerous
slightly alkaline
slower than average

1 You can hear a _____ diastolic murmur between heartbeats.

2 Analysis shows an _____ number of WBCs in the sample drawn from the vein.

3 We did a mid-stream collection and found a _____ pH of 8.0.

4 A _____ ventricular rate of 69 bpm indicating possible myocardial infarction.

5 We've had a look inside the duodenum and identified a _____ colony of H. pylori.

6 The Path lab's analysis of the sample says that you have a _____ mole on your mid-upper back.

2 Match each completed result in 1 with a test.

a Acidity of urine
b Biopsy
c Auscultation
d Blood test
e ECG / EKG (heart)
f Endoscopy

Project

Choose one illness from the list of the most common conditions treated in outpatients. Research the illness for facts and figures (numbers of patients, gender and ages of patients, average length of treatment, number of deaths, number of cures, etc.) and report back to the rest of the class.

- alcohol use disorders
- chickenpox
- dementia
- depression
- falls
- hepatitis
- HIV / AIDS
- influenza
- iron deficiency anaemia
- malaria
- osteoarthritis
- schizophrenia

Checklist

Assess your progress in this unit. Tick (✓) the statements which are true.

I can talk about different kinds of appointments

I can understand a letter from a nurse

I can use *used to do*, *be used to doing*, and *get used to doing*

I can understand a conversation as a nurse examines a child patient

I can talk about test result levels

Key words

Nouns
auscultation
cancellation
disregard
slot
stethoscope

Adjectives
delayed
double-booked
familiar
first come, first served
follow-up
out-of-hours
persistent
postponed
successive
vacant

Look back through this unit. Find five more words or expressions that you think are useful.

Speaking activities

Student A

Unit 2 p.12

Use your own name, age, and address.

Family history: mother has heart disease
Your medical history: childhood asthma
Appendectomy at age 14
You smoke ten cigarettes per day

Doubts about cardiac catheterization:

1 Invasive surgery should only be performed if it is really necessary. Is this operation necessary?
2 Cardiac catheterization is not a treatment – it is a test. It will not cure the pain.
3 There are many possible reasons for chest pain.
4 Possible complications: heart attacks, strokes, kidney damage, and haemorrhaging.

Unit 4 p.24

Read these sums aloud. Do not show them to your partner. After your partner has written them, invent two more of your own and repeat the practice.

a $43 + 7 - 2$

b $\frac{10}{5}$ ml = 2

c $52 \text{ mg} \times 3 \text{ mg} + 4 \text{ mg}$

d $27 - 13 \div 2$

e $1 \text{ kg} = 1000 \text{ g}$

Unit 4 p.25

1 Someone you love is near death from illness and the one drug that could save them is too expensive to buy. A local pharmacist refuses to sell it cheaper or accept payment later.

You could steal the money, steal the drug, or do nothing. What would you do? Explain your answer.

Would your answer be the same if the person who is dying was a stranger? Explain why.

2 You are working on a research project into HIV transmission. 1,000 pregnant women are tested for HIV. 140 women test positive. When they tell their partners, eleven of them are chased from their homes or replaced by another wife, seven are beaten, and one commits suicide.

You could advise participants not to tell their partners, insist they tell them in order to stop transmission of the disease, or do nothing. What would you do? Explain your answer.

Would your answer be different if the numbers were bigger or smaller? Explain why.

Unit 5 p.31

1 Read the descriptions of the eye-testing procedures below. Then perform the following eye tests on Student B. Keep talking to the 'patient' as you do so.

2 Discuss what feature of vision each one is testing.

1 Get the patient to sit in front of you, an arm's length away, and cover one eye. Imagine what the patient can see is divided in quarters, or 'quadrants', like a clock. Ask the patient to look straight ahead. Then hold up a number of fingers in one of the quadrants, and ask the patient to tell you how many fingers.

2 Ask the patient to fixate on a near or distant object. Cover one of the patient's eyes, then pause, and uncover it. Watch the eye as the patient fixates on the distant object again. It should quickly point in the same direction as the other eye.

Unit 15 p.106

Patient 1

On the telephone is a woman. She wants to make an appointment for her twelve-year-old child. Mother and daughter have missed the last two appointments; the first because they decided to go to the cinema instead, the second because they forgot.

Patient 2

In reception is a patient who is a heavy smoker. She has a bad cough, but has not stopped smoking despite doctors' warnings. An x-ray was taken last month, but the hospital has lost her records.

Unit 9 p.69

Tell Student B the information you have about Lewis Gavin. Speak naturally without reading out the notes. Note down Student B's information. When you both have all the information, discuss the case and try to work out what mistake the medical team made which caused his problems.

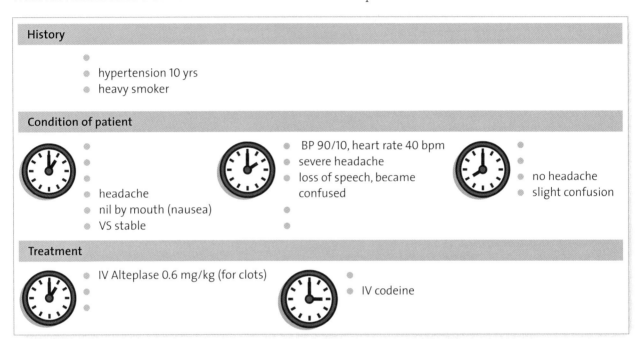

History
- hypertension 10 yrs
- heavy smoker

Condition of patient
- headache
- nil by mouth (nausea)
- VS stable
- BP 90/10, heart rate 40 bpm
- severe headache
- loss of speech, became confused
- no headache
- slight confusion

Treatment
- IV Alteplase 0.6 mg/kg (for clots)
- IV codeine

Unit 6 p.36

1 You and Student B are student nurses on placements in university medical centres. Call Student B and tell him / her about the patients below. Then listen to Student B's description of his / her patients and make notes. Arrange to do some research before talking again about suggested diagnoses.

Your patients

1
- 19-year-old woman
- very red cheeks
- worse in the morning
- had it several years, getting worse

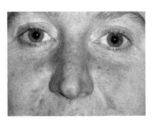

2
- 18-year-old man
- spots on back and chest
- got better then came back
- itchy at night
- sore throat two weeks ago

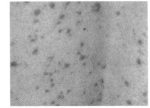

2 Now form a pair with another Student A. Look at the notes on three skin conditions on p.112. Discuss what condition you think Student B's patients have. When you have decided, call Student B with your suggestions.

Patient 1 _____

Patient 2 _____

Unit 9 p.73

Story A

A couple learned during pregnancy that their baby was missing most of her brain. She only had the brainstem, which controls basic functions such as breathing and heartbeat. The hospital made it clear that she could not survive without advanced life support, and at most would only be able to breathe. The couple are religious, and believe that it is wrong to take any life, including the life of an unborn baby.

Story B

A 27-year-old woman collapsed and fell into a coma, possibly as a result of an eating disorder. When she awoke, she was in a persistent vegetative state. This is where a person wakes and sleeps, and opens their eyes, but seems not to be aware of the world around them. After eight years in this state, her husband asked the hospital to remove her feeding tube. Her parents said that the hospital should continue to keep her alive, because she was conscious.

Story C

A 26-year-old woman was thrown through the windscreen of her car. She entered a persistent vegetative state. This is where a person wakes and sleeps, and opens their eyes, but seems not to be aware of the world around them. After four years her parents accepted that she would not recover and asked the hospital to remove the feeding tube. The hospital refused, saying that it had no evidence that the woman would have wanted to die in this situation.

Unit 6 p.36

Information for diagnosing Student B's patients

Erythema multiforme

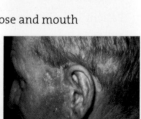

- most common in boys
- can be triggered by viruses, e.g. herpes simplex
- can be triggered by antibiotics
- itchy
- inflamed lesions inside nose and mouth

Discoid lupus erythematosus

- sores on exposed skin, especially face and head
- most common in young women
- sometimes runs in families
- strong sunlight worsens it
- cigarettes worsen it

Molluscum contagiosum

- pimples especially on trunk, shoulders, and thighs
- common in people with reduced immunity
- especially common in eczema sufferers
- spread by skin contact

Unit 11 p.81

1 You are about to have an eye operation. Tell the nurse you're worried about the things below.

- pain in operation
- pain afterwards
- vision no good afterwards
- long time off work

2 You are the nurse. Reassure the patient about his / her hernia operation using the information below.

- fully unconscious – anaesthetist monitors this
- straightforward operation – back here two hours from now
- able to have more children!
- able to do everything in a week except lift heavy objects

Student B

Unit 2 p.12

Cardiac catheterization

This is a diagnostic test done to get information about the heart. It takes three hours.

Procedure

Give the patient a mild sedative.

Insert IV line into a blood vessel in the arm, neck, or groin.

Insert dye into blood vessels.

Thread the catheter into the heart and take pictures.

Risk of serious complications: researchers say risk is 1 in 500.

Non-invasive alternatives are reported in medical journals, but they are very new and not widely used yet.

Unit 11 p.81

1 You are the nurse. Reassure the patient about his / her eye operation using the information below.

- eye drops – no pain
- discomfort possible – painkillers
- blurry vision possible
- work next week probably, if all OK

2 You are about to have a hernia operation. Tell the nurse you're worried about the things below.

- awake during operation
- might die
- not able to have more children?
- looking after six-year-old child

Unit 15 p.106

Patient 3

In reception is a patient who is worried about a slight, intermittent pain in his chest. He already has an appointment, but it is in four weeks' time and he wants an earlier one.

He has already been waiting for two hours.

Patient 4

On the telephone is a young man who is not ill, but needs a chest x-ray in order to start a new job. He says his new employers cannot wait and he must have the x-ray done now or lose the job.

Unit 4 p.24

Read these sums aloud. Do not show them to your partner. After your partner has written them, invent two more of your own and repeat the practice.

a $50 - \dfrac{25}{2}$

b $50 \times 2.5 = 125$

c 1.5 litres + 2.5 litres = 3.75 litres

d $x = \dfrac{y}{h}$

e $3\frac{1}{2} + 9\frac{3}{4} = 13\frac{1}{4}$

Unit 4 p.25

1 You go to the laboratory for a lesson on how drugs affect vital signs – knowledge that is in textbooks. You find that you have to give drugs to live rats and at the end of the experiments, you must kill them.

You could protest, get other students to join you, or keep quiet and do the experiment. You could even release the rats.

What would you do? Explain your answer.

Would your answer be the same if the animal was a dog? Explain why.

2 A fifteen-year-old girl is taking contraceptive pills but is keeping it a secret from her mother. One day her mother finds the pills and thinking that her daughter is taking illegal drugs, she comes to you to ask what they are.

You could tell her the truth, lie, or refuse to say anything.

What would you do? Explain your answer.

Would your answer be the same if you knew her mother was likely to be violent towards both you and the daughter? Explain why.

Unit 5 p.31

1 Read the descriptions of the eye-testing procedures below. Then perform the following eye tests on Student A. Keep talking to the 'patient' as you do so.

2 Discuss what feature of vision each one is testing.

1 Ask your patient to hold a pen in each hand at arm's length in front of their face.
   Ask them to touch the tips of the pens together.
   Repeat with one eye closed. Then the other eye closed.

2 Stand or sit one to two metres in front of your patient.
   Ask the patient to follow your finger with their eyes without moving their head.
   Move your finger in a cross or 'H' shape and check the patient's gaze in all directions.
   Ask the patient to count the number of fingers and briefly flash a number of fingers in each of the four corners.

Unit 6 p.36

You and Student A are student nurses on placements in university medical centres. Student A will call to describe two patients. Listen and make notes. Then describe your patients below. Arrange to do some research before talking again about suggested diagnoses.

Your patients

1 ● 21-year-old woman
   ● itchy rash, getting bigger
   ● painful sores inside mouth
   ● diarrhoea
   ● had cold sores recently

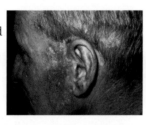

2 ● 20-year-old woman
   ● sores on face and head
   ● very bad in summer
   ● mother has it too

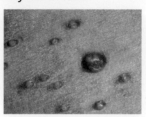

2 Now form a pair with another Student B. Look at the notes on three skin conditions on the right. Discuss what condition you think Student A's patients have. When you have decided, wait for Student A to call.

Patient 1 _____

Patient 2 _____

Unit 6 p.36

Information for diagnosing Student A's patients

Pityriasis rosea

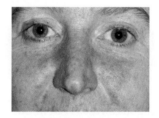

● mild, non-contagious
● common among children and young adults
● starts with single round spot, followed by a rash of coloured spots on the body and upper arms
● often fever, sore throat, and headache before skin symptoms develop

Rosacea

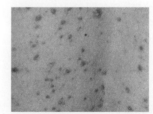

● especially on forehead, nose, and cheeks
● can be worsened by sun and wind
● spicy foods, caffeine, and alcohol can worsen it
● more common in females

Guttate psoriasis

● often triggered by strep throat 2–3 weeks before, or sometimes by chickenpox
● sometimes goes away then returns
● most common in children and young adults
● typically occurs on the back

Unit 7 p.45

You are Layla Hart's (the patient in *Listening*) specialist cancer nurse.
Read the information below. Then answer Layla's (Student A's) questions where you can.

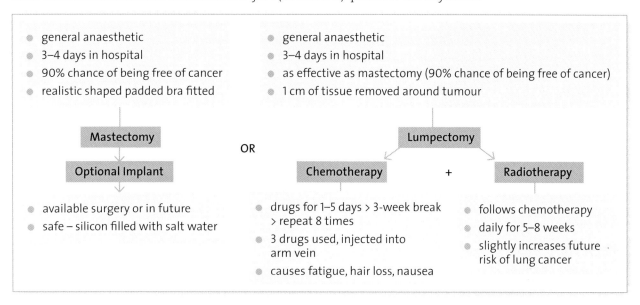

Unit 9 p.69

Tell Student A the information you have about Lewis Gavin. Speak naturally without reading out
the notes. Note down Student A's information. When you both have all the information, discuss
the case and try to work out what mistake the medical team made which caused his problems.

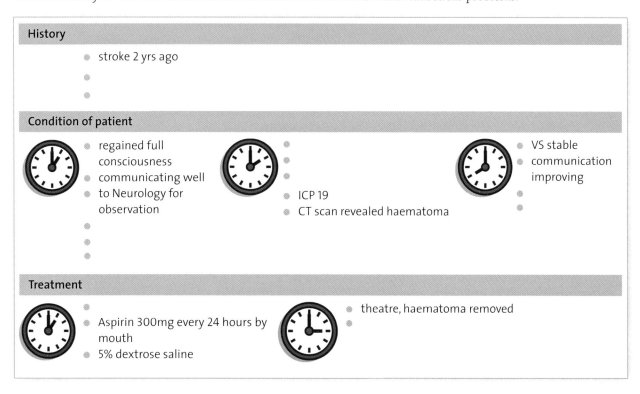

Grammar reference

1 Narrative tenses

Present Perfect

*They **have taken** him off the critical list.*
= subject + ***have / has*** + past participle

We use the Present Perfect to talk about an action that happened in a period of time from the past up to the present. It is commonly used to talk about a recent event, especially one that is relevant now. The Present Perfect can be used with *already*, *still*, and *yet*.

*We **haven't given** her any painkillers **yet**.*

Past Simple

We use the Past Simple to talk about a completed action in the past which has no relevance in the present.

*I **categorized** her as non-emergency.*
= subject + Past Simple

Past Continuous

Positive

I / He / She/ It	**was waiting**	for four hours.
You / We / They	**were waiting**	for four hours.

= subject + ***was / were*** + present participle

Negative

I / He / She / It	**wasn't responding**	to treatment.
You / We / They	**weren't responding**	to treatment.

= subject + ***was / were*** + not (***wasn't / weren't***) + present participle

Questions

Was	I / he / she / it	haemorrhaging?
Were	you / we / they	haemorrhaging?

= ***Was / Were*** + subject + present participle

Short answers

Yes,	I / he / she / it	**was.**
	you / we / they	**were.**
No,	I / he / she / it	**wasn't.**
	you / we / they	**weren't.**

Use

We use the Past Continuous to talk about an action that was in progress in the past. The Past Continuous and Past Simple are commonly used together when one action comes in the middle of a longer one. We can use time expressions such as *when* and *while* before the longer action.

Note: we can use *when* or *while* to introduce a Past Continuous clause.

***When / while** I was calling for an ambulance, the patient deteriorated.*

*The patient deteriorated **when / while** I was calling for an ambulance.*

Past Perfect

Positive

I / He / She/ It / You / We / They	***had waited***	for four hours.

= subject + ***had*** + past participle

Negative

I / He / She / It / You / We / They	***hadn't read***	the label.

= subject + ***had*** + ***not (hadn't)*** + past participle

Questions / **Short answers**

Questions	Short answers
Had I / he / she / it / you / we / they **crashed?**	Yes, I / he / she / it / you / we / they **had.**
	No, I / he / she / it / you / we / they **hadn't.**

= ***Had*** + subject + past participle

Use

We use the Past Perfect to talk about an action that happened before a point in the past.

***When** he reached the hospital, he **had stopped** bleeding.*
(= he stopped bleeding before he reached the hospital)

Note: if we use the Past Simple in both clauses, the sequence of events changes.

***When** he reached the hospital, he **stopped** bleeding.*
(= he stopped bleeding at the same time as he reached the hospital)

2 Reported speech

Reporting statements

When reporting what someone has said, we put the main verb into a past tense.

Tenses

Present Simple	→	Past Simple
Present Continuous	→	Past Continuous
Present Perfect	→	Past Perfect
Past Simple	→	Past Perfect

Modal verbs

must	→	*had to*
can	→	*could*
will	→	*would*

When reporting a statement, we use a reporting verb such as *say*, *explain*, or *tell*.

'This treatment is a temporary measure.' →
*The nurse **said** that the treatment was a temporary measure.*

Note: it may sometimes be necessary to change pronouns.

*'I'm referring **you** to a different department.'* →
*The doctor explained that she was referring **him** to a different department.*

'I took antidepressants when I was younger.' →
*She said that **she** had taken antidepressants when **she** was younger.*

Note: after *tell* we must use an object pronoun, such as *me, her, him, us, the doctor*, etc.

'I have never smoked.' Mr Marks said to the nurse. →
*Mr Marks **told the nurse** that he had never smoked.*

Reporting commands and instructions

In direct speech, we often use the imperative when giving a command or instruction.

In reported speech, we use the structure *tell* + object pronoun + infinitive with *to* for positive commands.

'Take one tablet after every meal.' →
*He **told me to take** one tablet after every meal.*

For negative commands, we use *tell* + object pronoun + *not* + infinitive with *to*.

'Don't take more than five tablets within a 24-hour period.' →
*He **told me not to take** more than five tablets within a 24-hour period.*

Reporting questions

yes / no questions

When reporting a *yes / no* question, we use *ask* and change the tense of the main verb. However, note the structure *if* + positive word order.

'Are you in a lot of pain?' →
*The doctor **asked if I was in a lot of pain**.*

wh- questions

When reporting a *wh*-question, we keep the question word, change the tense of the main verb, and use positive word order.

'Where are Miss Johansson's medical notes, Jane?' →
*She asked Jane **where Miss Johansson's medical notes were**.*

3 Modals and expressions for giving advice

We can use a variety of expressions to give advice. These include modal verbs such as *ought to* and *should* + infinitive. Both convey strong and / or urgent advice, and there is no difference in meaning between them.

Positive:	*You **ought to / should** take folic acid every day in early pregnancy.*
Negative:	*You **oughtn't to / shouldn't** smoke.*

Another way of giving strong advice is *you'd better (not)* + infinitive.

*If you start bleeding, **you'd better see** your doctor straight away.*

***You'd better not lift** heavy objects when pregnant.*

Other expressions that are less strong include:

- ***You may want to** + infinitive*
  You may want to avoid strenuous activity.
- ***It's (always) a good idea (not) to** + infinitive*
  It's always a good idea to have a balanced diet.
  It's always a good idea not to get too stressed.
- ***Try (not)** + infinitive with **to***
  Try to drink lots of fluids.
  Try not to push until I tell you to.
- ***I'd** + infinitive*

We often use *I'd* to give more personal advice. It means *If I were in your position*. It is common to add *if I were you* at the end of the clause.

***I'd cut down** on caffeine if I were you.*

4 Mathematical expressions

Multiplication

- *multiply by*

Multiply *4* **by** *10.* / *4* **multiplied by** *10 is 40.*

Another way to say *multiplied by* is *times*.

*4 **times** 10 is 40.*

Division

- *divide by*

Divide *126* **by** *3.* / *126* **divided by** *3 is 42.*

Another way to say *divided by* is *into*; however, it is necessary to change the order of the figures.

*3 **into** 126 is 42.*

Subtraction

- *subtract / take from*

*What do you get when you **subtract / take** 22.5 **from** 112.5?*

*22.5 **subtracted / taken from** 112.5 is 90.*

Another way to say *subtracted from* is *minus*. As with *into*, you need to change the order of the figures.

*112.5 **minus** 22.5 is 90.*

Addition

- *add to*

Add *41.7* **to** *36.3.* / *41.7* **added to** *36.3 is 78.*

Another way to say *added to* is *plus*.

*41.7 **plus** 36.3 is 78.*

Note: the words *times*, *into*, *minus*, and *plus* can't be used to replace the imperative form of the verb.

NOT ~~Times 4 by 10.~~

To talk about totals, the simplest way is to use *is*. Note: we never use the third person plural form of *be*.

NOT ~~41.7 added to 36.3 are 78.~~

Alternatives to *is* are *makes*, *equals*, *makes / gives a total of*, and *is equal to*.

*20 divided by 5 **makes** 4.*

*Three quarters minus a half **is equal to** a quarter.*

*Three quarters plus one eighth **makes a total of** seven eighths.*

5 Ability

- *can / can't* + infinitive

We use *can / can't* to talk about ability in the present.

***Can** you **see** the letters on the bottom line of the chart?*

*I **can't read** the numbers.*

- *could / couldn't* + infinitive

We use *could / couldn't* to talk about ability in the past.

*Once glasses were invented, people **could do** a lot more small-scale work.*

*Before glasses became widespread, many people **couldn't work** long hours.*

- *be able to* + infinitive

We use *be able to* in a number of tenses. In the present, *is / are able to* = *can*. In the Past Simple, *was / were able to* usually means the same as *could*. However, *was / were able to* also has a different sense. While *could* refers to general ability, *was / were able to* talks about the ability to do something in a specific set of circumstances or conditions.

*After the surgery, **I was able to** play football.*

Be able to expresses ability in other tenses:

Future: *We **won't be able to** give you the results until Thursday.*

Present Perfect: ***I've been able** to play football again since wearing contact lenses.*

Past Perfect: *She **hadn't been able to** do any close-up work before she had surgery.*

Note: we can't use *be able to* in continuous tenses.

NOT ~~I wasn't being able to~~ read for more than ten minutes.

- *manage to* + infinitive

We use *manage to* in a similar way to *be able to*, to talk about the ability to do something in certain circumstances. However, *manage to* suggests that a greater effort is required in order to achieve something. We can use *manage to* in a number of tenses.

*I **managed to read** for nearly an hour today without feeling tired.*

***Will** you **manage to** get to the hospital by yourself?*

We can't use *manage to* as an alternative to *can* or *could*.

NOT ~~Do you manage to see~~ the letters on the bottom line of the chart?

6 Modifying an adjective

We use adverbs of degree to modify adjectives in order to make an adjective stronger or weaker. These adverbs always go before the adjective.

Adverbs of degree

weaker		stronger
a bit	rather	very
a little	quite	really
a little bit	fairly	extremely
slightly	pretty	absolutely

Note: some adjectives refer to qualities that are gradable. For example, pain can be more or less severe. Other adjectives refer to non-gradable qualities, e.g. *fantastic, impossible, perfect, terrible, unbearable*. With non-gradable adjectives, the modifying adverb is used to emphasize the meaning of the adjective.

Absolutely is only used with non-gradable adjectives.

*The hospital's standard of care is **absolutely fantastic**.*

Comparative adjectives

We can use the following adverbs to make a comparative adjective weaker or stronger: *a lot, a little, a little bit, a bit, rather, slightly, far, much, very much*.

*The pain has become **a lot worse** recently.*

*The area is **a bit less sore** now.*

Superlative adjectives

We can use *easily the* + superlative and *by far the* + superlative to talk about an extreme situation.

*It was **easily the worst pain** he'd ever experienced.*

*This is **by far the most complicated** case I've come across.*

7 Articles

The way we use articles depends on whether the noun is countable or uncountable.

Countable nouns

With countable nouns, we use the article *a / an* when referring to a single item, and no article when referring to more than one.

Singular: *a biopsy, a hospital, an operation, a tumour*

Plural: *biopsies, hospitals, operations, tumours*

*He had **a biopsy** because there were **sores** on his leg.*

Uncountable nouns

With uncountable nouns, such as *cancer, damage, chemotherapy, news*, we never use the article *a / an*.

I underwent chemotherapy last year.

NOT   I underwent a chemotherapy last year.

Uncountable nouns do not have a plural form.

*I had **two courses of** chemotherapy last year.*

The article *the*

We can use *the* before countable and uncountable nouns to make it clear which particular object, person, or situation we are talking about.

Countable: *We found **a tumour. The tumour** is rather large, I'm afraid.*

In this sentence, we use *a* before *tumour* because we are talking about it for the first time. We then say *the tumour* because it is a tumour we already know about.

Uncountable: *The doctor has confirmed that I've got **cancer. The cancer** I've got doesn't have obvious symptoms, so I'm lucky that it was detected so quickly.*

In this sentence, we do not use *the* before *cancer* because we are talking about cancer in general. However, we go on to refer to *the cancer* because it indicates a particular example of cancer.

8 Explaining purpose and cause

Purpose

to + infinitive

*He stayed off work for six weeks **to** recover from his operation.*

Note: we don't use *to* + infinitive in the negative. Instead, we use *in order not to*.

in order (not) to + infinitive

In order (not) to is used in a similar way as *to* + infinitive, but it expresses a stronger purpose than *to* on its own.

*You need to keep the room cool **in order to** bring his temperature down.*

*We will reduce the dosage **in order not to** make the side effects worse.*

so that / so + clause

With *so that / so*, we can use a modal verb.

*The patient was repositioned **so that / so** he could breathe more easily.*

However, when *so* follows a comma, it is used to introduce an action that happens as a consequence of the previous clause.

*The patient isn't progressing as well as we'd hoped, **so** we're going to change his medication.*

which results in / resulting in + noun

Which results in and *resulting in* are used in a similar way to talk about purpose. Use a comma before them.

*The patient's blood pressure drops quickly, **resulting in** loss of consciousness.*

*The patient's blood pressure drops quickly, **which results in** loss of consciousness.*

Do not confuse these expressions with *as a result of*.

Cause

because, since, and *as* + clause

Because is the most common of these expressions, while *since* and *as* are slightly more formal.

*They performed a biopsy **because / since / as** the result of the test was inconclusive.*

We can reverse the order of the clauses. Note: we have to use a comma to separate the clauses. It is more common to use *since* and *as* at the beginning of the sentence.

***Because / Since / As** the result of the test was inconclusive, they performed a biopsy.*

The reason for / the cause of + noun phrase

These phrases are a stronger way of expressing cause.

***The reason for / the cause of** your high blood pressure is your stressful lifestyle.*
or
*Your stressful lifestyle is **the reason for / the cause of** your high blood pressure.*

because of / due to / owing to / as a result of + noun phrase

Although these expressions can be used either before or after the main verb, it is more common to use them after the main verb.

*He was getting headaches **because of / due to / owing to / as a result of** high blood pressure.*

9 First and Second Conditional

First Conditional

We use the First Conditional to talk about a possible future situation.

*If his operation **goes** well, he**'ll make** a full recovery.*

*If he takes the correct dosage, he **won't have** any side effects.*

= *If* + Present Simple + *will ('ll)* + infinitive
   if clause   main clause

Note: we can also use *should* in the main clause, if we want to sound less definite about the outcome.

*If everything goes well, he **should** regain consciousness within about half an hour.*

Note: we can reverse the order of the *if* clause and main clause. We do not use a comma when the main clause comes at the beginning of the sentence.

He should regain consciousness within about half an hour if everything goes well.

We can use *when* instead of *if*. *When* has a stronger sense than *if*, and means *only when* or *once*.

***When** she is able to sit up unaided, she will receive occupational therapy.*

*She will receive occupational therapy **when** she is able to sit up unaided.*

Second Conditional

We use the Second Conditional to talk about an imagined future situation.

*If they had more cycle paths, there **wouldn't be** so many accidents.*

= *If* + Past Simple + *would ('d) / would not (wouldn't)* + infinitive

We can also use *could* instead of *would* in the main clause. *Could = would be able to.*

*If he started exercising now, he **could** become fully mobile within a few weeks.*

As with the First Conditional, we can reverse the order of the clauses.

He could become fully mobile within a few weeks if he started exercising now.

Note: we can't use *when* with the Second Conditional.

NOT   ~~His blood pressure wouldn't be so high when he didn't smoke.~~

10 Verbs followed by *to* or *-ing* form

Verb + *to* + infinitive

These include *agree, decide, deserve, hope, learn, manage, offer, promise, refuse, seem,* and *want*.

*We **managed to** stabilize the patient.*

Verb + *-ing* form

These include *avoid, dislike, don't mind, enjoy, feel like, finish, give up, imagine, keep, practise, recommend,* and *stop*.

*He **doesn't mind waiting** for a cancellation.*

*Do you **feel like eating** anything?*

Some verbs can be followed by *to* or the *-ing* form, but with certain verbs this involves a change of meaning.

Verb + *to* or *-ing* form with no change in meaning

These include *begin, continue, hate, intend, like, love, prefer, start,* and *try*.

Note: after *would hate, would like, would love,* and *would prefer,* we use *to* + infinitive.

*I **would like to get** a second opinion.*

Verb + *to* or *-ing* form with a change in meaning

The verbs *try, remember,* and *forget* can also be used with either *to* or the *-ing* form, but they change their meaning in each case.

*He **tried to straighten** his arm, but was unable to. (try to + infinitive = make an attempt to do something)*

*We **tried moving** his bed next to an open window, but he still felt very warm. (try + -ing form = to test something out)*

***Remember to take** these tablets with every meal. (remember + to + infinitive = remember that you must take the tablets with every meal)*

*He **remembered arriving** at the hospital but nothing after that. (remember + -ing form = he remembers that he did something)*

*Don't **forget to use** hand-rub. (not forget + to + infinitive = remember that you must use hand-rub)*

*I'll never **forget seeing** the car coming straight towards me. (forget + -ing form = I saw the car and I'll never forget it)*

Verb + object + *to*

With some verbs, it is necessary to add an object. These include *advise, ask, encourage, forbid, help, invite,* *persuade, remind, recommend,* and *tell*.

*The doctor **asked me to** describe the symptoms.*

*They **advised me not to** do any physical activity for several days.*

Note: the position of *not* in the negative form.

NOT ~~They advised me to not do~~ ...

11 Future forms

will + infinitive

We use *will / won't* to talk about the future in general, and to make predictions, offers, or promises. The short form *'ll* is used in conversations. The negative form is *will not* or, more commonly, *won't*.

*The scar **will fade** over the next few months.*

*You **won't be** able to drive after the operation.*

be going to + infinitive

We use *be going to* to talk about intentions, schedules, or plans. A course of action has already been decided.

*I'm **going to** give you some pain relief.*

*Is the doctor **going to** see me today?*

should + infinitive

We can use *should* to mean 'probably' if it refers to an outcome with less certainty than *will*.

*The scar **should** fade over the next few months.*

may / might + infinitive

May and *might* have almost no difference in meaning. They are both used to talk about possibility.

*We **may / might have to** change your prescription.*

Note: we can't use modal verbs after these forms. We use *be able to* instead of *can* and *have to* instead of *must*.

NOT ~~You won't can talk~~ after the operation.

Present Simple

We can use the Present Simple after time expressions such as *when, as soon as, before,* and *after* in order to talk about a future situation.

The main clause can be in the Present Simple or the Future.

*I'll be with him **when** he **regains** consciousness.*

***After** I arrive in the morning, I **prepare** the theatre.*

*A patient has to sign a consent form **before** the hospital **can / is able to / will be able to** operate on him.*

Note: we can't use *will* in the time clause.

NOT   I'll be with him ~~when he will regain~~ consciousness.

12 Passive sentences

We use the Passive when we do not know who did an action or when it is not important to say who did it. If we want to say who did something (the agent), we can either use an Active or a Passive form. In the Passive, we use *by*.

Active:	The nurse on duty **writes** a report every day.
Passive:	A report **is written** every day by the nurse on duty.

Note: the Passive always focuses more on the action than on the agent.

Form

Present Simple Passive

We use this to talk about a regular activity in the present.

*Flowers **are not allowed** in some hospitals.*

= Present Simple of *be* + past participle

Past Simple Passive

We use this to talk about a complete action in the past.

*The procedure **was explained** in detail to the patient.*

= Past Simple of *be* + past participle

Present Continuous Passive

We use this to talk about an action that is in progress at the moment.

*Not enough **is being done** to stop the spread of hospital-acquired infections.*

= Present Continuous of *be* + past participle

Present Perfect Passive

We use this to talk about an action that has continued up to the present.

*Not enough people **have been treated** with this new drug for us to understand its effects.*

= Present Perfect of *be* + past participle

Future Passive

We use this to talk about a future action.

*Soap dispensers **will be cleaned** every day from tomorrow.*

= *will* + *be* + past participle

Most tenses used in the Active can be used in the Passive. The exception is the Present Perfect Continuous.

NOT   A new drug ~~has been being~~ developed.

We would use either:

Present Continuous Passive:	A new drug **is being developed**.
Present Perfect Passive:	A new drug **has been developed**.

Modal verbs in the Passive: *can*, *must*, etc.

We use *be* + past participle after *can, could, have to, may, might, must, ought to*, and *should*.

Modal verbs are commonly used in the Passive in official signs.

*Old dressings **should be wrapped** in a plastic bag.*

*Hands **must be air-dried** if no towels are available.*

13 Relative clauses

Defining and non-defining relative clauses

We use a relative clause as a means of joining two pieces of information together in one sentence. The two parts of the sentence are connected by one of the following relative pronouns:

- *who* to refer to a person or people
- *which* to talk about things or animals
- *where* to refer to places
- *whose* (= 'of who / of which') to talk about possession.

Note: we can use *that* instead of *who* or *which*.

There are two types of relative clause:

Defining relative clause

A defining relative clause helps us identify the person or thing we are talking about.
We do not use commas with this type of relative clause.

*The patient **who / that** was admitted late last night died this morning.*

*This is the place **where** they're going to build the annexe.*

*Is that the patient **whose** kidney transplant operation was postponed?*

Note: when the pronouns *who, which*, or *that* are the object of a defining relative clause, they can be removed with no change in meaning. However, when these pronouns are the subject of a defining relative clause, we can't remove them:

*At last, we're going to get **the new dialysis machine which** was promised.*

Non-defining relative clause

A non-defining relative clause tells us more information about people or things. The clause is not essential in order to understand the whole sentence. We can use *who* for people, *which* for things, and *where* for places. We can't use *that*. We must always use commas at the beginning and end of this type of relative clause:

*Here's a leaflet, **which** will help explain the procedure.*

*The doctor, **who** only qualified recently, works in the Renal unit.*

*The patient, **whose** kidney transplant operation was postponed, has been in a great deal of pain.*

Remember that we can never miss out the relative pronoun in non-defining relative clauses.

NOT   ~~The doctor, only qualified recently, ...~~

14 Present Perfect

Present Perfect Simple

See p.116.

Present Perfect Continuous

Positive

 We **have been monitoring** your condition.

= subject + *have / has* + *been* + *-ing* form

Negative

 You **haven't been eating** a healthy enough diet.

= subject + *have / has* + *not been* + *-ing* form

Questions

 Why **have** my headaches **been getting** worse recently?

= (question word +) *have / has* + *subject* + *been* + *-ing* form

Like the Present Perfect Simple, the Present Perfect Continuous is used to talk about an action that carries on up to the present. Sometimes we can use either tense without much difference in meaning, especially when we refer to a longer-term situation.

*He **has suffered** / **has been suffering** with a bad back for over ten years.*

*She**'s felt** / **has been feeling** like this for a number of years.*

In other cases, the Present Perfect Continuous emphasizes the fact that the action has continued up to the present, and may not be finished.

Compare:

*He's **been coming to terms** with the news that he has cancer.* (= he may or may not have finished coming to terms with the news)

*He's **come to terms** with the news that he has cancer.* (= he has finished coming to terms with the news)

15 used to do / be used to doing / get used to doing

used to + infinitive

We use *used to* + infinitive to talk about something that happened regularly in the past.

Positive:	People in Britain **used to pay** to see a doctor.
Negative:	I **didn't use to wait** so long for an appointment.
Questions:	**Did** you **use to work** in Endocrinology?

To talk about things we do regularly we use the Present Simple.

be used to + -ing form

We use *be used to* + *-ing* form in a number of tenses to talk about something that we are now comfortable about or familiar with.

Positive:	We**'re used to sitting** in an overcrowded waiting room.
Negative:	She **won't be used to being** in a wheelchair, so you'll have to help her.
Questions:	**Are** you **used to writing** with your left hand now?

get used to + -ing form

We use *get used to* + *-ing* form in a number of tenses to talk about becoming familiar with doing something.

Positive:	I**'m getting used to having** a catheter.
Negative:	We **haven't got used to living** in this climate.
Questions:	**Will** I **get used to working** nights?

We can also use *get used to* + noun to talk about familiarity with a person or thing.

*I haven't got used to **this climate**.*

Abbreviations

a.m.	morning
ABCDE (pain scale)	ask, believe, choose, deliver, empower
ABD	abdominal
agit	stir / shake
AMBO	ambulance
AMI	acute myocardial infarction (heart attack)
ATA	actual time of arrival
AXR	abdominal x-ray
BHT	blunt head trauma
bilat.	bilaterally (on both sides)
BM	bowel movement
BMI	body mass index
bpm / BPM	beats per minute / breaths per minute
BS	breathing sounds / bowel sounds
C	critical
c.f.	with food
c/o	complaining of
cap	capsule
CAPD	continuous ambulatory peritoneal dialysis
cat	category
CPR	cardiopulmonary resuscitation
CS	Caesarean section
CT	computerized tomography (scan)
CV	cardiovascular system
CVA	cerebrovascular accident (stroke)
CXR	chest x-ray
DM	diabetes mellitus
DNA	did not appear / attend
DoA	dead on arrival
DoB	date of birth
Dx / DX	diagnosis
ECG	electrocardiogram – heart scan
ECT	electroconvulsive therapy
EEG	electroencephalogram – brain scan

ETA	estimated time of arrival
EtOH	alcohol
F	female
FLACC pain scale	face, legs, activity, cry, consolability
FOBT	faecal occult blood test
Fx	fracture
g	gram
GCS	Glasgow coma scale
GI	gastrointestinal tract
GP	General Practitioner
h	hour
HTN	hypertension
ICU	Intensive Care Unit
ID	intradermal
IM	intramuscular
inj	injury
INJ	injection
JVP	jugular venous pressure
km	kilometre
L	litre
M/G/R	murmurs / gallops / rubs
mcg	microgram
mg	milligram
mm	millimetre
MRI	magnetic resonance imaging (scan)
MRSA	methycyllin resistant staphylococcus aureus
N	nausea
N/A	not appropriate
NICU	Neonatal Intensive Care Unit
NIPS	neonatal / infant pain scale
nmt	not more than
NPASS	neonatal pain, agitation, and sedation scale
NYD	not yet diagnosed
op	operation
OSG	overall stage grouping
p.m.	afternoon or evening
PD	peritoneal dialysis
PEP	post-exposure prophylaxis

PO	orally
POE	pain on exertion
pos	possible
PQRST	provocation and palliation, quality and quantity, region and radiation, severity and scale, timing and time of onset
prn	as needed
pt	patient
q2h	every two hours
qam	every day before noon
qd / QD	every day
qid	four times a day
qqh	every four hours
qs	a sufficient quantity
R	rectally / right
rep	repeat
RL	right lateral
RRR	regular rate and rhythm
RTA	road traffic accident
s.a.	use your own judgement
S/N	Staff Nurse
SHO	Senior House Officer
sl	slight
SOB	shortness of breath
SRN	State Registered Nurse (UK)
START	simple triage rapid treatment
tbsp	tablespoon
tds	three times daily
tid / TID	three times a day
TNM	tumour, node, metastasis
tsp	teaspoon
u	unit
u/s	ultrasound
UNK	unknown
URTI	upper respiratory tract infection
WBC	white blood cell
wk	week

Listening scripts

Unit 1

Listening

O = Operator, C = Caller,
D = Ambulance dispatcher

O Emergency services. Which service do you require?

C Ambulance, quick!

O Connecting you.

D Ambulance emergency. What number are you are calling from?

C There's been a terrible accident.

D OK, caller. Can you first give me your number so if we get cut off, I can call you back?

C I'm on a mobile. It's zero zero seven nine double three triple six.

D And where is the emergency?

C Here, just outside my house.

D It's OK sir, keep calm. I need to know where. Are you at the scene now?

C Yes.

D Where are you?

C I'm on Second Avenue in Newtown.

D Second Avenue, right. And your name?

C Alexander. Alexander Petit.

D OK, Alexander. Tell me what's happened.

C A lorry. It's a tanker. There was this terrible noise. A big crash and the shop wall fell down. The driver – he doesn't look good.

D Try to calm down, Alexander. Now let's take it slowly. You say that a tanker has crashed into a shop?

C Yes.

D In Second Avenue?

C Yes. Is an ambulance coming?

D It's on its way now, don't worry. But I need some information from you to give to the ambulance crew. Tell me who has been injured.

C The driver's been thrown out of his cab. He's not moving and I think someone in the shop has been hurt too. It's Mrs Williams, I think. A wall has fallen on her and there's a lot of blood coming from her head. She's not moving. The driver doesn't look good. My God! I think he's having a heart attack.

D What about the tanker? Do you know what it's carrying?

C No, but there's some liquid leaking from the back. It smells like petrol.

D Hello, Alexander?

C Hello. I can hear the ambulance now.

D Alexander, just stay on the line a little longer until it arrives. Now what I want you to do is ...

Writing

P = Police officer, N = Nurse

P Oh, Nurse. Do you have a moment? Could I talk to you about the accident last night?

N The RTA in Second Avenue?

P Yes, that's it. Can I speak to the lorry driver?

N You can't, I'm afraid. He died in the ambulance on the way in.

P Oh, I see. Cause of death?

N Myocardial infarction. He had a heart attack. The ambulance crew tried CPR but no luck, which is not surprising, considering his age and condition.

P How old was he?

N In his late fifties.

P So he wasn't very well? What makes you think that?

N He had a GTN spray in his pocket.

P GTN?

N Glyceryl Trinitrate – it's a medication for angina.

P I see. I'll make a note of that: Glyceryl Trinitrate. Do you think his medication could have affected his driving?

N It's possible, yes.

P What about the other casualty? That was a woman, according to my information.

N Yes, Mrs Williams. She was in her front room when the tanker crashed into the wall. She's in a critical condition. Multiple injuries; two fractured ribs, perforated liver, and lung contusion. She's in ICU.

P Can I talk to her?

N You'll have to ask the doctor about that.

P Right. I'm not getting very far, am I? What about witnesses? Who called for the ambulance?

N A neighbour. His name is Petit, I think. The dispatcher will have his details.

P Right.

N Do you know what caused the accident?

P It's hard to say at the moment. It was half past one in the morning. It was very quiet. The road is straight; there are no junctions. Suddenly the lorry swerved across the road and drove straight into a shop. Perhaps the driver fell asleep. Perhaps there's something wrong with the vehicle. I'm just guessing at the moment and we may never know.

Unit 2

Listening

a Yes, Mrs Oswald, there are medications available, but they will only control your symptoms, they won't get rid of the problem. Psychotherapy takes much longer, but it can sometimes cure. The third choice is ECT – electro-convulsive therapy. Many people are against it, but it can be highly effective and some patients, who have tried everything else, say it is the only thing to shine a light in their darkness.

b There can sometimes be bleeding with a biopsy, Mr de Jong. This is because an incision has to be made. We have to cut it open and get a sample of the tissue. There can be bleeding, but that's rare – about one in every two thousand. There's also a small danger of infection, but we do our best to prevent this.

c There is now no doubt that it's cancer and a hysterectomy – the surgical removal of your uterus – is the best chance for survival. We can't cure it so it's best to cut it out. We feel it's the best treatment option at this stage. Better than radiation or chemotherapy.

d I have to give you a local anaesthetic. Do you know what that is? No. Hussein, could you help me here? I want to explain to your mother that I want to give her something to make her eye numb so that I can get this thing out of her eye. Explain this to her, make sure she understands, and ask her if it's OK. Tell her that I'm not going to use a needle, but she must keep very still.

Language spot

My name is Akiko Tanaka and I'm twenty-three. My baby is due next month, but yesterday I started to get a pain in my lower back. This morning I was woken up by cramps. They're irregular, but they're very painful and I think the contractions have started early. Please don't contact the baby's father. My next of kin is my sister. Can you contact her?

Unit 3

Listening

M = Midwife, H = Hannah

a

M ... OK, I can see the top of the baby's head now, so give a gentle push, Hannah.

H Ooooooh.

M That's the way ... Now one more ... you can do it ... nearly there now ... just one more push ... and ... that's it ... well done ... and you've got a little baby girl.

b

M When did your labour start?

H My waters broke last night, and I started getting strong contractions early this morning.

M So that's about twelve hours ago. Well, you're seven centimetres dilated now, so I don't think we'll need to induce you. Now on your birth plan you've said you'd like gas and air as pain relief, yes?

H Yes, but if I can't bear the pain, I'd like an epidural.

M OK, well, you let me know how you're feeling ...

c

M She weighs just over eight pounds, and she's done fine in the tests.

H Her head's a funny shape.

M That's normal when forceps are used – the head will get into shape within a few days, and the bruising will disappear.

H Shouldn't she be crying more?

M Well, a strong cry is a sign of good lungs, but her breathing's nice and strong, so we don't have any worries about that.

d

M So, Hannah. you've had some bleeding, and you're in the 28th week – is that right?

H That's right. I've had a miscarriage before, so they thought I should have a scan.

M Right, well, the baby's moving fine, and it has a good strong heartbeat.

H That's a relief.

M The placenta looks just a little low, which is probably causing the bleeding. That should move up over the next few weeks. We'll bring you in in a month for another look, and meanwhile let us know if the bleeding gets heavier.

e

M The baby's presentation is perfect, with the head down. I know you want to push, Hannah, but don't push yet ... keep breathing ... take some gas and air if you need it ...

Language spot

E=Emma, N=Nina, D=Doctor

E Nina, can I have a word?

N Sure, what is it?

E I'm a bit concerned about Mrs Dent. The baby's heart rate has dropped to just under 100 bpm.

N Mm, that's outside the normal range. I think you ought to call the doctor.

E That's what I thought.

D You were right to call me. It's always a good idea to get help if you're concerned. How often have you been monitoring Mrs Dent?

E Every fifteen minutes.

D You'd better monitor continuously from now on, although the baby seems fine. You might want to take a pH measurement to double check for foetal distress – I'll leave that up to you.

E I will, yes, just to be sure.

D I'd give Mrs Dent some oxygen too – that won't do any harm. And try getting her to lie on her left side too. That may increase oxygen delivery slightly.

E I'll do that. And I'll call you if the heart rate goes down again.

D Yes, if it goes under 100. If it's a little slow, but over 100, you may want to think about amnioinfusion to raise the volume of fluid around the baby.

E Great, thanks, doctor.

D No problem.

Pronunciation

pathogen	stethoscope
national	prenatal
patient	frequency
basal	visible
labour	jaundice
perinatal	umbilical
benefits	survive
genitals	dilated
medical	vagina

Unit 4

Language spot

Exercise 3

a 3 milligrams plus 6 milligrams is equal to 9

b 4 millilitres into 36 millilitres is 9

c from 13 litres subtract 4 to leave 9

d 13 litres minus 4 is 9

e 6 milligrams added to 3 milligrams makes 9

f 3 milligrams times 3 is 9

g 36 millilitres divided by 4 equals 9

h 3 milligrams multiplied by 3 gives a total of 9

Exercise 4

a The dosage is 25 times 4 divided by 3

b The IV rate is calculated by dividing 500 by 4. That equals 125

c 40 units added to 10 gives a total of 50

d Divide 2 cc by four to get 0.5

e Multiply 1.5 mg by 0.5. That will give 0.75

f Take 25 from 60 to equal 35

g Subtract 52 from 100 to leave 48

h Give three 250 mg capsules to make a total dose of 750 mg

Listening

N=Nurse, P=Participant

N Good morning. I'm Sarah and I'm doing the monitoring this week. So I need to ask the usual questions and fill in the monitoring form.

P OK.

N Can I just get your details first? You are …?

P Mrs Brown.

N Right. And you're in Dr Kabowski's trial for the breast cancer drug?

P Yes, that's right.

N What dosage are you receiving?

P I'm on 15 milligrams a day.

N How is it going? Are there any improvements?

P No, I'm afraid not.

N Any deterioration?

P Deterioration? Yes. I would say so. This new drug is doing nothing for me.

N No?

P Dr Kabowski warned me at the start of the trial that I might not notice any benefits, and he was right. The pain is growing, so is the fatigue. I've completed the self-monitoring chart – here it is.

N Thanks. Let's see … you're having severe pain for nearly seventy-five per cent of the day?

P Yes.

N Are you experiencing any side effects from the medication?

P The pills leave a nasty taste in my mouth, but apart from that, no. It's a pity it's not working for me and I really don't understand what it all means. I mean, I fit Dr Kabowski's eligibility criteria all right; I'm a middle-aged woman and I've got breast cancer, but …

N Yes, I understand. Do you want to give it a little longer?

P Well, I've been coming here for six months now and the long journey here and the lack of results, well, it isn't worth it even though it's been great getting the extra check-ups and all the attention.

N Yes, I understand what you're saying, but you won't lose hope, will you? It's so important to be positive about your illness …

Unit 5

Listening

1

O = Ophthalmologist, T=Teri, D=Dean

O Teri, have a look at this and tell me what you see.

T The patient's eyes are bloodshot and watery.

O Yes, clearly an inflammation of the surface membrane.

T Do your eyes itch, Dean?

D Yes. I want to rub them all the time.

T Well, you mustn't do that.

O Has anyone else in your family got the same problem?

D Yes, my sister and my mum. They've both got it.

2

P1 = patient

O Have you been fighting?

P1 No, doctor, it was an accident. I fell out of a tree.

O You've got some nasty bruising around your eye. Have a closer look, Teri.

T I can see blood in the eye and something else, some foreign body embedded in the cornea, just next to the tear duct.

3

P2 = patient

O First of all, is there any pain?

P2 No, none at all, just blurred vision. I haven't been able to see well for over a year.

O Any ideas, Teri?

T Well, blurred vision is often the result of a clouding of the lens. You can see that from here.

O Do you get double vision – when you see two of everything?

P2 Sometimes I do, yes. I need a bright light to read and all colours look dull.

4

P3=patient

O So, tell me what happened.

P3 Well, I've gone almost completely blind in my right eye. If I close my left eye, I can't see much at all. At the best, everything looks misty and with haloes.

O Uh huh. Teri, can you describe the patient's right eye?

T The pupil is enlarged, oval-shaped, and bulging.

O OK. Let's find out about other symptoms. Do you ever get toothache?

P3 I do sometimes, yes.

O And nausea?

P3 Yes, that's right, I do.

Pronunciation

Exercise 1

optical illusion
depth perception

Exercise 3

1 light waves

2 diabetic retinopathy

3 electrical signals

4 eye condition

5 blood vessels

6 blurred vision

7 reading glasses

8 ocular movement

9 vision problems

10 optic nerve

11 pupil response

12 retinal detachment

13 surface membrane

14 eye test

15 visual acuity

Patient care

N = Practice nurse, P = Patient

1

N You need to be six metres from the chart, so could you stand here, please? Right, now I need you to cover your right eye. Good. Now, I'd like you to read the smallest line of letters that you can.

P P, E, C, F, D.

N Fine, will you cover the other eye for me, please? This time, can you read the same line of letters backwards?

P D, F, C, E, P.

N Right, now uncover both eyes. Try and read the next line down …

2

N Right, so I'm going to hold my finger in front of your nose, like this … about ten centimetres. Now I want you to look at the wall behind, please. OK, now look at my finger … and at the wall again. That's fine. Now keep looking at my finger … I'm going to move it towards your nose … and out again – keep looking at it – in … and out … right, that's fine. Now, can you cover one eye …

Unit 6

Listening

a

D=Doctor, I=Irena

D Mm, that looks nasty.

I Look, the skin's all purple and scaly here.

D That looks quite sore. Is it tender if I press it?

I Ah … yes, it is. It just doesn't seem to be getting better, doctor. It's getting worse, if anything.

D Yes, well, these can be slow to heal.

I What can you give me for it? Antibiotics?

D It's not infected, so antibiotics wouldn't do any good. These are caused by poor circulation, so you need to do everything you can to help the blood flow out of the leg.

I So I have to put my leg up when I sit down.

D That's right. But also take plenty of exercise and bandage the leg firmly every day – I'll show you how. That will also make it a bit less swollen. Make sure you change the bandage every day, so you don't get an infection. Have you been wearing compression stockings?

I No, I haven't.

D Well, I'll prescribe you some – they should help clear it up.

b

Z = Zak, D = Doctor

Z My wife made me come along because she says this looks a bit suspicious.

D Let's have a look. Have you always had this?

Z Yes, I have. But it used to be round, more or less. It seems to have changed over the last few months.

D Mm, the shape's fairly irregular, isn't it? And the edge is not clearly marked. How about the colour? Has that changed too?

Z It has, yes. It was always brown, but now it's much darker in parts.

D Right. And just feeling it with my finger, it feels quite hard and crusty on the top. Does it itch at all?

Z Yes, it's extremely itchy. It bleeds sometimes when I scratch it. Is it something to worry about?

D Well, it's certainly worth checking out, especially as you have really fair skin. What I'll do is make an appointment for you to have a biopsy, so they can have a look at the skin cells under the microscope.

c

D = Doctor, M = Mother of little boy

D So how's Josh's skin doing?

M It's much worse. It itches so much it drives him crazy. And now he's come out in little blisters.

D Yes, I can see. The skin is quite inflamed.

M It's even bleeding in some places, where he's scratched.

D Ah yes, that looks pretty sore.

M I'm worried about him. Is it going to carry on getting worse?

D No, in fact it will almost certainly get better when he gets older. But it will flare up from time to time. Watch what he eats, in case a particular food makes it worse, and try not to let him get too hot and sweaty.

M Is there anything we can do to make it less uncomfortable?

D I'll prescribe a topical corticosteroid cream for the itching. And keep his fingernails nice and short. Use moisturizing cream on the skin regularly to make it less dry and flaky, but don't use it where the skin is cracked, and avoid clothes made of scratchy materials such as wool.

Language spot

D=Doctor, P=Patient

D Mm, your scalp's still a bit inflamed, but actually it's much better than it was.

P Yes – it's my neck that's really sore. It's extremely itchy too, and it's got a lot worse this week. It was absolutely unbearable last night – easily the worst it's been.

D You've got to resist the urge to scratch, though, or it can get infected.

P I know, I know. It's very dry – that's the problem. I've tried creams from the chemist, but they don't seem to work.

D I'll prescribe you Topicon.

P Is that a barrier cream?

D Yes. It's really wonderful stuff. It's by far the best I've come across – fast-acting too.

P Let's hope so.

Pronunciation

1 I'm pretty disappointed with this cream.
2 My face is quite tender.
3 The treatment is fairly expensive.
4 I'm fairly confident this will work.
5 The wound is looking pretty good.
6 Your fingers are quite swollen.

Unit 7

Pronunciation

Exercise 1

N=Nurse, M=Maria

N Hello, Maria. Did you sleep better last night?

M Not really. The pain kept me awake.

N Did it? Oh dear. Where was the pain?

M In my leg.

N We'll give you more pain relief tonight.

Exercise 5

N=Nurse, P=Patient

N How are you feeling this morning?

P A bit low, to be honest.

N Are you? Aah. Would you like a chat about it?

P Well, I suppose so. Do you think it would help?

N I think so. You can tell me if anything's worrying you.

P OK then – that would be good.

Listening

L = Layla, D = Doctor

L So what's the news, doctor? Has it spread to my lymph glands?

D I'm afraid it has. But not to all the ones in the armpit. Only some of the ones we removed contained cancer cells.

L Oh … so it could be worse then.

D Yes, it certainly could.

L What was the tumour like?

D It was about 1.5 centimetres, so fairly small. And we also removed ten lymph nodes.

L Right. So what happens next then? Will I lose my breast?

D Different forms of treatment are possible. One is a full mastectomy, to remove the whole breast and some lymph nodes from the armpit. The alternative would be a lumpectomy, where just tissue from around the tumour and the lymph nodes are taken out.

L What's the advantage of a mastectomy?

D Well, it removes more tissue that could contain cancerous cells, so you could say it's safer.

L I don't like the thought of losing a breast.

D The other advantage is that the breast can be replaced with an implant, so your breast should end up looking as it does now.

L Oh, so what about the lumpectomy – is that more of a risk?

D You'd have a course of chemotherapy in addition to radiotherapy, to make sure that traces of cancer are removed. That can be pretty tough, though.

L You lose your hair, don't you? I don't want to do that …

D Yes, you do with chemotherapy, I'm afraid. Our cancer nurse would discuss ways of dealing with hair loss with you. There are pluses and minuses to the treatment, but I feel confident that whichever treatment you choose, it will get rid of the cancer.

L It's hard to think.

D Of course, you don't need to decide right now. I'm sure you've got lots of questions …

L No. I understand what you said, but my mind is blank. I can't think of any questions at the moment. I'll need a little time to take it in.

D Of course. I understand. Would you like to take a break, then we'll talk again?

L Yes, please.

Unit 8

Listening

N = Nurse (mentor), S = Student nurse

N Nadine Hartmann's colonoscopy and biopsy results have arrived from Pathology. I've got them here. Shall we go through them together?

S Right. I'll be glad of your help understanding them. Path lab reports are like a secret code!

N Like everything, they're easy when you know how. Look at this, for example, at the top of the page; 'polyp of sigmoid colon'.

S 'Polyp of sigmoid colon'?

N That's the specimen they analysed.

S I see – a polyp from her lower colon.

N So … it goes on … 'polyp of sigmoid colon, measuring nought point six by nought point four by nought point three centimetres'. That's the size of the specimen.

S Right.

N Next bit; 'mushroom-shaped specimen surrounded by mucus' – that's what the specimen looks like. Then it says; 'No evidence of stromal invasion.'

S What does that mean?

N That means there is no cancer.

S So does it give a diagnosis?

N Read what it says at the bottom of the page. Under 'Summary', it says 'Colon, sigmoid, endoscopic biopsy: tubular adenoma.'

S Let me work it out. The organ involved is the lower colon. That's where they got the biopsy using an endoscope. The diagnosis is a tubular adenoma.

N That's right; a benign tumour. She hasn't got cancer, but there is a danger of getting it in the future. The next thing we have to do is to write to Mrs Hartmann, explain all this, and arrange an appointment for her to see Dr Monroe to discuss treatment options.

Unit 9

Scrub up

1 He finds walking very difficult – he's had a few nasty falls. It's like he can't control his body any more.

2 The accident has affected the way she sees things. She doesn't recognize colours any more, and if something's moving, she can't see it at all. She sometimes sees the 'wrong' thing. Like the other day, she thought my umbrella was a big bird.

3 If he goes out alone, he always gets lost. He confuses right and left and has difficulty picking up objects. In fact, naming objects is also a problem.

4 Her memory's the biggest problem. Sometimes she looks at me and she just doesn't remember who I am. And she doesn't remember anything from one minute to the next. On the plus side, she likes my cooking better now because she's lost her sense of smell.

5 He's changed. He used to be very sociable, but now he's moody and prefers to be on his own. He can't handle everyday tasks such as cleaning his teeth – not only because he's lost the use of his right-hand side. He just seems to have forgotten how to do it.

Listening

Exercise 1

D=Doctor, N=Senior nurse

D Right, let's have a look at the patient and assess his GCS. Well, he hasn't opened his eyes at all, has he?

N No.

D OK. Let's see if he can hear me – Lewis. Lewis. Hello. Can you hear me? Yes. His eyes opened a little there. He can hear me. Hello, Lewis. Do you know where you are? You're in hospital. Can you remember what happened? Can you tell me your name? Mm, no – nothing there. Let's test his movements. Can you wiggle your fingers, Lewis? Was there a slight movement there?

N I didn't see anything, no.

D Right. What I'll do now is pinch him on the shoulder. Here goes … [N He's moving his hand …] … and he's trying to rub his shoulder. Good.

Exercise 2

D1, D2=Doctors

D1 He had a stroke two years ago, so that's almost certainly what it is.

D2 Yes, he's a high risk patient. His blood pressure's been very high, according to his wife.

D1 Mm. His blood pressure wouldn't be so high if he didn't smoke. How long ago did he collapse?

D2 About an hour.

D1 We need to act quickly. If we break up the clot now, that'll prevent further damage to the brain.

D2 He's regaining consciousness now.

D1 He should start to get better quickly if we give him a thrombolytic. We'll keep him under close observation tonight in case he has a relapse. If there's any change for the worse, page me.

D2 OK. He's looking much better.

D1 We'll do a CT scan tomorrow, and if that's clear, he should be able to go on the general ward.

Language spot

N1, N2 = Nurses

N1 How's Mr Rigg?

N2 If his operation goes well tomorrow, he'll make a full and speedy recovery.

N1 It's a straightforward procedure, isn't it?

N2 Yes, he's having a haematoma evacuated from his skull. He'll be home by the weekend, unless something unexpected happens.

N1 We spend too much time treating cyclists. There wouldn't be so many accidents if they had more cycle paths.

N2 And if cycle helmets were compulsory, there would be fewer brain injuries.

N1 Yes. This patient was lucky. At least he'll wear a helmet when he next rides his bike.

Pronunciation

1 His blood pressure would be lower if he didn't smoke.

2 She'd be healthier if she didn't eat so much.

3 If we break up the clot now, that'll prevent further damage to the brain.

4 If his operation goes well tomorrow, he'll make a full and speedy recovery.

5 If she were in pain, we'd give her morphine.

6 I'd work at the weekend if there were a staff shortage.

Unit 10

Listening

P = Presenter, A = Dr Adam Petrou

P First on today's show, we'll be talking about congestive heart failure, which affects around one million people in the UK. I have with me cardiologist Dr Adam Petrou … Adam, what is heart failure?

A Congestive heart failure occurs when the heart's ventricles are unable to pump enough blood to the body – the left one is usually the first to fail. This leaves the body short of oxygen, and also causes fluid to build up in the body's tissues and in the lungs.

P What are the common symptoms?

A It usually leaves sufferers extremely tired and breathless. The ankles often swell up, too.

P So what causes heart failure?

A Often, the heart has been damaged by a heart attack or by coronary heart disease, or simply by high blood pressure. These things can change the shape and thickness of the heart muscle, reducing its efficiency. Also, if the rhythm of the heart is irregular, over time this can cause heart failure.

P How is heart failure diagnosed?

A The best way is by echocardiogram, which is an ultrasound examination that gives us a clear image of the chambers of the heart in action.

P And the treatment?

A As with most heart problems, self-help is vital; by following an exercise programme, patients can greatly increase their energy and improve their breathing. Diuretics help reduce the fluid build-up, and make patients more comfortable too. The main drugs that work on the heart are ACE inhibitors and beta-blockers. ACE inhibitors dilate the blood vessels and bring down blood pressure. This reduces the pressure on the heart. Beta blockers have a calming effect on the heart – they keep it beating with an efficient, regular rhythm.

P And pacemakers can help with this too, can't they? Can you say a word about them?

A Yes, we do use pacemakers. These are small electrical devices that are implanted under the skin and attached to the heart by two wires. They send impulses that make sure the heart keeps a steady rhythm.

P So what's the prognosis for people with heart failure?

A The prognosis is not great – between 10 and 60 per cent of patients will die within a year of being diagnosed, so in many cases, the treatment aims to improve the quality of life rather than cure the problem.

P Dr Adam Petrou, thank you.

Writing

D = Doctor, M = Marie

D Hello. Marie Thomas?

M Yes, that's me.

D Hi, Mrs Thomas. Do you mind if a student observes the examination?

M No, that's fine.

D Great. So Mrs Thomas is 35.

M That's right.

D And can you tell us what the problem is?

M Well, the main thing is my breathing. I find it very hard to breathe when I go to bed. I have to stop to have a rest halfway up the stairs.

D I see. Does anything make it easier to breathe?

M Yes, it's easier if I sit up in bed, so that's how I sleep.

D How long have you had this problem?

M For about a year, I'd say. It's been bad for about two months.

D Do you have any pain?

M Yes. In the last three weeks or so, I've been getting pains down my left arm. I decided to come and see you when it got really bad.

D Can you describe the pains?

M Well, shooting pains, really. Starting at the top and going down to the bottom.

D OK. Any other problems?

M I've been sweating a lot, even though the weather's not hot.

D Have you been eating OK?

M No, not really. I've lost my appetite.

D Do you take exercise?

M No. I avoid doing exercise when possible. That's why I'm so overweight! I tried walking for ten minutes a day, but it almost killed me.

D We've got your weight here. 92 kilos. Do you drink?

M I enjoy having a glass of wine with dinner. That's all.

D Smoke?

M I'm afraid so – about a packet a day.

D Of course, I'd advise you to stop smoking.

M Yes, I know. My kids are always asking me to give up. I've tried to stop lots of times, but I haven't managed to kick the habit.

D Does anyone in your family have heart problems?

M Yes, my mother has angina, and my dad died of a heart attack.

D Any diabetes in the family?

M No.

D And your blood pressure was taken earlier and was … 160/80.

M I've always had high blood pressure.

D Right, I'm checking the ankles for oedema, and yes, they're very swollen. Now let's have a listen to your heart … and there are clear murmurs there. I'll have a listen to your lungs now. And I can hear abnormal sounds right and left. That sounds like there's some fluid there. And finally I'll listen to the abdomen. Bowel sounds present. If I press it, is there any tenderness?

M No – it's a bit swollen though.

D Yes, no masses, but some oedema.

Pronunciation

Exercise 2

1 Julia is an SRN.
2 This patient has a URTI.
3 A teacher gave the child CPR.
4 The driver of the car was DoA.
5 The hospital has no A&E department.

Exercise 3

1 I'm going to ask for an AXR.
2 The patient has a JVP of 5 cm.
3 She has a UTI and will need antibiotics.
4 Mr Musevi has a WBC of 45.

Unit 11

Listening

N = Nurse, T = Tori (patient), P = Porter

N Hello, Tori. How are you?

T I feel OK, but I'm very nervous.

N Are you? What's worrying you?

T Well, I'm worried that the anaesthetic won't be strong enough, and I'll be in pain, but won't be able to speak.

N I do know that anaesthetists monitor you very closely to make sure you're fully unconscious, but I've noted your worry. If you like, I'll ask the anaesthetist to explain exactly what he does.

T Yes, please – that would help.

N Now, the surgeon has talked to you about the hysterectomy procedure, hasn't he? Did he explain what he's going to do?

T Yes, he explained everything. And he marked where the operation will be. Look. I'm worried I'll have an ugly scar.

N It should leave quite a neat little scar actually, which will gradually fade away.

T I hope so.

N Now, you've signed the consent form, haven't you?

T Yes.

N I'll check that's here with your notes … good. Now I'll just talk you through what's going to happen next. In a moment I'm going to give you a pre-med. That's a liquid sedative that you drink. That'll make you feel nice and relaxed and sleepy.

T OK.

N After that we'll take you through to the theatre, and the anaesthetist will connect you up to the monitoring equipment, then he'll give you some drugs that'll send you to sleep. He'll ask you to count backwards from 100, and the next thing you'll see will be the recovery room. Is there anything you'd like to know?

T How will I feel when I wake up?

N You may feel a little sick or you might be really hungry – it varies from person to person. We'll give you pain relief while you're waking up, then when you're fully awake, you'll have a little pump – I've got one here – which you control yourself.

T How will I know when to use it?

N When you feel pain, you just press the button. Here, have a try.

T Seems easy enough.

N And I'll leave you some written instructions too.

T OK. So I won't have any pain at all then?

N Well, we normally express pain from zero, which is no pain, to ten which is unbearable pain. You shouldn't have more than two if you use the pump – that's very mild.

T Well, that doesn't sound too bad.

N No, it won't be. Right, so if you'd like to drink this pre-med. In about fifteen minutes an orderly will come and we'll go to theatre.

T OK, nurse – thanks.

P Hello, Tori.

T Yes?

P Hello. I'm going to take you to theatre. Can I just check your wristband? Victoria Hick 2-1-64 – that's you, is it?

T Yes.

P Lovely. And your notes are here … test results … and consent form, so we're ready.

Vocabulary

1 The patient was diagnosed with cervical cancer and we had to remove her womb.
2 We'll give you a local anaesthetic, then we'll insert a fibre-optic tube down through the mouth to see what's causing the pain.
3 The patient has a pneumothorax. I'm going to insert this needle between his ribs to release the air from around the lungs.
4 The remaining bowel is attached to an opening in the skin. Faeces then pass through this opening into a bag.
5 The burn is quite deep. We'll need to do a skin graft.
6 I'm going to make an incision in your stomach so that I can have a look at your ovaries.

Pronunciation

Exercise 1

1 colostomy	4 encephalography
2 tracheostomy	5 endoscope
3 encephalograph	6 endoscopy

Exercise 2

1 vasectomy	5 radiography
2 laparotomy	6 cardiograph
3 oesophagostomy	7 cystoscopy
4 microbiology	8 ophthalmoscope

Unit 12

Listening

V = Hospital visitor , N = Nurse

V Ah, Sister, I'm looking for my mother – Mrs Cohen. She was in this bed yesterday. Is everything all right?

N Oh, Mr Cohen, yes, don't worry, your mother is fine.

V Oh, I thought for one moment … Where is she?

N We've moved her to a single room.

V Why? What's wrong?

N She has an infection. It's potentially dangerous and highly contagious, you see. She's been isolated so that we can barrier nurse. All that means is that we are very strict about hygiene to prevent the infection spreading to other patients.

V What sort of infection? We were told she was having 'a routine operation'.

N It's a bug called Staphylococcus. It's something post-op patients of your mother's age are susceptible to. And in hospitals, where there are sick people, it can spread very easily.

V Does it mean I can't visit her?

N No, you're very welcome to visit. But you need to follow some basic hygiene procedures, OK? There's alcohol hand-rub in her room. Please could you, and all other visitors too, always use the hand-rub when you arrive and when you leave? And I mean *always*. Try very hard not to forget. There's a poster on the wall to remind you. Any hidden bugs you might be carrying will be killed off by the hand-rub. It's quicker and more hygienic than soap. Oh, and remember not to sit on her bed.

V Right, I'll remember. So this infection is contagious, is it?

N You won't catch it if you're healthy, no. But if you're not well, stay away until you're completely better. Any cuts you might have on your hands should be covered up. Anything that comes into direct contact with the patient is considered infected. So don't bring anything in to her room with you and don't take anything out.

V What, not even a bunch of flowers?

N No, not for the time being. You will see that the nurses are all wearing protective clothing, masks, and gloves, and we might ask you to do the same.

Unit 13

Listening

N = Nurse, P = Patient

N What does it say on the screen?

P It's blank.

N Well, switch it on then, Mr Mucci. The power switch is the black one in the bottom right-hand corner.

P Yes, I know. It is switched on.

N Is it plugged in? The power socket is directly under the screen.

P Oh, right. Sorry, nurse.

N OK. Now, the machine is plugged in and switched on?

P Yes.

N Good. On the screen you should now be able to see three function keys.

P Yes.

N The top one is 'drain', the middle one is 'fill' and the bottom one is 'dwell', right?

P Right, I see them.

N Press the button next to 'drain'. The green drain light above the screen should start flashing on and off. Is it?

P No.

N OK. Press the reset switch.

P That's the white one next to the power switch, isn't it?

N Yes. What do you see on the screen now?

P It says eighty eight minutes.

N That's the default setting. You need to change it to fifteen minutes. Use the timer arrows to the left of the screen to change the number. Do you see them?

P There are two timer arrows to the left of the screen.

N Press the down arrow and keep pressing until you see fifteen on the screen. OK?

P Yes, done.

N Now press the enter key which is just below the timer arrows. Has the stand-by light come on? That's the yellow one at the top of the machine.

P Yes.

N Good, we're getting there. Have the three function keys reappeared on the screen?

P Yes.

N Press 'drain'. The green start light at the top should come on and the other lights should go out.

P Yes.

N You're all ready to go. Press drain a second time. I can hear the alarm. What does it say on the screen?

P It says 'malfunction code 54.'

N That means there's a problem with the cartridge housing. OK, Mr Mucci, let's start again. Switch off the power and …

Speaking

D = Patient's daughter, W = Patient's wife

D How is he? How's Dad?

W Oh, the same. There's been no change.

D We've got to give it time.

W Time, Barbara? How much more time? He's been in this coma for eighty-three days now.

D I know, Mum.

W I spoke to Dr Williams this morning. He says the prognosis is not good. He says we should consider the possibility that even if your Dad wakes up, he will probably be a vegetable. He'll be conscious, but he won't be able to do anything for himself. Oh God! He wouldn't even be able to think.

D How does Dr Williams know that? He doesn't know that. You hear stories of people coming round after being in a coma for years.

W He's only alive now because of the respirator. If you switched that off, his body would die.

D On the other hand, he could wake up at any moment. It is possible that he could make a full recovery.

W Look, I don't even feel that this is him. I mean I know it is him, but he's just not in there. He's not aware, he doesn't feel anything. Your dad, he was always so full of life and he wouldn't want this. He would also want us to get on with our lives, wouldn't he? Not spend all our time sitting here; watching.

D Mum, you don't know this. Nobody has the right to make this decision, not you, not Dr Williams, no one.

W You're wrong. It means we've got to do the thinking for him. If we could ask him if he wanted to stay on this ventilator like this, what would he say?

D I think he'd say yes. He'd say, 'where there's life, there's hope.'

W There's another thing.

D What?

W Do you remember yesterday there was that terrible car accident? Remember all the ambulance sirens and everyone rushing around? Well, one of the victims is in that bed over there. She has severe internal injuries. The nurse told me earlier. Apparently they're waiting for donor organs and if they can't get them, she's going to die. She's twenty-one. It's such a shame, such a waste. And I was thinking …

D No, Mum!

W To save someone's life, Barbara? What would your dad say?

D He's my Dad. I don't care. I don't want to let him go. He needs us now, more than ever. He needs us to watch over him and take care of

him because I just know that one day soon he will, quite unexpectedly, open his eyes and call out for one of us.

Unit 14

Scrub up

N = Nurse Therapist, W= William

N William, I want you to have a look at these cards one by one and tell me what you see in them, OK? Just say what the cards look like. OK?

W OK.

N This is the first one. Take a moment. Say the first thing that comes to your mind.

W It looks like a turtle. It's been squashed. It's on a beach and it's trying to get to the sea, but it doesn't know which way to go and it gets squashed by a giant.

N Can you say why the giant squashed the turtle?

W Punishment.

N Punishment?

W For … I don't know … for being stupid.

Pronunciation

1	therapy	therapeutic
2	psychology	psychological
3	examine	examination
4	disabled	disability
5	trauma	traumatic
6	analysis	analytical
7	symptom	symptomatic
8	personal	personality

Listening

P = Psychiatrist, PN = Psychiatric nurse

P … so let's move quickly on to Daphne Duchamp. Daphne is forty-five and unmarried. She is suffering anxiety disorders. I believe she has been referred to us by her GP and now she's getting visits from a social worker and a psychiatric nurse. Barbara? Is that you?

PN Yes. I've made three home visits over the past two months.

P I want to hear about that and then decide if she's a suitable case for psychotherapy. Barbara, is she unable to function effectively?

PN Yes, Doctor. She is now housebound.

P I see. Take us through the case history, will you?

PN Daphne had her first panic attack in a shopping mall three years ago. Since then, she says, she has had them quite frequently. She describes feelings of sudden terror, accompanied by chest pain and trembling. The attacks are unpredictable and she says they happen whenever she goes out. As a result, she avoids any place she associates with the panic attacks, which is pretty well everywhere.

P She stays indoors all the time?

PN Yes. She is tense, tired, and full of worries. She shows obsessive tendencies, worrying about money (even though she has savings), about illness, and about germs – her house is spotless and smells of disinfectant. I also suspect she is beginning to drink a lot, though she tells me she has it under control.

P Anything else?

PN Not for the moment, Doctor, no.

P OK. It looks like fairly classic symptoms of agoraphobia, wouldn't you say? We've got the panic attacks, the patient's belief that the attacks could happen any time, and the onset of obsessive disorders and possible alcohol abuse. Agoraphobia is something that responds quite well to psychotherapy and desensitization so I'm going to arrange an outpatient's appointment with Dr Williams. Do you think she will go?

PN Probably, but only if she is accompanied.

P Will you be able to take her to the clinic?

PN Yes, certainly, if I'm on duty.

P Fine. Then I'll let you know.

Unit 15

Listening – Appointments diary

C = Consultant, R = Receptionist

C We've had a lot of problems with appointments today. Davina, you've been on the desk in Reception; could you run through the patients and tell us what you know?

R Yes, Doctor. The first problem was Natasha Alagaiah. She was your 9.30 appointment. She went to the wrong department, so when she finally got here it was already ten thirty. We could have fitted her in because we had a cancellation at midday, but she couldn't wait. Her appointment is just for a routine check-up so I rebooked her to see you on the fifth of September. The next problem was Serena Wilson at ten o'clock. Her appointment was to discuss her test results, but we have no record of them. I phoned Pathology, but nobody knew anything so the Practice Nurse took another sample and I made a new follow-up appointment.

C Mrs Hecker? She seemed annoyed when I saw her. Do you know what the problem was with her?

R I told her off, I'm afraid. She has missed her two previous appointments, but she never phoned up to cancel. She didn't seem to like me telling her about the difficulties this causes.

C OK. Then there was Celestina Dubois. She was very nervous because it was her initial appointment. I told her that we were going to be seeing a lot of each other over the next few months. Did she tell you all successive appointments will be weekly?

R Yes, Doctor. The next one is on the sixth of September. I got a phone call from Akira Sato who cancelled her twelve o'clock because she said she was too ill to get here on the bus and I notified the midwife who will make an out-of-hours visit.

C And Elsa Yager? I am rather worried and think we should keep an eye on her.

R Yes. I phoned admissions who confirmed that there is a vacant bed on the ward.

C Fine. So that just leaves Mrs Ba Ling.

R Yes. Ba Ling's appointment this morning was postponed from last week when we found she was double-booked.

C Oh yes, I remember.

Listening – Examining a child

N = Nurse, L = Lisa, M = Patient's mother

N So, Lisa, your mum tells me you've been feeling a lot better since the operation and that the pain in your chest has gone. Is that right?

L Yes.

N No more fainting?

L No.

N Great! Mum? How is Lisa in herself? Generally happy?

M She's full of life; sometimes I can't get her to sit down.

N That's a very good sign. She's a good colour – there's no sign of blueness, is there?

M No.

N Lisa, I'm going to have a little look at your chest and a listen to your heart, OK?

L OK.

N Now, let's start with your back. Could you take off your T-shirt for me? That's it. I'm going to feel around so tell me if my hands are cold. Are they OK?

L They're not cold.

N Good. Just lean forward a little. That's it, good girl. Breathe out for me. Just hold for a moment. Good. OK, breathe in. Fine. Does this hurt, Lisa, if I press here?

L No.

N Here?

L No.

N Mum? Have you noticed any tenderness? Has Lisa complained of any pains in her chest, back, or abdomen?

M No.

N Well, everything seems fine here. Lie back on the couch, Lisa. Is that comfortable?

L Yes.

N I'm going to use this. You've seen these things before, haven't you?

L Yes.

N Do you know what it's called?

L It's a stethoscope.

N That's right, it's a stethoscope. OK. I'm going to listen to your heart ... good ... good ... fine! Now turn on to your left side. No, the other way, that's your right. OK. Good. Has she shown any signs of extreme tiredness, Mum?

M She was exhausted last week after her school sports day, weren't you, Lisa?

L Yes, a bit.

N Did you run in a race?

L Yes.

N Did you win? That's the important thing.

M She came second, didn't you, Lisa?

L Yes.

N Did you? Well done! You wouldn't have been able to do that a year ago, would you?

L No.

N And how long did she feel like that?

M For about two hours.

N I see. Now sit upright, Lisa. Good. Lean forward for me and I'll listen to your back. Breathe out ... and hold. Excellent. No murmurs from your heart, everything seems to be going very well.

Unit 7 Scrub up Answers

1 13%
2 33%
3 25%
4 Men:

1	lung	4	colorectal
2	stomach	5	oesophagus
3	liver		

Women:

1	breast	4	colorectal
2	lung	5	cervical
3	stomach		

Glossary

Vowels

iː	br**ee**ch	ʊ	double-b**oo**ked	aɪ	ang**i**na
i	flak**y**	uː	hall**u**cination	aʊ	dr**ow**siness
ɪ	**i**nduce	u	c**u**taneous	ɔɪ	paran**oi**a
e	s**e**nsory	ʌ	bl**u**nt	ɪə	carr**ier**
æ	**a**cne	ɜː	h**e**rnia	eə	Caes**a**rean
ɑː	h**a**rmful	ə	en**e**ma	ʊə	epid**u**ral
ɒ	sl**o**t	ɚ	sed**a**te		
ɔː	m**o**rbid	əʊ	embry**o**		

Consonants

p	**p**ancreas	f	**f**oetus	h	**h**ygiene
b	**b**iopsy	v	**v**ision	m	**m**alignant
t	**t**ransplant	θ	ste**th**oscope	n	**n**ephrology
d	**d**ialysis	ð	wi**th**drawal	ŋ	scarri**ng**
k	**c**onsent	s	**s**tress	l	**l**oneliness
ɡ	**g**rave	z	authori**z**ation	r	**r**atio
tʃ	dis**ch**arge	ʃ	feveri**sh**	j	so**l**uble
dʒ	conta**g**ious	ʒ	ca**s**ualty	w	**w**itness

absorption /əbˈsɔːpʃn/ *n* the process of a liquid, gas, or other substance being taken in

accuracy /ˈækjərəsi/ *n* the ability to do something skilfully without making mistakes

acne /ˈækni/ *n* a skin condition, mainly affecting young people, that produces many spots on the face

amniotic fluid /ˌæmnɪɒtɪk ˈfluːɪd/ *n* the liquid that surrounds a baby inside the mother's womb (= the organ in women in which babies develop before they are born)

amputation /ˌæmpjuˈteɪʃn/ *n* the removal of an arm, leg, etc. by cutting it off in an operation

angina /ænˈdʒaɪnə/ *n* severe pain in the chest caused by a low supply of blood to the heart

antibody /ˈæntibɒdi/ *n* a protein produced in the body to fight disease

anus /ˈeɪnəs/ *n* the opening in a person's bottom through which solid waste leaves the body

apathetic /ˌæpəˈθetɪk/ *adj* without energy and showing no interest or enthusiasm

asepsis /eɪˈsepsɪs/ *n* the absence of bacteria, viruses, and other organisms that could cause disease

assess /əˈses/ *v* to make a judgement about a patient's physical or mental health

atria /ˈeɪtriə/ *n* the two upper spaces in the heart, used in the first stage of sending the blood around the body

atypical /ˌeɪˈtɪpɪkl/ *adj* not typical or usual

auditory /ˈɔːdətri/ *adj* connected with hearing

auscultation /ˌɔːskəlˈteɪʃn/ *n* the process of listening, usually with a stethoscope, to sounds inside the body

authorization /ˌɔːθəraɪˈzeɪʃn/ *n* official permission

balance /ˈbæləns/ *n* the ability to keep steady with an equal amount of weight on each side of the body

beta blockers /ˈbiːtə ˌblɒkəz/ *n* drugs used to control heart rhythm and blood pressure

bilaterally /ˌbaɪˈlætərəli/ *adv* on both sides

bile duct /ˈbaɪl dʌkt/ *n* a tube in the body that carries bile (= a greenish brown liquid that helps digestion of fat)

biopsy /ˈbaɪɒpsi/ *n* the removal and examination of tissue from a patient's body, in order to find out more about their disease

birth plan /ˈbɜːθ plæn/ *n* a document written by a woman who is going to give birth, describing what kind of medical treatment she wants

bladder /ˈblædə(r)/ *n* an organ like a bag in which liquid waste (= urine) collects before it is passed out of the body

bloodshot /ˈblʌdʃɒt/ *adj* (of eyes) with the part that is usually white full of red lines because of lack of sleep, etc.

blunt /blʌnt/ *adj* (used about an injury) caused by an object without a sharp edge or point, for example blunt head trauma

blurred vision /ˌblɜːd ˈvɪʒn/ *n* the inability to see clearly

breathlessness /ˈbreθləsnəs/ *n* difficulty in breathing

breech /briːtʃ/ *adj* used to describe a birth in which the baby's bottom or feet come out of the mother first

build up /bɪld ˈʌp/ *v* to form or develop

Caesarean /siˈzeəriən/ *n* an operation in which an opening is cut in a woman's abdomen (= the part of the body below the chest) in order to take out a baby

cancellation /ˌkænsəˈleɪʃn/ *n* an appointment, a meeting, etc. that has been arranged but will now not happen

carcinogen /kɑːˈsɪnədʒən/ *n* a substance that can cause cancer

carrier /'kæriə(r)/ *n* a person or animal that carries a disease and is able to infect others but does not have any symptoms of the disease

casualty /'kæʒuəlti/ *n* a person who is injured or killed in an accident

catheter /'kæθitə(r)/ *n* a thin tube that is put into the body, usually in order to remove liquids such as urine

cerebral /'serəbrəl/ *adj* relating to the brain

chemotherapy /ˌkiːməʊ'θerəpi/ *n* the treatment of disease, especially cancer, with the use of chemical substances

clinical trial /ˌklɪnɪkl 'traɪəl/ *n* the process of testing a new drug on humans

collapse /kə'læps/ *v* to fall down because you are very ill, often becoming unconscious

colon /'kəʊlən/ *n* the main part of the large intestine, which absorbs water from waste that passes through it

colour-blindness /'kʌlə̩blaɪndnəs/ *n* the inability to see the difference between colours such as red and green

commit suicide /kəˌmɪt 'suːɪsaɪd/ *v* to deliberately kill yourself

complaint /kəm'pleɪnt/ *n* a medical problem or symptom

complex /'kɒmpleks/ *adj* complicated and difficult

complications /ˌkɒmplɪ'keɪʃnz/ *n* new problems that make treatment of an illness more complicated and difficult

compulsory /kəm'pʌlsəri/ *adj* used about something that must be done because of a law or a rule

congestive heart failure /kənˌdʒestɪv 'hɑːt ˌfeɪljə(r)/ *n* a serious condition in which the heart is unable to pump enough blood to the body

consent /kən'sent/ *n* permission to do something

contagious /kən'teɪdʒəs/ *adj* (used about a disease) spread through physical contact

contractions /kən'trækʃnz/ *n* sudden tightening movements of the muscles around a woman's womb when she is giving birth

contraindication /ˌkɒntrəˌɪndɪ'keɪʃn/ *n* a possible reason for not giving someone a particular drug or medical treatment

conventional surgery /kən'venʃənl ̩sɜːdʒəri/ *n* operations in which a patient's body is cut open using the standard techniques and equipment

cranial /'kreɪniəl/ *adj* relating to the bone structure that surrounds and protects the brain (= the cranium)

creativity /ˌkriːeɪ'tɪvəti/ *n* the ability and the imagination to create new things

critical /'krɪtɪkl/ *adj* (used in triage) extremely serious, needing to be dealt with immediately

crusty /'krʌsti/ *adj* (used about the skin) having a hard outer layer

cutaneous /kjuː'teɪniəs/ *adj* connected with the skin

defecation /ˌdefə'keɪʃn/ *n* the process of getting rid of solid waste from the body through the **anus**

delayed /dɪ'leɪd/ *adj* happening or arriving later than planned

depth perception /'depθ pəˌsepʃn/ *n* the ability to judge distances in space using your sense of vision

detect /dɪ'tekt/ *v* to discover or notice something

dialysis /daɪ'æləsɪs/ *n* a process for taking waste substances out of the blood of people with damaged kidneys

diastole /daɪ'æstəli/ *n* the stage of the heartbeat when the heart muscle relaxes and the heart fills with blood

dietary /'daɪətəri/ *adj* concerning the food that you eat and drink regularly

dilated /daɪ'leɪtɪd/ *adj* widened; opened

discharge /'dɪstʃɑːdʒ/ *n* a thick substance that comes out from a part of the body, such as an infected eye

discomfort /dɪs'kʌmfət/ *n* a feeling of slight pain or of being physically uncomfortable

disfigurement /dɪs'fɪgəmənt/ *n* damage to a person's physical appearance

disregard /ˌdɪsrɪ'gɑːd/ *n* lack of consideration for other people

DNA /ˌdiː en 'eɪ/ *n* deoxyribonucleic acid (= the chemical in cells that carries genetic information)

donor /'dəʊnə(r)/ *n* a person who gives a part of their body (when alive or dead) to be used in medical treatment

dosage /'dəʊsɪdʒ/ *n* the amount of a medicine that should be taken

double-booked /ˌdʌbl 'bʊkt/ *adj* (used about an appointment, slot, etc.) promised to two different people by mistake

drain /dreɪn/ *v* to make liquid flow away from something

dwell /dwel/ *v* (used about the liquid in **dialysis**) to remain in the patient's body

electrode /ɪ'lektrəʊd/ *n* one of several electrical devices that are placed on a patient's body to measure electrical activity, for example when examining the heart

eligibility /ˌelɪdʒə'bɪləti/ *n* the ability to have or to do something because you are the right age, sex, etc.

elimination /ɪˌlɪmɪ'neɪʃn/ *n* the removal of waste products from the blood

embolism /'embəlɪzəm/ *n* a condition in which a blood clot or an air bubble blocks an artery

embryo /'embriəʊ/ *n* a human egg in the first eight weeks of development

enema /'enəmə/ *n* a procedure in which liquid is put into the body through the **anus** in order to clean out the intestine

epidemic /ˌepɪ'demɪk/ *n* a situation in which a serious disease spreads very quickly and infects many people in a particular community

epidural /ˌepɪ'djʊərəl/ *n* an injection into the lower part of the back so that no pain is felt below the waist

ethical /'eθɪkl/ *adj* connected with principles about what is right and wrong

exertion /ɪg'zɜːʃn/ *n* physical or mental effort

eyesight /'aɪsaɪt/ *n* the ability to see

familiar /fə'mɪliə(r)/ *adj* (used about a job, task, etc.) well known to you; not unusual

feverish /'fiːvərɪʃ/ *adj* suffering from a fever

first come, first served /ˌfɜːst 'kʌm ˌfɜːst 'sɜːvd/ *adj* used to describe a system in which people are dealt with strictly in the order in which they arrive

flaky /'fleɪki/ *adj* (used about the skin) coming off in small, thin pieces

flash on and off /ˌflæʃ ɒn ənd 'ɒf/ *v* (used about a light on a machine) to shine and then stop shining repeatedly as a signal that something is happening

flatulence /'flætjʊləns/ *n* gas produced in your body when digesting food and released through the mouth or **anus**

foetus /'fiːtəs/ *n* an unborn baby more than eight weeks after fertilization

follow-up /'fɒləʊ ʌp/ *adj* (used about a meeting with a doctor) taking place after an operation in order to check on the condition of the patient

full-blown /ˌfʊl 'bləʊn/ *adj* having all the characteristics of a disease

go off /gəʊ 'ɒf/ *v* (used about an alarm) to start ringing or making a noise

grave /greɪv/ *adj* (used about a person's medical condition) very serious, requiring intensive care

haematoma /ˌhiːmə'təʊmə/ *n* a solid swelling, consisting of blood that has become thick

haemorrhage /'hemərɪdʒ/ *v* to lose blood heavily from a broken blood vessel, especially from an injury inside the body

hallucination /hə‚luːsɪˈneɪʃn/ *n* the experience of seeing or hearing something that is not really there; the object seen or heard in this way

halo /ˈheɪləʊ/ *n* a circle of light, seen around bright objects

harmful /ˈhɑːmfl/ *adj* causing injury to a person's health or state of mind

heart murmurs /ˈhɑːt ‚mɜːməz/ *n* sounds made by the heart that are not normal

hernia /ˈhɜːniə/ *n* a condition in which part of an organ is pushed through a weak part of a wall inside the body

hygiene /ˈhaɪdʒiːn/ *n* the practice of keeping things clean in order to prevent illness and disease

impairment /ɪmˈpeəmənt/ *n* the state of having a physical or mental condition which means that part of your body or brain does not work correctly

incision /ɪnˈsɪʒn/ *n* a cut made during an operation

incurable /ɪnˈkjʊərəbl/ *adj* (used about an illness or disease) not able to be cured

induce /ɪnˈdjuːs/ *v* to deliberately make a woman start to give birth by giving her drugs

inflamed /ɪnˈfleɪmd/ *adj* (used about a part of the body) red and sore because of infection or injury

ingestion /ɪnˈdʒestʃən/ *n* the act of taking food, etc. into your body, usually by swallowing

initial /ɪˈnɪʃl/ *adj* happening at the beginning; first

inoculation /ɪ‚nɒkjuˈleɪʃn/ *n* the process of protecting a person against a particular disease by injecting them with a vaccine (= a mild form of the disease)

intelligence /ɪnˈtelɪdʒəns/ *n* the ability to learn, understand, and think about things

intention /ɪnˈtenʃn/ *n* what you plan or aim to do

intracranial /‚ɪntrəˈkreɪniəl/ occurring inside the skull

intravenous /‚ɪntrəˈviːnəs/ *adj* (used about drugs, an injection, etc.) going into a vein

invasion /ɪnˈveɪʒn/ *n* the movement of a disease from one cell or area of the body to another

isolation /‚aɪsəˈleɪʃn/ *n* the separation of a patient with an infectious disease from other patients

judgement /ˈdʒʌdʒmənt/ *n* the ability to make sensible decisions after carefully considering the best thing to do

keyhole surgery /ˈkiːhəʊl ‚sɜːdʒri/ *n* operations in which only very small cuts are made in the patient's body

load up /ləʊd ˈʌp/ *v* to fill a machine with something so that it is ready to use

loneliness /ˈləʊnlinəs/ *n* a feeling of unhappiness because you have no friends or people to talk to

long-sightedness /‚lɒŋ ˈsaɪtɪdnəs/ *n* the inability to see things clearly if they are close to you

lymph nodes /ˈlɪmf nəʊdz/ *n* small organs that prevent harmful substances from entering the blood and which produce white blood cells

malfunction /‚mælˈfʌŋkʃn/ *n* (used about a machine or piece of equipment) a failure to work correctly

malignant /məˈlɪɡnənt/ *adj* (used to describe cancer) able to spread to other parts of the body

metastasis /mɪˈtæstəsɪs/ *n* the spread of cancer to new areas of the body through the lymphatic or blood system

metastasized /mɪˈtæstəsaɪzd/ *adj* (used about cancer) having already spread to other areas of the body

miscarriage /ˈmɪskærɪdʒ/ *n* giving birth to a baby before it is fully developed so that it is not able to survive

moisturizing cream /ˈmɔɪstʃəraɪzɪŋ ‚kriːm/ *n* a cream that is used to make the skin less dry

morbid /ˈmɔːbɪd/ *adj* not healthy; diseased

motor response /ˈməʊtə rɪ‚spɒns/ the ability of the patient to respond to a command by moving part of the body

mucous membrane /ˈmjuːkəs ‚membreɪn/ *n* a thin layer of skin that covers the inside of the mouth, nose, intestines, etc. and which produces mucus (= a thick liquid)

myocardial infarction /maɪəʊ‚kɑːdɪəl ɪnˈfɑːkʃn/ *n* the death of an area of heart muscle, caused by a block in its blood supply

nephrology /neˈfrɒlədʒi/ *n* the area of medicine concerned with the kidneys

obsession /əbˈseʃn/ *n* a state in which a person continuously thinks about one particular thing or person in a way that is not normal

ocular /ˈɒkjələ(r)/ *adj* relating to the eyes

oedema /ɪˈdiːmə/ *n* a condition in which liquid collects in the spaces inside the body and makes it swell

oesophagus /iˈsɒfəɡəs/ *n* the tube in the body through which food passes from the mouth to the stomach

optimum /ˈɒptɪməm/ *adj* the best possible; producing the best results

oral /ˈɔːrəl/ *adj* relating to the mouth

organ /ˈɔːɡən/ *n* a part of the body that has a particular purpose, such as the heart or lungs

out-of-hours /‚aʊt əv ˈaʊəz/ *adj* (used about a service, an appointment, etc.) not taking place during normal working hours

pacemaker /ˈpeɪsmeɪkə(r)/ *n* an electronic device that is put inside a person's body to help their heart beat regularly

palpitations /‚pælpɪˈteɪʃnz/ *n* a physical condition in which your heart beats unusually fast

pancreas /ˈpæŋkriəs/ *n* an organ near the stomach that produces a liquid that helps the body to digest food

pandemic /pænˈdemɪk/ *n* a disease that spreads over a whole country or the whole world

paranoia /‚pærəˈnɔɪə/ *n* a mental condition in which a person wrongly believes that other people want to harm them, or that they are an extremely important person, etc.

participant /pɑːˈtɪsɪpənt/ *n* a person who is taking part in an experiment, a test, etc.

perception /pəˈsepʃn/ *n* the way you notice things, especially with the senses

peritoneal /‚perɪtəˈniəl/ *adj* of the membrane (= very thin layer of tissue) on the inside of the area below the chest, covering the stomach and other organs

persistent /pəˈsɪstənt/ *adj* continuing to do the same thing or to behave in the same way

phobia /ˈfəʊbiə/ *n* an extreme and unreasonable fear of something

placenta /pləˈsentə/ *n* the organ in a mother's body that feeds and protects a baby before it is born

plague /pleɪɡ/ *n* any infectious disease that kills a lot of people

post-operative /ˈpəʊst ‚ɒpərətɪv/ *adj* connected with the period after an operation

postponed /pəˈspəʊnd/ *adj* (used about an appointment, etc.) arranged to take place at a later time or date

precision /prɪˈsɪʒn/ *n* the quality of being exact and precise, for example a precision instrument

presentation /‚prezn̩ˈteɪʃn/ *n* the position of a baby in the mother's body just before birth

presenting symptoms /prɪˈzentɪŋ ‚sɪmptəmz/ *n* the symptoms that cause a patient to go to a doctor for help

prognosis /prɒɡˈnəʊsɪs/ *n* a prediction, based on medical evidence, of the likely development of an illness

prophylaxis /‚prɒfɪˈlæksɪs/ *n* action taken to prevent disease

pulmonary veins /ˈpʌlmənəri veɪnz/ *n*

veins that carry blood containing oxygen from the lungs to the heart

pupil response /'pju:pl rɪˌspɒns/ n the reaction of the pupil (= the small round black area at the centre of the eye) to bright light

pus /pʌs/ n a thick yellow or green liquid that is produced in an infected wound

radiotherapy /ˌreɪdiəʊ'θerəpi/ n the treatment of cancer or other disease using radiation

ramp /ræmp/ n a slope that can be moved, used when putting a patient in an ambulance

ratio /'reɪʃiəʊ/ n the relationship between two quantities, represented by two numbers that show how much larger one quantity is than the other

re-evaluate /ˌri:ɪ'væljueɪt/ v to form a new opinion of the amount, value, or quality of something after thinking about it again

referral /rɪ'fɜ:rəl/ n sending a patient who needs special help to see an expert in that area of medicine

regime /reɪ'ʒi:m/ n a course of medical treatment that you follow in order to improve your health

rejection /rɪ'dʒekʃn/ n the process after a transplant in which the body does not accept the new organ and starts to attack it

remission /rɪ'mɪʃn/ n a period during which an illness temporarily improves and the patient seems to get better

reveal /rɪ'vi:l/ v to show something that was previously hidden

rinse off /rɪns ɒf/ v to remove soap, etc. from your skin by washing it with water

round-the-clock /ˌraʊnd ðə 'klɒk/ adj all day; twenty-four hour

run out /rʌn 'aʊt/ v to use up or finish a supply of something

rupture /'rʌptʃə(r)/ n the tearing or bursting apart of an organ, for example the amniotic sac during childbirth

salivary glands /sə'laɪvəri glænz/ n small organs that produce a liquid in your mouth that helps you to swallow food

scaly /'skeɪli/ adj (used about the skin) hard and dry, with small pieces that come off

scarring /'skɑ:rɪŋ/ n marks that are left on the skin after it has healed

schizophrenia /ˌskɪtsə'fri:niə/ n a serious mental illness in which a person's thoughts, feelings, and behaviour are not connected with reality

score /skɔ:(r)/ n the number of points that someone gets in a particular scale of measurement

screen /skri:n/ v to examine a person to find out if they have a particular illness

secretion /sɪ'kri:ʃn/ n the production of liquid substances by parts of the body

sedate /sɪ'deɪt/ v to give a patient drugs so that they sleep or become more calm

self-harm /self 'hɑ:m/ n the act of deliberately injuring yourself, for example by cutting yourself, as a result of having emotional or mental problems

semi-urgent /'semi ˌɜ:dʒənt/ adj (used in triage) not likely to die, needing to be dealt with within one hour

senile /'si:naɪl/ adj connected with old age

sensitivity /ˌsensə'tɪvəti/ n the quality of having an unusually strong physical reaction to something

sensory /'sensəri/ adj connected with the physical senses

short-sightedness /ˌʃɔ:t 'saɪtɪdnəs/ n the inability to see things clearly if they are far away from you

shut down /ʃʌt 'daʊn/ v (used about a machine) to stop or switch off automatically

significant /sɪg'nɪfɪkənt/ adj large or important enough to have an effect or to be noticed

site /saɪt/ n a place or location

skin graft /'skɪn grɑ:ft/ n an operation in which healthy skin is taken from one part of the body and placed over another area that has been burned or damaged

slot /slɒt/ n a period of time in a schedule, for example when a patient can arrange to meet a doctor

soluble /'sɒljəbl/ adj able to dissolve in a liquid

stable /'steɪbl/ adj (used about a person's medical condition) not becoming worse; under control

staging /'steɪdʒɪŋ/ n a system used to judge how far a cancer has developed; a diagnosis based on this system

stethoscope /'steθəskəʊp/ n an instrument used to listen to a person's heart and breathing

stool /stu:l/ n a piece of solid waste from a person's body

stress /stres/ n pressure or worry caused by work, emotional problems, etc.

success rate /sək'ses ˌreɪt/ n the number of people who are cured by a particular treatment, used to judge if it is an effective cure

successive /sək'sesɪv/ adj (used about appointments, etc.) following one after the other; future, subsequent

survivable /sə'vaɪvəbl/ adj (used about an injury, illness, etc.) able to be survived

synthetic /sɪn'θetɪk/ adj made by combining chemicals rather than produced naturally; artificial

tendency /'tendənsi/ n if someone has a particular tendency, they often behave or act in that particular way

terminal /'tɜ:mɪnl/ adj (used about an illness) not able to be cured and leading to death

tolerance /'tɒlərəns/ n the inability to receive any benefit from a particular medicine because your body has become used to it

topical cream /'tɒpɪkl kri:m/ n cream that is applied to a localized part of the body and is used to treat certain skin conditions, such as eczema

transmission /træns'mɪʃn/ n the act or process of passing a disease from one person to another

transplant /'trænsplɑ:nt/ n a medical operation in which a damaged organ is replaced with one taken from another person

turn into /tɜ:n 'ɪntʊ/ v to change into; to become

uterine /'ju:təraɪn/ adj relating to the uterus (= the organ in women in which babies develop)

vacant /'veɪkənt/ adj (used about a slot) available; not taken

venous /'vi:nəs/ adj relating to veins

ventricles /'ventrɪklz/ n the two lower spaces in the heart that pump blood to the lungs or around the body

vision /'vɪʒn/ n the ability to see

visual acuity /ˌvɪʒuəl ə'kju:əti/ n the ability to see clearly

visual field /ˌvɪʒuəl 'fi:ld/ n the total area that you can see without moving your head

waters /'wɔ:təz/ n the liquid inside a woman's body that breaks (= passes out of her) just before the baby is born

withdrawal /wɪð'drɔ:əl/ n behaviour in which a person wants to be alone and shows no interest in other people or things

witness /'wɪtnəs/ n a person who sees a crime or an accident and is able to describe what happened

OXFORD
UNIVERSITY PRESS

Great Clarendon Street, Oxford OX2 6DP

Oxford University Press is a department of the University of Oxford.
It furthers the University's objective of excellence in research, scholarship,
and education by publishing worldwide in

Oxford New York

Auckland Cape Town Dar es Salaam Hong Kong Karachi
Kuala Lumpur Madrid Melbourne Mexico City Nairobi
New Delhi Shanghai Taipei Toronto

With offices in

Argentina Austria Brazil Chile Czech Republic France Greece
Guatemala Hungary Italy Japan Poland Portugal Singapore
South Korea Switzerland Thailand Turkey Ukraine Vietnam

OXFORD and OXFORD ENGLISH are registered trade marks of
Oxford University Press in the UK and in certain other countries

© Oxford University Press 2008

The moral rights of the author have been asserted

Database right Oxford University Press (maker)

First published 2008

2012 2011 2010 2009 2008

10 9 8 7 6 5 4 3 2 1

ISBN: 978 0 19 456988 0

Printed in Spain by Orymu S.A.

ACKNOWLEDGEMENTS

Artwork sourced by: Suzanne Williams/Pictureresearch.co.uk

Illustrations by: Emma Dodd pp 12, 13, 104, 108; Mark Duffin pp 5, 19, 22, 28,
62, 94; Andy Hammond p 83; Andy Parker p 103; Tony Sigley p 4; Amanda
Williams pp 44, 50, 74, 75, 93

Cover image courtesy: Getty Images (Geoff Brightling).

*We would also like to thank the following for permission to reproduce the following
photographs:* Alamy pp 8 (Australian outback/Ethel Davies/ImageState),
8 (helicopter/Annette Price/H2O Photography), 19 (forceps/Jupiterimages/
Ablestock), 24 (Tim Hill), 27 (citrus fruits/Nick Carman/The Anthony Blake
Photo Library), 27 (deadly nightshade/Konrad Zelazowski), 29 (3/Robert Slade/
Manor Photography), 29 (4/James Ambler), 32 (Snellen chart/Simon Belcher),
32 (African woman/Alan Gignoux), 34 (mole/Don Garbera/Phototake Inc.),
36 (teenager/Angela Hampton Picture Library), 40 (smoking/Peter Titmuss),
42 (crab/Lynx/Iconotec), 43, 46 (Charmaine Peterson/Dieter Melhorn),
52 (accident on motorway/Alvey & Towers Picture Library), 54 (J Marshall/
Tribaleye Images), 55 (capsules and tablets /WidStock), 55 (IV fluid and
catheter/David Taylor), 90 (quack doctor/neal and molly jansen), 106 (Libby
Welch); The Bridgeman Art Library p 77 (William Harvey/by Paul Rainer,
(20th century)/Private Collection, © Look and Learn); Corbis pp 7 (police
officer/Peter Dazeley/zefa), 10 (smoker/Katja Ruge/zefa), 19 (Mango
Productions), 22 (elderly man /Claire Artman/zefa), 22 (crying baby/Brigitte
Sporrer/zefa), 22 (woman with red top/Norbert Huettermann/zefa), 34 (tattoos/
Jodi Hilton), 34 (Geisha/Karen Kasmauski), 40 (radioactivity symbol/Roger
Ressmeyer), 41 (Larry Williams), 49 (Ole Graf/zefa), 58 (T & L/Image Point FR),
68 (chatting/Michael Prince), 68 (driving/Bruce Benedict/Transtock),
68 (sleeping/Elke Van De Velde/zefa), 68 (jigsaw/Birgid Allig/zefa), 77 (nurse/
Jose Luis Pelaez, Inc.), 90 (plague victims/Bettmann), 98 (woman), 108 (René
Laënnec/Bettmann); Dorling Kindersley pp 6, 48 (diagram); Getty Images pp
5 (Reza Estakhrian/Stone), 10 (elderly woman/Macduff Everton/The Image
Bank), 10 (boy/Nick Dolding/Taxi), 15 (Reza Estakhrian/Stone+), 16 (foetus/
Nucleus Medical Art, Inc.), 17 (Hans Neleman/Riser), 22 (young man/Eric
Tucker/Stone+), 27 (betel nut palm/Fredrick & Laurence Arvidsson/Dorling
Kindersley), 29 (2/Dan McCoy/Rainbow/Science Faction), 34 (boy sweating/Zia
Soleil/Iconica), 34 (goose pimples/Ebby May/The Image Bank), 34 (mother
and baby /Julia Smith/Riser), 36 (skin diagram/Dea Picture Library), 38 (snowy
landscape/Matthias Breiter/Minden Pictures), 46 (Lal Bibi/Zubin Shroff/Stone+),
47 (Lester Lefkowitz/Stone), 53 (Seiya Kawamoto/Taxi), 61 (David Hanover/
Stone), 72 (Michael J. Fox/Mark Wilson), 88 (hand dispenser/Christopher
Furlong), 96 (ERproductions Ltd/Blend Images); Mary Evans Picture Library
p 90 (plague doctor); Mediscan Medical Images p 34 (eczema); PA Photos
p 38 (woman with burn mask/Matthew Fearn/PA Archive); Courtesy of
www.pemed.com p 37; Photolibrary.com p 52 (cardiac arrest/Stockbyte);
Punchstock pp 7 (nurse/Mike Powell/Digital Vision), 11 (UpperCut Images),
14 (ER Productions/Brand X), 16 (sperm fertilizing an egg /Steve Taylor/Digital
Vision), 22 (baby with dummy/GoGo Images Corporation), 23 (Larry Williams
Associates/Corbis Super RF), 25 (male nurse with green overall/Jose Luis Pelaez
Inc/Blend Images), 30 (George Doyle/Stockbyte), 31 (test glasses/Banana Stock),
34 (reading braille/George Doyle/Stockbyte), 44 (doctor and patient/Keith
Brofsky/Photodisc), 46 (Jim Pear/Jack Hollingsworth/Photodisc), 46 (Hapreet
Singh/81a), 46 (Miss Weinberger/Somos/Veer), 48 (boy/Elke Van de Velde/
Photodisc), 52 (tower block/Andrew Ward/Life File/Photodisc), 52 (park
railings/Dorling Kindersley), 55 (medicine and spoon/Jupiterimages/Comstock
Images), 55 (hypodermic syringe/Image Source Black), 62 (moodboard),
68 (smelling a flower/Plattform/Johner Images Royalty-Free), 68 (dancing/ans
Neleman/zefa), 69 (Radius Images), 71 (wrecked car/pixtal), 72 (nurse/Jon
Feingersh/Blend Images), 74 (Don Farrall/Photodisc), 75 (Dorling Kindersley),
76 (Don Hammond/Design Pics Inc.), 78 (Dynamic Graphics/Jupiterimages/
Creatas), 79 (salad), 79 (burger/Foodcollection), 80 (operation/Stockbyte),
80 (surgical instruments/PhotoLink/Photodisc), 83 (Fancy), 88 (nurse talking
/Purestock), 94 (Radius Images), 100 (Sami Sarkis/Photographer's Choice RF),
105 (UpperCut Images), 108 (nurse/Corbis Premium RF); Reuters p 84 (Gopal
Chitrakar); Rex Features pp 25 (drug testing/Sipa Press), 44 (Jerri Nielsen),
50 (Garo/Phanie), 63 (Alix/Phanie); Science Photo Library pp 12 (National
Library Of Medicine), 13 (Lea Paterson), 16 (divided cells/Michel Delarue,
ISM), 20 (pregnant women/Ian Hooton), 20 (birthing pool/Eddie Lawrence),
26 (Francoise Sauze), 27 (poppy/Philippe Psaila), 29 (eye cross-section/John
Daugherty), 29 (1/Paul Parker), 31 (colour/David Nicholls), 31 (vision/David
Nicholls), 34 (leg ulcer/Dr P. Marazzi), 38 (silver coated dressing/Dr P. Marazzi),
40 (DNA/Pasieka), 40 (lung cancer scan/Scott Camazine), 40 (virus/Centre For
Infections), 40 (cells dividing/Steve Gschmeissner), 42 (x-ray/Zephyr),
68 (brain/Pasieka), 71 (CT scanner /GustoImages), 82 (Steve Gschmeissner),
95 (haemodialysis machine/BSIP, Beranger), 95 (peritoneal dialysis machine/
Antonia Reeve), 101 (Will Mcintyre), 111 (rosacea/Dr P. Marazzi), 111 (guttate
psoriasis/CNRI), 112 (erythema multiforme/Dr P. Marazzi), 112 (discoid lupus
erythematosus/CNRI), 112 (molluscum contagiosum/Dr P. Marazzi),
112 (cardiac catheterisation/K.Glaser), 114 (rosacea/Dr P. Marazzi),
114 (erythema multiforme/Dr P. Marazzi), 114 (guttate psoriasis/CNRI),
114 (discoid lupus erythematosus/CNRI), 114 (molluscum contagiosum/
Dr P. Marazzi); Science & Society Picture Library pp 32 (historic glasses/Science
Museum), 32 (Science Museum), 98 (ink blot/Science Museum); Still Pictures
pp 18 (Jorgen Schytte), 32 (child eyesight patient/Adrian Arbib); Wellcome
Images p 108 (Laënnec stethoscope/Wellcome Library, London)

*The author and publisher would like to thank the following people who assisted in the
development of this title:* Paul Henderson and Mary Wilson, IFAGE, Fondation
pour la Formation des Adultes, Geneva; Christine Tracey; and Elizabeth
Ulrich, RN, MSN, The Language Company, Baden.

Special thanks are also due to: Rowena Deans RN, Nick Canham, Suraya Grice,
Amalina Grice, Ahmad Suffian Arshad, Salmah Malik and the nursing staff at
Calderdale Royal Hospital.